# Trustworthy Online Controlled Experiments

A Practical Guide to A/B Testing

Getting numbers is easy; getting numbers you can trust is hard. This practical guide by experimentation leaders at Google, LinkedIn, and Microsoft will teach you how to accelerate innovation using trustworthy online controlled experiments, or A/B tests. Based on practical experiences at companies that each runs more than 20,000 controlled experiments a year, the authors share examples, pitfalls, and advice for students and industry professionals getting started with experiments, plus deeper dives into advanced topics for experienced practitioners who want to improve the way they and their organizations make data-driven decisions.

Learn how to:

- Use the scientific method to evaluate hypotheses using controlled experiments
- Define key metrics and ideally an Overall Evaluation Criterion
- Test for trustworthiness of the results and alert experimenters to violated assumptions
- Interpret and iterate quickly based on the results
- Implement guardrails to protect key business goals
- Build a scalable platform that lowers the marginal cost of experiments close to zero
- Avoid pitfalls such as carryover effects, Twyman's law, Simpson's paradox, and network interactions
- Understand how statistical issues play out in practice, including common violations of assumptions

RON KOHAVI is a vice president and technical fellow at Airbnb. This book was written while he was a technical fellow and corporate vice president at Microsoft. He was previously director of data mining and personalization at Amazon. He received his PhD in Computer Science from Stanford University. His papers have more than 40,000 citations and three of them are in the top 1,000 most-cited papers in Computer Science.

DIANE TANG is a Google Fellow, with expertise in large-scale data analysis and infrastructure, online controlled experiments, and ads systems. She has an AB from Harvard and an MS/PhD from Stanford, with patents and publications in mobile networking, information visualization, experiment methodology, data infrastructure, data mining, and large data.

YA XU heads Data Science and Experimentation at LinkedIn. She has published several papers on experimentation and is a frequent speaker at top-tier conferences and universities. She previously worked at Microsoft and received her PhD in Statistics from Stanford University.

"At the core of the Lean Methodology is the scientific method: Creating hypotheses, running experiments, gathering data, extracting insight and validation or modification of the hypothesis. A/B testing is the gold standard of creating verifiable and repeatable experiments, and this book is its definitive text."
— Steve Blank, Adjunct professor at Stanford University, father of modern entrepreneurship, author of *The Startup Owner's Manual* and *The Four Steps to the Epiphany*

"This book is a great resource for executives, leaders, researchers or engineers looking to use online controlled experiments to optimize product features, project efficiency or revenue. I know firsthand the impact that Kohavi's work had on Bing and Microsoft, and I'm excited that these learnings can now reach a wider audience."
— Harry Shum, EVP, Microsoft Artificial Intelligence and Research Group

"A great book that is both rigorous and accessible. Readers will learn how to bring trustworthy controlled experiments, which have revolutionized internet product development, to their organizations"
— Adam D'Angelo, Co-founder and CEO of Quora and former CTO of Facebook

"This book is a great overview of how several companies use online experimentation and A/B testing to improve their products. Kohavi, Tang and Xu have a wealth of experience and excellent advice to convey, so the book has lots of practical real world examples and lessons learned over many years of the application of these techniques at scale."
— Jeff Dean, Google Senior Fellow and SVP Google Research

"Do you want your organization to make consistently better decisions? This is the new bible of how to get from data to decisions in the digital age. Reading this book is like sitting in meetings inside Amazon, Google, LinkedIn, Microsoft. The authors expose for the first time the way the world's most successful companies make decisions. Beyond the admonitions and anecdotes of normal business books, this book shows what to do and how to do it well. It's the how-to manual for decision-making in the digital world, with dedicated sections for business leaders, engineers, and data analysts."
— Scott Cook, Intuit Co-founder & Chairman of the Executive Committee

"Online controlled experiments are powerful tools. Understanding how they work, what their strengths are, and how they can be optimized can illuminate both specialists and a wider audience. This book is the rare combination of technically authoritative, enjoyable to read, and dealing with highly important matters"
— John P.A. Ioannidis, Professor of Medicine, Health Research and Policy, Biomedical Data Science, and Statistics at Stanford University

"Which online option will be better? We frequently need to make such choices, and frequently err. To determine what will actually work better, we need rigorous controlled experiments, aka A/B testing. This excellent and lively book by experts from Microsoft, Google, and LinkedIn presents the theory and best practices of A/B testing. A must read for anyone who does anything online!"
— Gregory Piatetsky-Shapiro, Ph.D., president of KDnuggets, co-founder of SIGKDD, and LinkedIn Top Voice on Data Science & Analytics.

"Ron Kohavi, Diane Tang and Ya Xu are the world's top experts on online experiments. I've been using their work for years and I'm delighted they have now teamed up to write the definitive guide. I recommend this book to all my students and everyone involved in online products and services."

– Erik Brynjolfsson, Professor at MIT and Co-Author of
*The Second Machine Age*

"A modern software-supported business cannot compete successfully without online controlled experimentation. Written by three of the most experienced leaders in the field, this book presents the fundamental principles, illustrates them with compelling examples, and digs deeper to present a wealth of practical advice. It's a "must read"!

– Foster Provost, Professor at NYU Stern School of Business & co-author of the
best-selling *Data Science for Business*

"In the past two decades the technology industry has learned what scientists have known for centuries: that controlled experiments are among the best tools to understand complex phenomena and to solve very challenging problems. The ability to design controlled experiments, run them at scale, and interpret their results is the foundation of how modern high tech businesses operate. Between them the authors have designed and implemented several of the world's most powerful experimentation platforms. This book is a great opportunity to learn from their experiences about how to use these tools and techniques."

– Kevin Scott, EVP and CTO of Microsoft

"Online experiments have fueled the success of Amazon, Microsoft, LinkedIn and other leading digital companies. This practical book gives the reader rare access to decades of experimentation experience at these companies and should be on the bookshelf of every data scientist, software engineer and product manager."

– Stefan Thomke, William Barclay Harding Professor, Harvard Business School,
Author of *Experimentation Works: The Surprising Power of Business Experiments*

"The secret sauce for a successful online business is experimentation. But it is a secret no longer. Here three masters of the art describe the ABCs of A/B testing so that you too can continuously improve your online services."

– Hal Varian, Chief Economist, Google, and author of
*Intermediate Microeconomics: A Modern Approach*

"Experiments are the best tool for online products and services. This book is full of practical knowledge derived from years of successful testing at Microsoft Google and LinkedIn. Insights and best practices are explained with real examples and pitfalls, their markers and solutions identified. I strongly recommend this book!"

– Preston McAfee, former Chief Economist and VP of Microsoft

"Experimentation is the future of digital strategy and 'Trustworthy Experiments' will be its Bible. Kohavi, Tang and Xu are three of the most noteworthy experts on experimentation working today and their book delivers a truly practical roadmap for digital experimentation that is useful right out of the box. The revealing case studies they conducted over many decades at Microsoft, Amazon, Google and LinkedIn are organized into easy to understand practical lessens with tremendous depth and clarity. It should be required reading for any manager of a digital business."

– Sinan Aral, David Austin Professor of Management,
MIT and author of *The Hype Machine*

"Indispensable for any serious experimentation practitioner, this book is highly practical and goes in-depth like I've never seen before. It's so useful it feels like you get a superpower. From statistical nuances to evaluating outcomes to measuring long term impact, this book has got you covered. Must-read."

– Peep Laja, top conversion rate expert, Founder and Principal of CXL

"Online experimentation was critical to changing the culture at Microsoft. When Satya talks about "Growth Mindset," experimentation is the best way to try new ideas and learn from them. Learning to quickly iterate controlled experiments drove Bing to profitability, and rapidly spread across Microsoft through Office, Windows, and Azure."

– Eric Boyd, Corporate VP, AI Platform, Microsoft

"As an entrepreneur, scientist, and executive I've learned (the hard way) that an ounce of data is worth a pound of my intuition. But how to get good data? This book compiles decades of experience at Amazon, Google, LinkedIn, and Microsoft into an accessible, well-organized guide. It is the bible of online experiments."

– Oren Etzioni, CEO of Allen Institute of AI and
Professor of Computer Science at University of Washington

"Internet companies have taken experimentation to an unprecedented scale, pace, and sophistication. These authors have played key roles in these developments and readers are fortunate to be able to learn from their combined experiences."

– Dean Eckles, KDD Career Development Professor in Communications and
Technology at MIT and former scientist at Facebook

"A wonderfully rich resource for a critical but under-appreciated area. Real case studies in every chapter show the inner workings and learnings of successful businesses. The focus on developing and optimizing an "Overall Evaluation Criterion" (OEC) is a particularly important lesson."

– Jeremy Howard, Singularity University, founder of fast.ai,
and former president and chief scientist of Kaggle

"There are many guides to A/B Testing, but few with the pedigree of Trustworthy Online Controlled Experiments. I've been following Ronny Kohavi for eighteen years and find his advice to be steeped in practice, honed by experience, and tempered by doing laboratory work in real world environments. When you add Diane Tang, and Ya Xu to the mix, the breadth of comprehension is unparalleled. I challenge you to compare this tome to any other - in a controlled manner, of course."

– Jim Sterne, Founder of Marketing Analytics Summit and
Director Emeritus of the Digital Analytics Association

"An extremely useful how-to book for running online experiments that combines analytical sophistication, clear exposition and the hard-won lessons of practical experience."

– Jim Manzi, Founder of Foundry.ai, Founder and former CEO and
Chairman of Applied Predictive Technologies, and author of *Uncontrolled:
The Surprising Payoff of Trial-and-Error for Business, Politics, and Society*

"Experimental design advances each time it is applied to a new domain: agriculture, chemistry, medicine and now online electronic commerce. This book by three top experts is rich in practical advice and examples covering both how and why to experiment online and not get fooled. Experiments can be expensive; not knowing what works can cost even more."

– Art Owen Professor of Statistics, Stanford University

"This is a must read book for business executives and operating managers. Just as operations, finance, accounting and strategy form the basic building blocks for business, today in the age of AI, understanding and executing online controlled experiments will be a required knowledge set. Kohavi, Tang and Xu have laid out the essentials of this new and important knowledge domain that is practically accessible."

– Karim R. Lakhani, Professor and Director of Laboratory for
Innovation Science at Harvard, Board Member, Mozilla Corp.

"Serious 'data-driven' organizations understand that analytics aren't enough; they must commit to experiment. Remarkably accessible and accessibly remarkable, this book is a manual and manifesto for high-impact experimental design. I found its pragmatism inspirational. Most importantly, it clarifies how culture rivals technical competence as a critical success factor."

– Michael Schrage, research fellow at MIT's Initiative on the
Digital Economy and author of *The Innovator's Hypothesis:
How Cheap Experiments Are Worth More than Good Ideas*

"This important book on experimentation distills the wisdom of three distinguished leaders from some of the world's biggest technology companies. If you are a software engineer, data scientist, or product manager trying to implement a data-driven culture within your organization, this is an excellent and practical book for you."

– Daniel Tunkelang, Chief Scientist at Endeca and former Director of
Data Science and Engineering at LinkedIn

"With every industry becoming digitized and data-driven, conducting and benefiting from controlled online experiments becomes a required skill. Kohavi, Tang and Yu provide a complete and well-researched guide that will become necessary reading for data practitioners and executives alike."

– Evangelos Simoudis, Co-founder and Managing Director Synapse Partners;
author of *The Big Data Opportunity in Our Driverless Future*

"The authors offer over 10 years of hard-fought lessons in experimentation, in the most strategic book for the discipline yet"

– Colin McFarland, Director Experimentation Platform at Netflix

"The practical guide to A/B testing distills the experiences from three of the top minds in experimentation practice into easy and digestible chunks of valuable and practical concepts. Each chapter walks you through some of the most important considerations when running experiments - from choosing the right metric to the benefits of institutional memory. If you are looking for an experimentation coach that balances science and practicality, then this book is for you."

– Dylan Lewis, Experimentation Leader, Intuit

"The only thing worse than no experiment is a misleading one, because it gives you false confidence! This book details the technical aspects of testing based on insights from some of the world's largest testing programs. If you're involved in online experimentation in any capacity, read it now to avoid mistakes and gain confidence in your results."

- Chris Goward, Author of *You Should Test That!*,
Founder and CEO of Widerfunnel

"This is a phenomenal book. The authors draw on a wealth of experience and have produced a readable reference that is somehow both comprehensive and detailed at the same time. Highly recommended reading for anyone who wants to run serious digital experiments."

- Pete Koomen, Co-founder, Optimizely

"The authors are pioneers of online experimentation. The platforms they've built and the experiments they've enabled have transformed some of the largest internet brands. Their research and talks have inspired teams across the industry to adopt experimentation. This book is the authoritative yet practical text that the industry has been waiting for."

– Adil Aijaz, Co-founder and CEO, Split Software

# Trustworthy Online Controlled Experiments

# Experiments

## A Practical Guide to A/B Testing

RON KOHAVI

*Microsoft*

DIANE TANG

*Google*

YA XU

*LinkedIn*

CAMBRIDGE
UNIVERSITY PRESS

# CAMBRIDGE
## UNIVERSITY PRESS

Shaftesbury Road, Cambridge CB2 8EA, United Kingdom

One Liberty Plaza, 20th Floor, New York, NY 10006, USA

477 Williamstown Road, Port Melbourne, VIC 3207, Australia

314–321, 3rd Floor, Plot 3, Splendor Forum, Jasola District Centre,
New Delhi – 110025, India

103 Penang Road, #05-06/07, Visioncrest Commercial, Singapore 238467

Cambridge University Press is part of Cambridge University Press & Assessment,
a department of the University of Cambridge.

We share the University's mission to contribute to society through the pursuit of
education, learning and research at the highest international levels of excellence.

www.cambridge.org
Information on this title: www.cambridge.org/9781108724265
DOI: 10.1017/9781108653985

First published 2020 (version 7, September 2024)

Printed in the United States of America by Books International, Virginia

*A catalogue record for this publication is available from the British Library.*

*Library of Congress Cataloging-in-Publication Data*
Names: Kohavi, Ron, author. | Tang, Diane, 1974– author. | Xu, Ya, 1982– author.
Title: Trustworthy online controlled experiments : a practical guide to A/B testing /
Ron Kohavi, Diane Tang, Ya Xu.
Description: Cambridge, United Kingdom ; New York, NY : Cambridge University Press,
2020. | Includes bibliographical references and index.
Identifiers: LCCN 2019042021 (print) | LCCN 2019042022 (ebook) | ISBN 9781108724265
(paperback) | ISBN 9781108653985 (epub)
Subjects: LCSH: Social media. | User-generated content–Social aspects.
Classification: LCC HM741 .K68 2020 (print) | LCC HM741 (ebook) | DDC 302.23/1–dc23
LC record available at https://lccn.loc.gov/2019042021
LC ebook record available at https://lccn.loc.gov/2019042022

ISBN 978-1-108-72426-5 Paperback

# Contents

*Preface – How to Read This Book*        *page* xv
*Acknowledgments*        xvii

PART I INTRODUCTORY TOPICS FOR EVERYONE    1

**1**    **Introduction and Motivation**    3
    Online Controlled Experiments Terminology    5
    Why Experiment? Correlations, Causality, and Trustworthiness    8
    Necessary Ingredients for Running Useful Controlled Experiments    10
    Tenets    11
    Improvements over Time    14
    Examples of Interesting Online Controlled Experiments    16
    Strategy, Tactics, and Their Relationship to Experiments    20
    Additional Reading    24

**2**    **Running and Analyzing Experiments: An End-to-End Example**    26
    Setting up the Example    26
    Hypothesis Testing: Establishing Statistical Significance    29
    Designing the Experiment    32
    Running the Experiment and Getting Data    34
    Interpreting the Results    34
    From Results to Decisions    36

**3**    **Twyman's Law and Experimentation Trustworthiness**    39
    Misinterpretation of the Statistical Results    40
    Confidence Intervals    43
    Threats to Internal Validity    43
    Threats to External Validity    48

|  |  |  |
|---|---|---|
| | Segment Differences | 52 |
| | Simpson's Paradox | 55 |
| | Encourage Healthy Skepticism | 57 |
| **4** | **Experimentation Platform and Culture** | 58 |
| | Experimentation Maturity Models | 58 |
| | Infrastructure and Tools | 66 |
| | PART II SELECTED TOPICS FOR EVERYONE | 79 |
| **5** | **Speed Matters: An End-to-End Case Study** | 81 |
| | Key Assumption: Local Linear Approximation | 83 |
| | How to Measure Website Performance | 84 |
| | The Slowdown Experiment Design | 86 |
| | Impact of Different Page Elements Differs | 87 |
| | Extreme Results | 89 |
| **6** | **Organizational Metrics** | 90 |
| | Metrics Taxonomy | 90 |
| | Formulating Metrics: Principles and Techniques | 94 |
| | Evaluating Metrics | 96 |
| | Evolving Metrics | 97 |
| | Additional Resources | 98 |
| | SIDEBAR: Guardrail Metrics | 98 |
| | SIDEBAR: Gameability | 100 |
| **7** | **Metrics for Experimentation and the Overall Evaluation Criterion** | 102 |
| | From Business Metrics to Metrics Appropriate for Experimentation | 102 |
| | Combining Key Metrics into an OEC | 104 |
| | Example: OEC for E-mail at Amazon | 106 |
| | Example: OEC for Bing's Search Engine | 108 |
| | Goodhart's Law, Campbell's Law, and the Lucas Critique | 109 |
| **8** | **Institutional Memory and Meta-Analysis** | 111 |
| | What Is Institutional Memory? | 111 |
| | Why Is Institutional Memory Useful? | 112 |
| **9** | **Ethics in Controlled Experiments** | 116 |
| | Background | 116 |
| | Data Collection | 121 |
| | Culture and Processes | 122 |
| | SIDEBAR: User Identifiers | 123 |

PART III COMPLEMENTARY AND ALTERNATIVE
TECHNIQUES TO CONTROLLED EXPERIMENTS                     125

10   **Complementary Techniques**                          127
     The Space of Complementary Techniques               127
     Logs-based Analysis                                 128
     Human Evaluation                                    130
     User Experience Research (UER)                      131
     Focus Groups                                        132
     Surveys                                             132
     External Data                                       133
     Putting It All Together                             135

11   **Observational Causal Studies**                     137
     When Controlled Experiments Are Not Possible        137
     Designs for Observational Causal Studies            139
     Pitfalls                                            144
     SIDEBAR: Refuted Observational Causal Studies       147

PART IV ADVANCED TOPICS FOR BUILDING AN
EXPERIMENTATION PLATFORM                                 151

12   **Client-Side Experiments**                          153
     Differences between Server and Client Side          153
     Implications for Experiments                        156
     Conclusions                                         161

13   **Instrumentation**                                  162
     Client-Side vs. Server-Side Instrumentation         162
     Processing Logs from Multiple Sources               164
     Culture of Instrumentation                          165

14   **Choosing a Randomization Unit**                    166
     Randomization Unit and Analysis Unit                168
     User-level Randomization                            169

15   **Ramping Experiment Exposure: Trading Off Speed,
     Quality, and Risk**                                 171
     What Is Ramping?                                    171
     SQR Ramping Framework                               172
     Four Ramp Phases                                    173
     Post Final Ramp                                     176

16   **Scaling Experiment Analyses**                                177
     Data Processing                                                177
     Data Computation                                               178
     Results Summary and Visualization                             180

     PART V ADVANCED TOPICS FOR ANALYZING
     EXPERIMENTS                                                    183

17   **The Statistics behind Online Controlled Experiments**       185
     Two-Sample t-Test                                              185
     p-Value and Confidence Interval                               186
     Normality Assumption                                          187
     Type I/II Errors and Power                                    189
     Bias                                                          191
     Multiple Testing                                              191
     Fisher's Meta-analysis                                        192

18   **Variance Estimation and Improved Sensitivity: Pitfalls
     and Solutions**                                               193
     Common Pitfalls                                               193
     Improving Sensitivity                                         196
     Variance of Other Statistics                                  198

19   **The A/A Test**                                              200
     Why A/A Tests?                                                200
     How to Run A/A Tests                                          205
     When the A/A Test Fails                                       207

20   **Triggering for Improved Sensitivity**                       209
     Examples of Triggering                                        209
     A Numerical Example (Kohavi, Longbotham et al. 2009)          212
     Optimal and Conservative Triggering                           213
     Overall Treatment Effect                                      214
     Trustworthy Triggering                                        215
     Common Pitfalls                                               216
     Open Questions                                                217

21   **Sample Ratio Mismatch and Other Trust-Related
     Guardrail Metrics**                                           219
     Sample Ratio Mismatch                                         219
     Debugging SRMs                                                222

| 22 | **Leakage and Interference between Variants** | 226 |
| | Examples | 227 |
| | Some Practical Solutions | 230 |
| | Detecting and Monitoring Interference | 234 |
| 23 | **Measuring Long-Term Treatment Effects** | 235 |
| | What Are Long-Term Effects? | 235 |
| | Reasons the Treatment Effect May Differ between Short-Term and Long-Term | 236 |
| | Why Measure Long-Term Effects? | 238 |
| | Long-Running Experiments | 239 |
| | Alternative Methods for Long-Running Experiments | 241 |
| | *References* | 246 |
| | *Index* | 266 |

# Preface

## *How to Read This Book*

*If we have data, let's look at data.*
*If all we have are opinions, let's go with mine*
                              *— Jim Barksdale, Former CEO of Netscape*

Our goal in writing this book is to share practical lessons from decades of experience running online controlled experiments at scale at Amazon and Microsoft (Ron), Google (Diane), and Microsoft and LinkedIn (Ya). While we are writing this book in our capacity as individuals and not as representatives of Google, LinkedIn, or Microsoft, we have distilled key lessons and pitfalls encountered over the years and provide guidance for both software platforms and the corporate cultural aspects of using online controlled experiments to establish a data-driven culture that informs rather than relies on the HiPPO (Highest Paid Person's Opinion) (R. Kohavi, HiPPO FAQ 2019). We believe many of these lessons apply in the online setting, to large or small companies, or even teams and organizations within a company. A concern we share is the need to evaluate the trustworthiness of experiment results. We believe in the skepticism implied by Twyman's Law: *Any figure that looks interesting or different is usually wrong*; we encourage readers to double-check results and run validity tests, especially for breakthrough positive results. Getting numbers is easy; getting numbers you can trust is hard!

Part I is designed to be read by everyone, regardless of background, and consists of four chapters.

- Chapter 1 is an overview of the benefits of running online controlled experiments and introduces experiment terminology.
- Chapter 2 uses an example to run through the process of running an experiment end-to-end.
- Chapter 3 describes common pitfalls and how to build experimentation trustworthiness, and

- Chapter 4 overviews what it takes to build an experiment platform and scale online experimentation.

Parts II through V can be consumed by everyone as needed but are written with a focus on a specific audience. Part II contains five chapters on fundamentals, such as Organizational Metrics. The topics in Part II are recommended for everyone, especially leaders and executives. Part III contains two chapters that introduce techniques to complement online controlled experiments that leaders, data scientists, engineers, analysts, product managers, and others would find useful for guiding resources and time investment. Part IV focuses on building an experimentation platform and is aimed toward engineers. Finally, Part V digs into advanced analysis topics and is geared toward data scientists.

Our website, https://experimentguide.com, is a companion to this book. It contains additional material, errata, and provides an area for open discussion. The authors intend to donate all proceeds from this book to charity.

# Acknowledgments

We would like to thank our colleagues who have worked with us throughout the years. While too numerous to name individually, this book is based on our combined work, as well as others throughout the industry and beyond researching and conducting online controlled experiments. We learned a great deal from you all, thank you.

On writing the book, we'd like to call out Lauren Cowles, our editor, for partnering with us throughout this process. Cherie Woodward provided great line editing and style guidance to help mesh our three voices. Stephanie Grey worked with us on all diagrams and figures, improving them in the process. Kim Vernon provided final copy-editing and bibliography checks.

Most importantly, we owe a deep debt of gratitude to our families, as we missed time with them to work on this book. Thank you to Ronny's family: Yael, Oren, Ittai, and Noga, to Diane's family: Ben, Emma, and Leah, and to Ya's family: Thomas, Leray, and Tavis. We could not have written this book without your support and enthusiasm!

**Google:** Hal Varian, Dan Russell, Carrie Grimes, Niall Cardin, Deirdre O'Brien, Henning Hohnhold, Mukund Sundararajan, Amir Najmi, Patrick Riley, Eric Tassone, Jen Gennai, Shannon Vallor, Eric Miraglia, David Price, Crystal Dahlen, Tammy Jih Murray, Lanah Donnelly and all who work on experiments at Google.

**LinkedIn:** Stephen Lynch, Yav Bojinov, Jiada Liu, Weitao Duan, Nanyu Chen, Guillaume Saint-Jacques, Elaine Call, Min Liu, Arun Swami, Kiran Prasad, Igor Perisic, and the entire Experimentation team.

**Microsoft:** Omar Alonso, Benjamin Arai, Jordan Atlas, Richa Bhayani, Eric Boyd, Johnny Chan, Alex Deng, Andy Drake, Aleksander Fabijan, Brian Frasca, Scott Gude, Somit Gupta, Adam Gustafson, Tommy Guy, Randy Henne, Edward Jezierski, Jing Jin, Dongwoo Kim, Waldo Kuipers, Jonathan Litz, Sophia Liu, Jiannan Lu, Qi Lu, Daniel Miller, Carl Mitchell, Nils

Pohlmann, Wen Qin, Thomas Schreiter, Harry Shum, Dan Sommerfield, Garnet Vaz, Toby Walker, Michele Zunker, and the Analysis & Experimentation team.

Special thanks to Maria Stone and Marcus Persson for feedback throughout the book, and Michelle N. Meyer for expert feedback on the ethics chapter

Others who have given feedback include: Adil Aijaz, Jonas Alves, Alon Amit, Kevin Anderson, Joel Barajas, Houman Bedayat, Beau Bender, Bahador Biglari, Stuart Buck, Jike Chong, Jed Chou, Pavel Dmitriev, Yurong Fan, Georgi Georgiev, Ilias Gerostathopoulos. Matt Gershoff, William Grosso, Aditya Gupta, Rajesh Gupta, Shilpa Gupta, Kris Jack, Jacob Jarnvall, Dave Karow, Slawek Kierner, Pete Koomen, Dylan Lewis, Bryan Liu, David Manheim, Colin McFarland, Tanapol Nearunchron, Dheeraj Ravindranath, Aaditya Ramdas, Andre Richter, Jianhong Shen, Gang Su, Anthony Tang, Lukas Vermeer, Rowel Willems, Yu Yang, and Yufeng Wang.

Thank you to the many who helped who are not named explicitly.

# PART I

Introductory Topics for Everyone

# 1

# Introduction and Motivation

One accurate measurement is worth more than a thousand expert opinions
– *Admiral Grace Hopper*

In 2012, an employee working on Bing, Microsoft's search engine, suggested changing how ad headlines display (Kohavi and Thomke 2017). The idea was to lengthen the title line of ads by combining it with the text from the first line below the title, as shown in Figure 1.1.

Nobody thought this simple change, among the hundreds suggested, would be the best revenue-generating idea in Bing's history!

The feature was prioritized low and languished in the backlog for more than six months until a software developer decided to try the change, given how easy it was to code. He implemented the idea and began evaluating the idea on real users, randomly showing some of them the new title layout and others the old one. User interactions with the website were recorded, including ad clicks and the revenue generated from them. This is an example of an A/B test, the simplest type of controlled experiment that compares two variants: A and B, or a *Control and a Treatment*.

A few hours after starting the test, a revenue-too-high alert triggered, indicating that something was wrong with the experiment. The Treatment, that is, the new title layout, was generating too much money from ads. Such "too good to be true" alerts are very useful, as they usually indicate a serious bug, such as cases where revenue was logged twice (double billing) or where only ads displayed, and the rest of the web page was broken.

For this experiment, however, the revenue increase was valid. Bing's revenue increased by a whopping 12%, which at the time translated to over $100M annually in the US alone, without significantly hurting key user-experience metrics. The experiment was replicated multiple times over a long period.

3

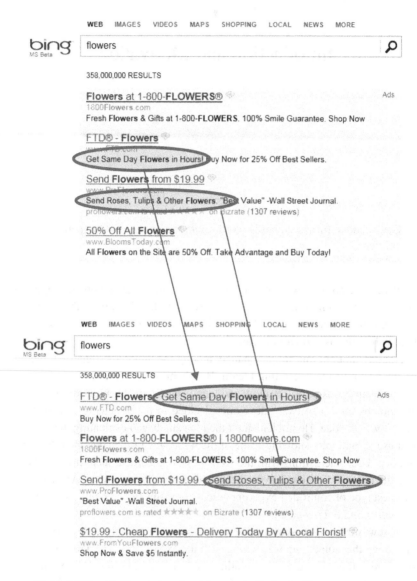

Figure 1.1  An experiment changing the way ads display on Bing

The example typifies several key themes in online controlled experiments:

- It is hard to assess the value of an idea. In this case, a simple change worth over $100M/year was delayed for months.
- Small changes can have a big impact. A $100M/year return-on-investment (ROI) on a few days' work for one engineer is about as extreme as it gets.

- Experiments with big impact are rare. Bing runs over 10,000 experiments a year, but simple features resulting in such a big improvement happen only once every few years.
- The overhead of running an experiment must be small. Bing's engineers had access to ExP, Microsoft's experimentation system, which made it easy to scientifically evaluate the idea.
- The overall evaluation criterion (OEC, described more later in this chapter) must be clear. In this case, revenue was a key component of the OEC, but revenue alone is insufficient as an OEC. It could lead to plastering the web site with ads, which is known to hurt the user experience. Bing uses an OEC that weighs revenue against user-experience metrics, including Sessions per user (are users abandoning or increasing engagement) and several other components. The key point is that user-experience metrics did not significantly degrade even though revenue increased dramatically.

The next section introduces the terminology of controlled experiments.

## Online Controlled Experiments Terminology

Controlled experiments have a long and fascinating history, which we share online (Kohavi, Tang and Xu 2019). They are sometimes called A/B tests, A/B/n tests (to emphasize multiple variants), field experiments, randomized controlled experiments, split tests, bucket tests, and flights. In this book, we use the terms *controlled experiments* and *A/B tests* interchangeably, regardless of the number of variants.

Online controlled experiments are used heavily at companies like Airbnb, Amazon, Booking.com, eBay, Facebook, Google, LinkedIn, Lyft, Microsoft, Netflix, Twitter, Uber, Yahoo!/Oath, and Yandex (Gupta et al. 2019). These companies run thousands to tens of thousands of experiments every year, sometimes involving millions of users and testing everything, including changes to the user interface (UI), relevance algorithms (search, ads, personalization, recommendations, and so on), latency/performance, content management systems, customer support systems, and more. Experiments are run on multiple channels: websites, desktop applications, mobile applications, and e-mail.

In the most common online controlled experiments, users are randomly split between variants in a persistent manner (a user receives the same variant in multiple visits). In our opening example from Bing, the Control was the original display of ads and the Treatment was the display of ads with longer

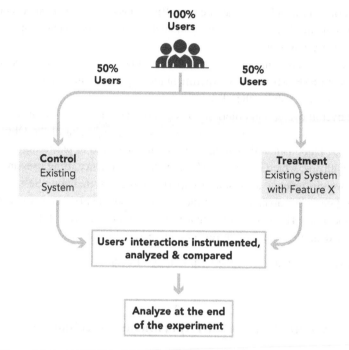

Figure 1.2 A simple controlled experiment: An A/B Test

titles. The users' interactions with the Bing web site were instrumented, that is, monitored and logged. From the logged data, metrics are computed, which allowed us to assess the difference between the variants for each metric.

In the simplest controlled experiments, there are two variants: Control (A) and Treatment (B), as shown in Figure 1.2.

We follow the terminology of Kohavi and Longbottom (2017), and Kohavi, Longbottom et al. (2009) and provide related terms from other fields below. You can find many other resources on experimentation and A/B testing at the end of this chapter under Additional Reading.

**Overall Evaluation Criterion (OEC):** A quantitative measure of the experiment's objective. For example, your OEC might be active days per user, indicating the number of days during the experiment that users were active (i.e., they visited and took some action). Increasing this OEC implies that users are visiting your site more often, which is a great outcome. The OEC must be measurable in the short term (the duration of an experiment) yet believed to causally drive long-term strategic objectives (see *Strategy, Tactics, and their Relationship to Experiments* later in this chapter and Chapter 7). In the case of a search engine, the OEC can be a combination of usage (e.g., sessions-per-user), relevance (e.g., successful sessions, time to success), and advertisement revenue (not all search engines use all of these metrics or only these metrics).

In statistics, this is often called the *Response* or *Dependent* variable (Mason, Gunst and Hess 1989, Box, Hunter and Hunter 2005); other synonyms are *Outcome*, *Evaluation* and *Fitness Function* (Quarto-vonTivadar 2006). Experiments can have multiple objectives and analysis can use a balanced scorecard approach (Kaplan and Norton 1996), although selecting a single metric, possibly as a weighted combination of such objectives is highly desired and recommended (Roy 2001, 50, 405−429).

We take a deeper dive into determining the OEC for experiments in Chapter 7.

**Parameter:** A controllable experimental variable that is thought to influence the OEC or other metrics of interest. Parameters are sometimes called *factors* or *variables*. Parameters are assigned *values*, also called *levels*. In simple A/B tests, there is commonly a single parameter with two values. In the online world, it is common to use univariable designs with multiple values (such as, A/B/C/D). Multivariable tests, also called *Multivariate Tests* (MVTs), evaluate multiple parameters (variables) together, such as font color and font size, allowing experimenters to discover a global optimum when parameters interact (see Chapter 4).

**Variant:** A user experience being tested, typically by assigning values to parameters. In a simple A/B test, A and B are the two variants, usually called Control and Treatment. In some literature, a variant only means a Treatment; we consider the Control to be a special variant: the existing version on which to run the comparison. For example, in case of a bug discovered in the experiment, you would abort the experiment and ensure that all users are assigned to the Control variant.

**Randomization Unit:** A pseudo-randomization (e.g., hashing) process is applied to units (e.g., users or pages) to map them to variants. Proper randomization is important to ensure that the populations assigned to the different variants are similar statistically, allowing causal effects to be determined with high probability. You must map units to variants in a persistent and independent manner (i.e., if user is the randomization unit, a user should consistently see the same experience, and the assignment of a user to a variant should not tell you anything about the assignment of a different user to its variant). It is very common, and we highly recommend, to use *users* as a randomization unit when running controlled experiments for online audiences. Some experimental designs choose to randomize by pages, sessions, or user-day (i.e., the experiment remains consistent for the user for each 24-hour window determined by the server). See Chapter 14 for more information.

Proper randomization is critical! If the experimental design assigns an equal percentage of users to each variant, then each user should have an equal chance of being assigned to each variant. Do not take randomization lightly. The examples below demonstrate the challenge and importance of proper randomization.

- The RAND corporation needed random numbers for Monte Carlo methods in the 1940s, so they created a book of a million random digits generated using a pulse machine. However, due to skews in the hardware, the original table was found to have significant biases and the digits had to re-randomized in a new edition of the book (RAND 1955).
- Controlled experiments were initially used in medical domains. The US Veterans Administration (VA) conducted an experiment (drug trial) of streptomycin for tuberculosis, but the trials failed because physicians introduced biases and influenced the selection process (Marks 1997). Similar trials in Great Britain were done with blind protocols and were successful, creating what is now called a watershed moment in controlled trials (Doll 1998).

No factor should be allowed to influence variant assignment. Users (units) cannot be distributed "any old which way" (Weiss 1997). It is important to note that random does not mean "haphazard or unplanned, but a deliberate choice based on probabilities" (Mosteller, Gilbert and McPeek 1983). Senn (2012) discusses some myths of randomization.

## Why Experiment? Correlations, Causality, and Trustworthiness

Let's say you're working for a subscription business like Netflix, where X% of users churn (end their subscription) every month. You decide to introduce a new feature and observe that churn rate for users using that feature is X%/2, that is, half. You might be tempted to claim causality; the feature is reducing churn by half. This leads to the conclusion that if we make the feature more discoverable and used more often, subscriptions will soar. Wrong! Given the data, no conclusion can be drawn about whether the feature reduces or increases user churn, and both are possible.

An example demonstrating this fallacy comes from Microsoft Office 365, another subscription business. Office 365 users that see error messages and experience crashes have lower churn rates, but that does not mean that Office 365 should show more error messages or that Microsoft should lower code

Figure 1.3 A simple hierarchy of evidence for assessing the quality of trial design (Greenhalgh 2014)

quality, causing more crashes. It turns out that all three events are caused by a single factor: usage. Heavy users of the product see more error messages, experience more crashes, and have lower churn rates. Correlation does not imply causality and overly relying on these observations leads to faulty decisions.

In 1995, Guyatt et al. (1995) introduced the hierarchy of evidence as a way to grade recommendations in medical literature, which Greenhalgh expanded on in her discussions on practicing evidence-based medicine (1997, 2014). Figure 1.3 shows a simple hierarchy of evidence, translated to our terminology, based on Bailar (1983, 1). Randomized controlled experiments are the gold standard for establishing causality. Systematic reviews, that is, meta-analysis, of controlled experiments provides more evidence and generalizability.

More complex models, such as the *Levels of Evidence* by the Oxford Centre for Evidence-based Medicine are also available (2009).

The experimentation platforms used by our companies allow experimenters at Google, LinkedIn, and Microsoft to run tens of thousands of online controlled experiments a year with a high degree of trust in the results. We believe online controlled experiments are:

- The best scientific way to establish causality with high probability.
- Able to detect small changes that are harder to detect with other techniques, such as changes over time (sensitivity).

- Able to detect unexpected changes. Often underappreciated, but many experiments uncover surprising impacts on other metrics, be it performance degradation, increased crashes/errors, or cannibalizing clicks from other features.

A key focus of this book is highlighting potential pitfalls in experiments and suggesting methods that improve trust in results. Online controlled experiments provide an unparalleled ability to electronically collect reliable data at scale, randomize well, and avoid or detect pitfalls (see Chapter 11). We recommend using other, less trustworthy, methods, including observational studies, when online controlled experiments are not possible.

## Necessary Ingredients for Running Useful Controlled Experiments

Not every decision can be made with the scientific rigor of a controlled experiment. For example, you cannot run a controlled experiment on mergers and acquisitions (M&A), as we cannot have both the merger/acquisition and its counterfactual (no such event) happening concurrently. We now review the necessary technical ingredients for running useful controlled experiments (Kohavi, Crook and Longbotham 2009), followed by organizational tenets. In Chapter 4, we cover the experimentation maturity model.

1. There are experimental units (e.g., users) that can be assigned to different variants with no interference (or little interference); for example, users in Treatment do not impact users in Control (see Chapter 22).
2. There are enough experimental units (e.g., users). For controlled experiments to be useful, we recommend thousands of experimental units: the larger the number, the smaller the effects that can be detected. The good news is that even small software startups typically get enough users quickly and can start to run controlled experiments, initially looking for big effects. As the business grows, it becomes more important to detect smaller changes (e.g., large web sites must be able to detect small changes to key metrics impacting user experience and fractions of a percent change to revenue), and the sensitivity improves with a growing user base.
3. Key metrics, ideally an OEC, are agreed upon and can be practically evaluated. If the goals are too hard to measure, it is important to agree on surrogates (see Chapter 7). Reliable data can be collected, ideally cheaply and broadly. In software, it is usually easy to log system events and user actions (see Chapter 13).

4. Changes are easy to make. Software is typically easier to change than hardware; but even in software, some domains require a certain level of quality assurance. Changes to a recommendation algorithm are easy to make and evaluate; changes to software in airplane flight control systems require a whole different approval process by the Federal Aviation Administration (FAA). Server-side software is much easier to change than client-side (see Chapter 12), which is why calling services from client software is becoming more common, enabling upgrades and changes to the services to be done more quickly and using controlled experiments.

Most non-trivial online services meet, or could meet, the necessary ingredients for running an agile development process based on controlled experiments. Many implementations of software+services could also meet the requirements relatively easily. Thomke wrote that organizations will recognize maximal benefits from experimentation when it is used in conjunction with an "innovation system" (Thomke 2003). Agile software development is such an innovation system.

When controlled experiments are not possible, modeling could be done, and other experimental techniques might be used (see Chapter 10). The key is that if controlled experiments can be run, they provide the most reliable and sensitive mechanism to evaluate changes.

## Tenets

There are three key tenets for organizations that wish to run online controlled experiments (Kohavi et al. 2013):

1. The organization wants to make data-driven decisions and has formalized an OEC.
2. The organization is willing to invest in the infrastructure and tests to run controlled experiments and ensure that the results are trustworthy.
3. The organization recognizes that it is poor at assessing the value of ideas.

### Tenet 1: The Organization Wants to Make Data-Driven Decisions and Has Formalized an OEC

You will rarely hear someone at the head of an organization say that they don't want to be data-driven (with the notable exception of Apple under Steve Jobs, where Ken Segall claimed that "we didn't test a single ad. Not for print, TV, billboards, the web, retail, or anything" (Segall 2012, 42). But measuring the incremental benefit to users from new features has cost, and objective measurements typically show that progress is not as rosy as initially envisioned. Many organizations will not spend the resources required to define and measure progress. It is often easier to generate a plan, execute against it, and declare success, with the key metric being: "percent of plan delivered," ignoring whether the feature has any positive impact to key metrics.

To be data-driven, an organization should define an OEC that can be easily measured over relatively short durations (e.g., one to two weeks). Large organizations may have multiple OECs or several key metrics that are shared with refinements for different areas. The hard part is finding metrics measurable in a short period, sensitive enough to show differences, and that are predictive of long-term goals. For example, "Profit" is not a good OEC, as short-term theatrics (e.g., raising prices) can increase short-term profit, but may hurt it in the long run. Customer lifetime value is a strategically powerful OEC (Kohavi, Longbottom et al. 2009). We cannot overemphasize the importance of agreeing on a good OEC that your organization can align behind; see Chapter 6.

The terms "data-informed" or "data-aware" are sometimes used to avoid the implication that a single source of data (e.g., a controlled experiment) "drives" the decisions (King, Churchill and Tan 2017, Knapp et al. 2006). We use data-driven and data-informed as synonyms in this book. Ultimately, a decision should be made with many sources of data, including controlled experiments, surveys, estimates of maintenance costs for the new code, and so on. A data-driven or a data-informed organization gathers relevant data to drive a decision and inform the HiPPO (Highest Paid Person's Opinion) rather than relying on intuition (Kohavi 2019).

## Tenet 2: The Organization Is Willing to Invest in the Infrastructure and Tests to Run Controlled Experiments and Ensure That Their Results Are Trustworthy

In the online software domain (websites, mobile, desktop applications, and services) the necessary conditions for controlled experiments can be met through software engineering work (see *Necessary Ingredients for Running Useful Controlled Experiments*): it is possible to reliably randomize users; it is possible to collect telemetry; and it is relatively easy to introduce software changes, such as new features (see Chapter 4). Even relatively small websites have enough users to run the necessary statistical tests (Kohavi, Crook and Longbotham 2009).

Controlled experiments are especially useful in combination with Agile software development (Martin 2008, K. S. Rubin 2012), Customer Development process (Blank 2005), and MVPs (Minimum Viable Products), as popularized by Eric Ries in *The Lean Startup* (Ries 2011).

In other domains, it may be hard or impossible to reliably run controlled experiments. Some interventions required for controlled experiments in medical domains may be unethical or illegal. Hardware devices may have long lead times for manufacturing and modifications are difficult, so controlled experiments with users are rarely run on new hardware devices (e.g., new mobile phones). In these situations, other techniques, such as *Complementary Techniques* (see Chapter 10 ), may be required when controlled experiments cannot be run.

Assuming you can run controlled experiments, it is important to ensure their trustworthiness. When running online experiments, getting numbers is easy; getting numbers you can trust is hard. Chapter 3 is dedicated to trustworthy results.

### Tenet 3: The Organization Recognizes That It Is Poor at Assessing the Value of Ideas

Features are built because teams believe they are useful, yet in many domains most ideas fail to improve key metrics. Only one third of the ideas tested at Microsoft improved the metric(s) they were designed to improve (Kohavi, Crook and Longbotham 2009). Success is even harder to find in well-optimized domains like Bing and Google, whereby some measures' success rate is about 10–20% (Manzi 2012).

Fareed Mosavat, Slack's Director of Product and Lifecycle tweeted that with all of Slack's experience, only about 30% of monetization experiments show positive results; "if you are on an experiment-driven team, get used to, at best, 70% of your work being thrown away. Build your processes accordingly" (Mosavat 2019).

Avinash Kaushik wrote in his Experimentation and Testing primer (Kaushik 2006) that "80% of the time you/we are wrong about what a customer wants." Mike Moran (Moran 2007, 240) wrote that Netflix considers 90% of what they try to be wrong. Regis Hadiaris from Quicken Loans wrote that "in the five years I've been running tests, I'm only about as correct in guessing the results as a major league baseball player is in hitting the ball. That's right – I've been doing this for 5 years, and I can only 'guess' the outcome of a test about 33% of the time!" (Moran 2008). Dan McKinley at Etsy (McKinley 2013) wrote "nearly everything fails" and for features, he wrote "it's been humbling to realize how rare it is for them to succeed on the first attempt. I strongly suspect that this experience is universal, but it is not universally recognized or acknowledged." Finally, Colin McFarland wrote in the book *Experiment!* (McFarland 2012, 20) "No matter how much you think it's a no-brainer, how much research you've done, or how many competitors are doing it, sometimes, more often than you might think, experiment ideas simply fail."

Not every domain has such poor statistics, but most who have run controlled experiments in customer-facing websites and applications have experienced this humbling reality: *we are poor at assessing the value of ideas.*

## Improvements over Time

In practice, improvements to key metrics are achieved by many small changes: 0.1% to 2%. Many experiments only impact a segment of users, so you must dilute the impact of a 5% improvement for 10% of your users, which results in a much smaller impact (e.g., 0.5% if the *triggered* population is similar to the rest of the users); see Chapter 3. As Al Pacino says in the movie *Any Given Sunday*, "...winning is done inch by inch."

## Google Ads Example

In 2011, Google launched an improved ad ranking mechanism after over a year of development and incremental experiments (Google 2011). Engineers developed and experimented with new and improved models for measuring the quality score of ads within the existing ad ranking mechanism, as well as with changes to the ad auction itself. They ran hundreds of controlled experiments and multiple iterations; some across all markets, and some long term in specific markets to understand the impact on advertisers in more depth. This large backend change – and running controlled experiments – ultimately validated how planning multiple changes and layering them together improved the user's experience by providing higher quality ads, and improved their advertiser's experience moving towards lower average prices for the higher quality ads.

## Bing Relevance Example

The Relevance team at Bing consists of several hundred people tasked with improving a single OEC metric by 2% every year. The 2% is the sum of the Treatment effects (i.e., the delta of the OEC) in all controlled experiments that shipped to users over the year, assuming they are additive. Because the team runs thousands of experiment Treatments, and some may appear positive by chance (Lee and Shen 2018), credit towards the 2% is assigned based on a replication experiment: once the implementation of an idea is successful, possibly after multiple iterations and refinements, a *certification* experiment is run with a single Treatment. The Treatment effect of this certification experiment determines the credit towards the 2% goal. Recent development suggests shrinking the Treatment effect to improve precision (Coey and Cunningham 2019).

## Bing Ads Example

The Ads team at Bing has consistently grown revenue 15−25% per year (eMarketer 2016), but most improvements were done inch-by-inch. Every month a "package" was shipped, the results of many experiments, as shown in Figure 1.4. Most improvements were small, some monthly packages were even known to be negative, as a result of space constraints or legal requirements.

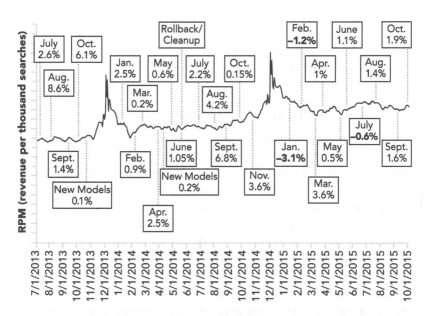

(*) Numbers have been perturbed for obvious reasons

Figure 1.4 Bing Ad Revenue over Time (y-axis represents about 20% growth/ year). The specific numbers are not important

It is informative to see the seasonality spikes around December when purchase intent by users rises dramatically, so ad space is increased, and revenue per thousand searches increases.

## Examples of Interesting Online Controlled Experiments

Interesting experiments are ones where the absolute difference between the expected outcome and the actual result is large. If you thought something was going to happen and it happened, then you haven't learned much. If you thought something was going to happen and it didn't, then you've learned something important. And if you thought something minor was going to happen, and the results are a major surprise and lead to a breakthrough, you've learned something highly valuable.

The Bing example at the beginning of this chapter and those in this section are uncommon successes with surprising, highly positive, results. Bing's attempt to integrate with social networks, such as Facebook and Twitter, are an example of expecting a strong result and not seeing it – the effort was abandoned after many experiments showed no value for two years.

While sustained progress is a matter of continued experimentation and many small improvements, as shown in the section *Bing Ads Example*, here are several examples highlighting large surprising effects that stress how poorly we assess the value of ideas.

## UI Example: 41 Shades of Blue

Small design decisions can have significant impact, as both Google and Microsoft have consistently shown. Google tested 41 gradations of blue on Google search results pages (Holson 2009), frustrating the visual design lead at the time. However, Google's tweaks to the color scheme ended up being substantially positive on user engagement (note that Google does not report on the results of individual changes) and led to a strong partnership between design and experimentation moving forward. Microsoft's Bing color tweaks similarly showed that users were more successful at completing tasks, their time-to-success improved, and monetization improved to the tune of over \$10 M annually in the United States (Kohavi et al. 2014, Kohavi and Thomke 2017).

While these are great examples of tiny changes causing massive impact, given that a wide sweep of colors was done, it is unlikely that playing around with colors in additional experiments will yield more significant improvements.

You could save $30 today with the Amazon Visa® Card:

Your current subtotal:     $32.20
Amazon Visa discount: - $30.00     ● Find out how
Your new subtotal:     $2.20

Save $30 off your first purchase, earn 3% rewards, get a 0% APR*, and pay no annual fee.

Figure 1.5  Amazon's credit card offer with savings on cart total

## Making an Offer at the Right Time

In 2004, Amazon placed a credit-card offer on the home page. It was highly profitable but had a very low click-through rate (CTR). The team ran an experiment to move the offer to the shopping cart page that the user sees after adding an item, showing simple math highlighting the savings the user would receive, as shown in Figure 1.5 (Kohavi et al. 2014).

Since users adding an item to the shopping cart have clear purchase intent, this offer displays at the right time. The controlled experiment demonstrated that this simple change increased Amazon's annual profit by tens of millions of dollars.

## Personalized Recommendations

Greg Linden at Amazon created a prototype to display personalized recom-mendations based on items in the user's shopping cart (Linden 2006, Kohavi, Longbottom et al. 2009). When you add an item, recommendations come up; add another item, new recommendations show up. Linden notes that while the prototype looked promising, "a marketing senior vice-president was dead set against it," claiming it would distract people from checking out. Greg was "forbidden to work on this any further." Nonetheless, he ran a controlled experiment, and the "feature won by such a wide margin that not having it live was costing Amazon a noticeable chunk of change. With new urgency, shopping cart recommendations launched." Now multiple sites use cart recommendations.

## Speed Matters a LOT

In 2012, an engineer at Microsoft's Bing made a change to the way JavaScript was generated, which shortened the HTML sent to clients significantly, resulting in improved performance. The controlled experiment showed a surprising number of improved metrics. They conducted a follow-on experiment to estimate the impact on server performance. The result showed that performance improvements also significantly improve key user metrics, such as success rate and time-to-success, and each 10 millisecond performance improvement (1/30th of the speed of an eye blink) pays for the fully loaded annual cost of an engineer (Kohavi et al. 2013).

By 2015, as Bing's performance improved, there were questions about whether there was still value to performance improvements when the server was returning results in under a second at the 95th percentile (i.e., for 95% of the queries). The team at Bing conducted a follow-on study and key user metrics still improve significantly. While the relative impact on revenue was somewhat reduced, Bing's revenue improved so much during the time that each millisecond in improved performance was worth more than in the past; every four milliseconds of improvement funded an engineer for a year! See Chapter 5 for in-depth review of this experiment and the criticality of performance.

Performance experiments were done at multiple companies with results indicating how critical performance is. At Amazon, a 100-millisecond slow-down experiment decreased sales by 1% (Linden 2006b, 10). A joint talk by speakers from Bing and Google (Schurman and Brutlag 2009) showed the significant impact of performance on key metrics, including distinct queries, revenue, clicks, satisfaction, and time-to-click.

## Malware Reduction

Ads are a lucrative business and "freeware" installed by users often contains malware that pollutes pages with ads. Figure 1.6 shows what a resulting page from Bing looked like to a user with malware. Note that multiple ads (high-lighted in red) were added to the page (Kohavi et al. 2014).

Not only were Bing ads removed, depriving Microsoft of revenue, but low-quality ads and often irrelevant ads displayed, providing a poor user experience for users who might not have realized why they were seeing so many ads.

Microsoft ran a controlled experiment with 3.8 million users potentially impacted, where basic routines that modify the DOM (Document Object Model) were overridden to allow only limited modifications from trusted sources (Kohavi et al. 2014). The results showed improvements to all of Bing's key metrics, including Sessions per user, indicating that users visited more often or churned less. In addition, users were more successful in their searches, quicker to click on useful links, and annual revenue improved by several million dollars. Also, page-load time, a key performance metric we previously discussed, improved by hundreds of milliseconds for the impacted pages.

Figure 1.6  Bing page when the user has malware shows multiple ads

## Backend Changes

Backend algorithmic changes are often overlooked as an area to use controlled experiments (Kohavi, Longbottom et al. 2009), but it can yield significant results. We can see this both from how teams at Google, LinkedIn, and Microsoft work on many incremental small changes, as we described above, and in this example involving Amazon.

Back in 2004, there already existed a good algorithm for making recommendations based on two sets. The signature feature for Amazon's

Figure 1.7 Amazon search for "24" with and without BBS

recommendation was "People who bought item X bought item Y," but this was generalized to "People who *viewed* item X bought item Y" and "People who viewed item X *viewed* item Y." A proposal was made to use the same algorithm for "People who *searched* for X bought item Y." Proponents of the algorithm gave examples of underspecified searches, such as "24," which most people associate with the TV show starring Kiefer Sutherland. Amazon's search was returning poor results (left in Figure 1.7), such as CDs with 24 Italian Songs, clothing for 24-month old toddlers, a 24-inch towel bar, and so on. The new algorithm gave top-notch results (right in Figure 1.7), returning DVDs for the show and related books, based on what items people actually purchased after searching for "24." One weakness of the algorithm was that some items surfaced that did not contain the words in the search phrase; however, Amazon ran a controlled experiment, and despite this weakness, this change increased Amazon's overall revenue by 3% – hundreds of millions of dollars.

## Strategy, Tactics, and Their Relationship to Experiments

When the necessary ingredients for running online controlled experiments are met, we strongly believe they should be run to inform organizational decisions at all levels from strategy to tactics.

Strategy (Porter 1996, 1998) and controlled experiments are synergistic. David Collis of Lean Strategy wrote that "rather than suppressing entrepreneurial behavior, effective strategy encourages it – by identifying the bounds within which innovation and experimentation should take place" (Collis 2016). He defines a *lean strategy process*, which guards against the extremes of both rigid planning and unrestrained experimentation.

Well-run experiments with appropriate metrics complement business strategy, product design, and improve operational effectiveness by making the organization more data driven. By encapsulating strategy into an OEC, controlled experiments can provide a great feedback loop for the strategy. Are the ideas evaluated with experiments improving the OEC sufficiently? Alternatively, surprising results from experiments can shine a light on alternative strategic opportunities, leading to pivots in those directions (Ries 2011). Product design decisions are important for coherency and trying multiple design variants provides a useful feedback loop to the designers. Finally, many tactical changes can improve the operational effectiveness, defined by Porter as "performing similar activities better than rivals perform them" (Porter 1996).

We now review two key scenarios.

### Scenario 1: You Have a Business Strategy and You Have a Product with Enough Users to Experiment

In this scenario, experiments can help hill-climb to a local optimum based on your current strategy and product:

- Experiments can help identify areas with high ROI: those that improve the OEC the most, relative to the effort. Trying different areas with MVPs can help explore a broader set of areas more quickly, before committing significant resources.
- Experiments can also help with optimizations that may not be obvious to designers but can make a large difference (e.g., color, spacing, performance).
- Experiments can help continuously iterate to better site redesigns, rather than having teams work on complete site redesigns that subject users to primacy effects (users are *primed* in the old feature, i.e., used to the way it works) and commonly fail not only to achieve their goals, but even fail to achieve parity with the old site on key metrics (Goward 2015, slides 22–24, Rawat 2018, Wolf 2018, Laja 2019).
- Experiments can be critical in optimizing backend algorithms and infrastructure, such as recommendation and ranking algorithms.

Having a strategy is critical for running experiments: the strategy is what drives the choice of OEC. Once defined, controlled experiments help accelerate innovation by empowering teams to optimize and improve the OEC. Where we have seen experiments misused is when the OEC is not properly chosen. The metrics chosen should meet key characteristics and not be game-able (see Chapter 7).

At our companies, not only do we have teams focused on how to run experiments properly, but we also have teams focused on metrics: choosing metrics, validating metrics, and evolving metrics over time. Metric evolution will happen both due to your strategy evolving over time but also as you learn more about the limitations of your existing metrics, such as CTR being too gameable and needing to evolve. Metric teams also work on determining which metrics measurable in the short term drive long-term objectives, since experiments usually run over a shorter time frame. Hauser and Katz (1998) wrote that "the firm must identify metrics that the team can affect today, but which, ultimately, will affect the firm's long-term goals" (see Chapter 7).

Tying the strategy to the OEC also creates *Strategic Integrity* (Sinofsky and Iansiti 2009). The authors point out that "Strategic integrity is not about crafting brilliant strategy or about having the perfect organization: It is about getting the right strategies done by an organization that is aligned and knows how to get them done. It is about matching top-down-directed perspectives with bottom-up tasks." The OEC is the perfect mechanism to make the strategy explicit and to align what features ship with the strategy.

Ultimately, without a good OEC, you are wasting resources – think of experimenting to improve the food or lighting on a sinking cruise ship. The weight of passenger safety term in the OEC for those experiments should be extremely high – in fact, so high that we are not willing to degrade safety. This can be captured either via high weight in the OEC, or, equivalently, using passenger safety as a guardrail metric (see Chapter 21). In software, the analogy to the cruise ship passenger safety is software crashes: if a feature is increasing crashes for the product, the experience is considered so bad, other factors pale in comparison.

Defining guardrail metrics for experiments is important for identifying what the organization is *not* willing to change, since a strategy also "requires you to make tradeoffs in competing – to choose what not to do" (Porter 1996). The ill-fated Eastern Air Lines flight 401 crashed because the crew was focused on a burned-out landing gear indicator light, and failed to notice that the autopilot was accidentally disengaged; altitude, a key guardrail metric, gradually decreased and the plane crashed in the Florida Everglades in 1972, resulting in 101 fatalities (Wikipedia contributors, Eastern Air Lines Flight 401 2019).

Improvements in operational efficiencies can provide long-term differentiated advantage, as Porter noted in a section titled "Japanese Companies Rarely have Strategies" (1996) and Varian noted in his article on Kaizen (2007).

## Scenario 2: You Have a Product, You Have a Strategy, but the Results Suggest That You Need to Consider a Pivot

In Scenario 1, controlled experiments are a great tool for hill climbing. If you think of the multi-dimensional space of ideas, with the OEC as the "height" that is being optimized, then you may be making steps towards a peak. But sometimes, either based on internal data about the rate of change or external data about growth rates or other benchmarks, you need to consider a pivot: jumping to a different location in the space, which may be on a bigger hill, or changing the strategy and the OEC (and hence the shape of the terrain).

In general, we recommend always having a portfolio of ideas: most should be investments in attempting to optimize "near" the current location, but a few radical ideas should be tried to see whether those jumps lead to a bigger hill. Our experience is that most big jumps fail (e.g., big site redesigns), yet there is a risk/reward tradeoff: the rare successes may lead to large rewards that compensate for many failures.

When testing radical ideas, how you run and evaluate experiments changes somewhat. Specifically, you need to consider:

- The duration of experiments. For example, when testing a major UI redesign, experimental changes measured in the short term may be influenced by primacy effects or change aversion. The direct comparison of Treatment to Control may not measure the true long-term effect. In a two-sided marketplace, testing a change, unless sufficiently large, may not induce an effect on the marketplace. A good analogy is an ice cube in a very cold room: small increases to room temperature may not be noticeable, but once you go over the melting point (e.g., 32 Fahrenheit), the ice cube melts. Longer and larger experiments, or alternative designs, such as the country-level experiments used in the Google Ads Quality example above, may be necessary in these scenarios (see also Chapter 23).
- The number of ideas tested. You may need many different experiments because each experiment is only testing a specific tactic, which is a component of the overall strategy. A single experiment failing to improve the OEC may be due to the specific tactic being poor, not necessarily indicating that the overall strategy is bad. Experiments, by design, are testing specific hypotheses, while strategies are broader. That said, controlled experiments help refine the strategy, or show its ineffectiveness and encourage a pivot (Ries 2011). If many tactics evaluated through controlled experiments fail, it may be time to think about Winston Churchill's saying: "However beautiful the strategy, you should occasionally look at the results." For about two years, Bing had a strategy of integrating with social media, particularly

Facebook and Twitter, opening a third pane with social search results. After spending over $25 million on the strategy with no significant impact to key metrics, the strategy was abandoned (Kohavi and Thomke 2017). It may be hard to give up on a big bet, but economic theory tells us that failed bets are sunk costs, and we should make a forward-looking decision based on the available data, which is gathered as we run more experiments.

Eric Ries uses the term "achieved failure" for companies that successfully, faithfully, and rigorously execute a plan that turned out to have been utterly flawed (Ries 2011). Instead, he recommends:

> The Lean Startup methodology reconceives a startup's efforts as experiments that test its strategy to see which parts are brilliant and which are crazy. A true experiment follows the scientific method. It begins with a clear hypothesis that makes predictions about what is supposed to happen. It then tests those predictions empirically.

Due to the time and challenge of running experiments to evaluate strategy, some, like Sinofsky and Iansiti (2009) write:

> ... product development process as one fraught with risk and uncertainty. These are two very different concepts ... We cannot reduce the uncertainty – you don't know what you don't know.

We disagree: the ability to run controlled experiments allows you to significantly reduce uncertainty by trying a Minimum Viable Product (Ries 2011), getting data, and iterating. That said, not everyone may have a few years to invest in testing a new strategy, in which case you may need to make decisions in the face of uncertainty.

One useful concept to keep in mind is EVI: Expected Value of Information from Douglas Hubbard (2014), which captures how additional information can help you in decision making. The ability to run controlled experiments allows you to significantly reduce uncertainty by trying a Minimum Viable Product (Ries 2011), gathering data, and iterating.

## Additional Reading

There are several books directly related to online experiments and A/B tests (Siroker and Koomen 2013, Goward 2012, Schrage 2014, McFarland 2012, King et al. 2017). Most have great motivational stories but are inaccurate on the statistics. Georgi Georgiev's recent book includes comprehensive statistical explanations (Georgiev 2019).

The literature related to controlled experiments is vast (Mason et al. 1989, Box et al. 2005, Keppel, Saufley and Tokunaga 1992, Rossi, Lipsey and Freeman 2004, Imbens and Rubin 2015, Pearl 2009, Angrist and Pischke 2014, Gerber and Green 2012).

There are several primers on running controlled experiments on the web (Peterson 2004, 76–78, Eisenberg 2005, 283–286, Chatham, Temkin and Amato 2004, Eisenberg 2005, Eisenberg 2004); (Peterson 2005, 248–253, Tyler and Ledford 2006, 213–219, Sterne 2002, 116–119, Kaushik 2006).

A multi-armed bandit is a type of experiment where the experiment traffic allocation can be dynamically updated as the experiment progresses (Li et al. 2010, Scott 2010). For example, we can take a fresh look at the experiment every hour to see how each of the variants has performed, and we can adjust the fraction of traffic that each variant receives. A variant that appears to be doing well gets more traffic, and a variant that is underperforming gets less.

Experiments based on multi-armed bandits are usually more efficient than "classical" A/B experiments, because they gradually move traffic towards winning variants, instead of waiting for the end of an experiment. While there is a broad range of problems they are suitable for tackling (Bakshy, Balandal and Kashin 2019), some major limitations are that the evaluation objective needs to be a single OEC (e.g., tradeoff among multiple metrics can be simply formulated), and that the OEC can be measured reasonably well between re-allocations, for example, click-through rate vs. sessions. There can also be potential bias created by taking users exposed to a bad variant and distributing them unequally to other winning variants.

In December 2018, the three co-authors of this book organized the First Practical Online Controlled Experiments Summit. Thirteen organizations, including Airbnb, Amazon, Booking.com, Facebook, Google, LinkedIn, Lyft, Microsoft, Netflix, Twitter, Uber, Yandex, and Stanford University, sent a total of 34 experts, which presented an overview and challenges from breakout sessions (Gupta et al. 2019). Readers interested in challenges will benefit from reading that paper.

# 2

# Running and Analyzing Experiments

## *An End-to-End Example*

The fewer the facts, the stronger the opinion
– *Arnold Glasow*

In Chapter 1, we reviewed what controlled experiments are and the importance of getting real data for decision making rather than relying on intuition. The example in this chapter explores the basic principles of designing, running, and analyzing an experiment. These principles apply to wherever software is deployed, including web servers and browsers, desktop applications, mobile applications, game consoles, assistants, and more. To keep it simple and concrete, we focus on a website optimization example. In Chapter 12, we highlight the differences when running experiments for *thick clients*, such as native desktop and mobile apps.

## Setting up the Example

Our concrete example is a fictional online commerce site that sells widgets. There are a wide range of changes we can test: introducing a new feature, a change to the user interface (UI), a back-end change, and so on.

In our example, the marketing department wants to increase sales by sending promotional emails that include a coupon code for discounts on the widgets. This change is a potential business model change, as the company has not previously offered coupons. However, an employee at the company recently read about Dr. Footcare losing significant revenue after adding a coupon code (Kohavi, Longbottom et al. 2009, section 2.1) and also read that *removing* coupon codes is a positive pattern on GoodUI.org (Linowski 2018). Given these external data, there is concern that adding the coupon code field to checkout will degrade revenue, even if there are no coupons, that is, just the fact of users seeing this field will slow them down, and cause them to search for codes, or even abandon.

We want to evaluate the impact of simply adding a coupon code field. We can use a fake door or painted door approach (Lee 2013) – the analogy is that we build a fake door or paint it on a wall and see how many people try to open it. In this case, we implement the trivial change of adding a coupon code field to the checkout page. We do not implement a true coupon code system, as there are no codes available. Whatever the user enters, the system says: "Invalid Coupon Code." Our goal is simply to assess the impact on revenue by having this coupon code field and evaluate the concern that it will distract people from checking out. As this is a simple change, we will test two UI implementations. It is common to test several Treatments simultaneously to evaluate an idea versus an implementation. In this case, the idea is adding coupon code, while the implementation is a specific UI change.

This simple A/B test is a critical step in assessing the feasibility of the new business model.

When translating this proposed UI change into a hypothesis, it is useful to think about the online shopping process as a funnel, shown in Figure 2.1. A customer starts at the home page, browses through a few widgets, adds a widget to the cart, starts the purchase process, and finally completes a purchase. Of course, the idea of a funnel is simplistic; customers rarely complete the steps in a consistently linear fashion. There is a lot of back-and-forth swirl between states as well as repeat visitors who skip intermediate steps. However, this simple model is useful in thinking through experiment design and analysis, as experiments commonly target improving a particular step in the funnel (McClure 2007).

For our experiment, we are adding a coupon code field to the checkout page, and we are testing two different UIs, as shown in Figure 2.2, and would like to evaluate the impact (if any) on revenue. Our hypothesis is: "Adding a coupon code field to the checkout page will degrade revenue."

To measure the impact of the change, we need to define goal metrics, or success metrics. When we have just one, we can use that metric directly as our *OEC* (see Chapter 7). One obvious choice for this experiment might be revenue. Note that even though we want to increase overall revenue, we do not recommend using the sum of revenue itself, as it depends on the number of users in each variant. Even if the variants are allocated with equal traffic, the actual number of users may vary due to chance. We recommend that key metrics be normalized by the actual sample sizes, making *revenue-per-user* a good OEC.

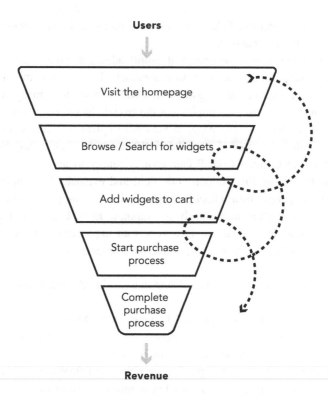

Figure 2.1 A user online shopping funnel. Users may not progress linearly through a funnel, but instead skip, repeat or go back-and-forth between steps

The next critical question is to determine which users to consider in the denominator of the revenue-per-user metric:

- **All users who visited the site.** This is valid; however, it is noisy because it includes users who never initiated checkout, where the change was made. We know that users who never initiated checkout could not be impacted by our change. Excluding these users will result in a more sensitive A/B test (see Chapter 20).
- **Only users who complete the purchase process.** This choice is incorrect, as it assumes that the change will impact the amount purchased, not the percentage of users who complete the purchase. If more users purchase, revenue-per-user may drop even though total revenue increases.
- **Only users who start the purchase process.** This is the best choice, given where the change is in the funnel. We include all potentially affected users, but no unaffected users (users who never start checking out) who dilute our results.

**Control**                           **Treatment 1**

**Treatment 2**

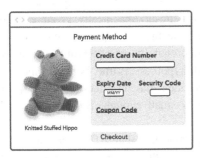 

Figure 2.2 (1) Control: the old checkout page. (2) Treatment one: coupon or gift code field below credit card information (3) Treatment two: coupon or gift code as a popup

Our more refined hypothesis becomes "Adding a coupon code field to the checkout page will degrade revenue-per-user for users who start the purchase process."

## Hypothesis Testing: Establishing Statistical Significance

Before we can design, run, or analyze our experiment, let us go over a few foundational concepts relating to statistical hypothesis testing.

First, we characterize the metric by understanding the baseline *mean* value and the *standard error* of the mean, in other words, how variable the estimate of our metric will be. We need to know the variability to properly size our experiment and calculate statistical significance during analysis. For most metrics we measure the mean, but we can also choose other summary statistics, such as percentiles. The sensitivity, or ability to detect statistically significant differences, improves with lower standard errors of the mean. This can typically be achieved by allocating more traffic to the variants or running the experiment longer because the number of users typically grows over time. The latter, however, may not be as effective after the first couple of weeks as unique user growth is sub-linear due to repeat users while some metrics themselves have a "growing" variance over time (Kohavi et al. 2012).

When we run an experiment, instead of characterizing a metric for a single sample, we instead have multiple samples. Specifically, in controlled experiments, we have one sample for the *Control* and one sample for each *Treatment*. We quantitatively test whether the difference between a pair of Treatment and Control samples is unlikely, given the *Null hypothesis* that the means are the same. If it is unlikely, we reject the Null hypothesis and claim that the difference is statistically significant. Specifically, given revenue-per-user estimates from the Control and Treatment samples, we compute the *p-value* for the difference, which is the probability of observing such difference or more extreme assuming the Null hypothesis is true. We reject the Null hypothesis and conclude that our experiment has an effect (or the result is statistically significant) if the p-value is small enough. But what is small enough?

The scientific standard is to use a p-value less than 0.05, meaning that if there is truly no effect, we can correctly infer there is no effect 95 out of 100 times. Another way to examine whether the difference is statistically significant is by checking whether the *confidence interval* overlaps with zero. A 95% confidence interval is the range that covers the true difference 95% of the time, and for fairly large sample sizes it is usually centered around the observed delta between the Treatment and the Control with an extension of 1.96 standard errors on each side. Figure 2.3 shows the equivalence of the two views.

*Statistical power* is the probability of detecting a meaningful difference between the variants when there really is one (statistically, reject the null when there is a difference). Practically speaking, you want enough power in your experiment to be able to conclude with high probability whether your experiment has resulted in a change bigger than what you care about. Usually, we get more power when the sample size is larger. It is common practice to design experiments for 80–90% power. Chapter 17 further discusses the statistical details.

While "statistical significance" measures how likely the result you observe or more extreme could have happened by chance assuming the null, not all statistically significant results are practically meaningful. How big of a difference, in this case for revenue-per-user, actually matters to us from a business perspective? In other words, what change is *practically significant*?

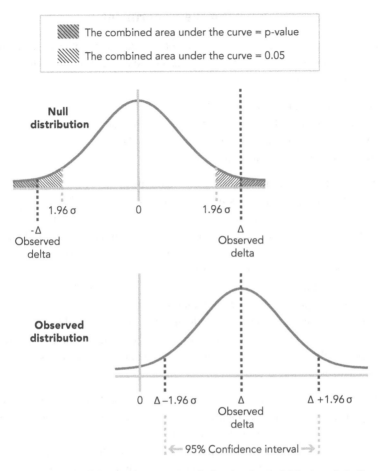

Figure 2.3 Top: Using p-value to assess whether the observed delta is statistically significant. If p-value is less than 0.05, we declare that the difference is statistically significant. Bottom: The equivalent view of using 95% confidence interval $[\varDelta - 1.96\,\sigma, \varDelta + 1.96\,\sigma]$ to assess statistical significance. If zero lies outside of the confidence interval, we declare significance

Establishing this substantive boundary is important for understanding whether the difference is worth the costs of making the change. If your website generates billions of dollars, like Google and Bing, then a 0.2% change is practically significant. In comparison, a startup may consider even a 2% change too small, because they are looking for changes that improve by 10% or more. For our example, let's state that from a business perspective, a 1% or larger increase in revenue-per-user is a change that matters or is practically significant.

## Designing the Experiment

We are now ready to design our experiment. We have a hypothesis, a practical significance boundary, and we have characterized our metric. We will use this set of decisions to finalize the design:

1. What is the randomization unit?
2. What population of randomization units do we want to target?
3. How large (size) does our experiment need to be?
4. How long do we run the experiment?

For now, let's assume that *users* is our randomization unit. Chapter 14 discusses alternatives, but *users* is by far the most common choice.

Targeting a specific population means that you only want to run the experiment for users with a particular characteristic. For example, you are testing out new text but only have the new text in a few languages; in this case, you could only target users with their interface locale set to those languages. Other common targeting attributes include geographic region, platform, and device type. Our example assumes we are targeting all users.

The size of the experiment (for us, the number of users) has direct impact on the precision of the results. If you want to detect a small change or be more confident in the conclusion, run a larger experiment with more users. Here are some changes we might consider:

- If we use *purchase indicator* (i.e., did the user purchase yes/no, without regard to the purchase amount) instead of using *revenue-per-user* as our OEC, the standard error will be smaller, meaning that we will not need to expose the experiment to as many users to achieve the same sensitivity.
- If we increase our practical significance level, saying that we no longer care about detecting a 1% change, but only bigger changes, we could reduce the sample size because bigger changes are easier to detect.
- If we want to use a lower p-value threshold such as 0.01 to be more certain that a change occurred before we reject the Null hypothesis, we need to increase the sample size.

Here are a few other considerations when deciding experiment size:

- How safe is the experiment? For large changes where you are uncertain about how users might react, you may want to start with a smaller proportion of the users first. This rationale should not impact the choice of the final experiment size but may instead impact the ramp-up tactics (see Chapter 15 for more details).

- Does this experiment need to share traffic with other experiments, and if so, how do you balance traffic requirements? At a high level, if you have other changes to test, you can choose to either run those changes at the same time or sequentially. If you must divide traffic among several simultaneous tests, each test will end up with a smaller amount of traffic. In Chapter 4, we talk about running tests as a single layer or overlapping, and more importantly, how to build a proper infrastructure to scale all experiments.

Another big question is how long to run the experiment. Here are other factors to consider:

- **More users**: In the online experiments, because users trickle into experiments over time, the longer the experiment runs, the more users the experiment gets. This usually results in increased statistical power (exceptions happen if the metric being measured accumulates, e.g., number of sessions, and the variance also increases; see Chapter 18 for details). The user accumulation rate over time is also likely to be sub-linear given that the same user may return: if you have N users on day one, you will have fewer than 2N users after two days since some users visit on both days.
- **Day-of-week effect**: You may have a different population of users on weekends than weekdays. Even the same user may behave differently. It is important to ensure that your experiment captures the weekly cycle. We recommend running experiments for a minimum of one week.
- **Seasonality**: There can be other times when users behave differently that are important to consider, such as holidays. If you have a global user base, US as well as non-US holidays may have an effect. For example, selling gift cards may work well during the Christmas season but not as well during other times of the year. This is called *external validity*; the extent to which the results can be generalized, in this case to other periods of time.
- **Primacy and novelty effects**: There are experiments that tend to have a larger or smaller initial effect that takes time to stabilize. For example, users may try a new flashy button and discover it is not useful, so clicks on the button will decrease over time. On the other hand, features that require adoption take time to build an adopter base.

Our experiment design is now as follows:

1. The randomization unit is a user.
2. We will target all users and analyze those who visit the checkout page.
3. To have 80% power to detect at least a 1% change in revenue-per-user, we will conduct a power analysis to determine size.

4. This translates into running the experiment for a minimum of four days with a 34/33/33% split among Control/Treatment one/Treatment two. We will run the experiment for a full week to ensure that we understand the day-of-week effect, and potentially longer if we detect novelty or primacy effects.

In general, overpowering an experiment is fine and even recommended, as sometimes we need to examine segments (e.g., geographic region or platform) and to ensure that the experiment has sufficient power to detect changes on several key metrics. For example, we may have enough power to detect revenue impact across all users, but not enough power if we want to look at users in Canada only. Also note that while we have chosen approximately equal sizes for Control and Treatments, if the number of Treatments increases, you may consider increasing the size of the Control to be larger than that of Treatments (see Chapter 18 for more discussion).

## Running the Experiment and Getting Data

Now let us run the experiment and gather the necessary data. Here we give you a brief overview of the pieces involved and provide more detail in *Scaling Experimentation: Digging into Variant Assignment* in Chapter 4.

To run an experiment, we need both:

- **Instrumentation** to get logs data on how users are interacting with your site and which experiments those interactions belong to (see Chapter 13).
- **Infrastructure** to be able to run an experiment, ranging from experiment configuration to variant assignment. See Chapter 4 *Experimentation Platform and Culture* for more detail.

Once you have run the experiment and gathered the logs data with the necessary instrumentation, it is time to process the data, compute the summary statistics, and visualize the results (see Chapter 4 and Chapter 16).

## Interpreting the Results

We have data from our experiment! Before we look at the revenue-per-user results, let's run some sanity checks to make sure the experiment was run properly.

Table 2.1 *Results on revenue-per-user from the checkout experiment.*

| | Revenue-per-user, Treatment | Revenue-per-user, Control | Difference | p-value | Confidence Interval |
|---|---|---|---|---|---|
| **Treatment One vs. Control** | $3.12 | $3.21 | −$0.09 (−2.8%) | 0.0003 | [−4.3%, −1.3%] |
| **Treatment Two vs. Control** | $2.96 | $3.21 | −$0.25 (−7.8%) | 1.5e-23 | [−9.3%, −6.3%] |

There are many ways for bugs to creep in that would invalidate the experiment results. To catch them, we'll look at the *guardrail metrics* or *invariants*. These metrics should not change between the Control and Treatment. If they change, any measured differences are likely the result of other changes we made rather than the feature being tested.

There are two types of invariant metrics:

1. Trust-related guardrail metrics, such as expecting the Control and Treatment samples to be sized according to the configuration or that they have the same cache-hit rates.
2. Organizational guardrail metrics, such as latency, which are important to the organization and expected to be an invariant for many experiments. In the checkout experiment, it would be very surprising if latency changed.

If these sanity checks fail, there is probably a problem with the underlying experiment design, infrastructure, or data processing. See Chapter 21 for more information.

After running the sanity checks based on the guardrail metrics, we are ready to look at the results (Table 2.1).

Because the p-value for both Treatments is less than 0.05, we reject the Null hypothesis that Treatment and Control have the same mean.

So, what does this mean? Well, it means that we confirmed the pattern that adding a coupon code to the UI will decrease revenue. If we dig into the numbers further, the results indicate that the decrease is because fewer users complete the purchase process. Thus, any marketing email that sends out coupon codes needs to recoup not just the implementation cost of adding coupon processing and maintenance, but also the negative impact of adding the coupon code in the first place. Since the marketing model estimated a small revenue increase for the targeted users, but the A/B test shows a significant revenue decrease to all users, the decision is made to scrap the idea of introducing promotion codes. A/B testing with a painted door saved us a large effort!

## From Results to Decisions

The goal of running A/B tests is to gather data to drive decision making. A lot of work goes into ensuring that our results are repeatable and trustworthy so that we make the right decision. Let's walk through the decision-making process for a few different cases that could come up.

For each case, we have the results from the experiment, and our goal is to translate the results into a launch/no-launch decision. The reason to stress the decision-making part is because a decision needs to take into consideration both the conclusion from the measurement and the broader context, such as:

- Do you need to make tradeoffs between different metrics? For example, if user engagement goes up, but revenue goes down, should you launch? Another example is if CPU utilization increases, the cost of running your service may outweigh the benefit of the change.
- What is the cost of launching this change? This includes both the:
  - Cost to fully build out the feature before launch. Some features may have been fully built before experimenting. In those cases, the cost of going from 1% to 100% launch is zero. This is not always the case. As in our example, implementing the painted door was cheap, but the cost of implementing a full coupon system is expensive.
  - Cost for ongoing engineering maintenance after launch, since it may be more costly to maintain new code. New code tends to have more bugs and be less well tested for edge cases. If the new code introduces more complexity, it may also add friction and cost to build new changes on top of it.

    If the cost is high, you must ensure that the expected gain can cover it. In those situations, make sure that your practical significance boundary is high enough to reflect that. Conversely, if the cost is low or even zero, you may choose to launch any change that is positive, in other words, your practical significance boundary is low.
- What is the downside of making wrong decisions? Not all decisions are equal and not all mistakes are equal. There may be no downside of launching a change that has no impact, but the opportunity cost can be high if we forego a change that has impact, and vice versa. For example, you may be testing two possible headline offers on your site, and the offer itself will

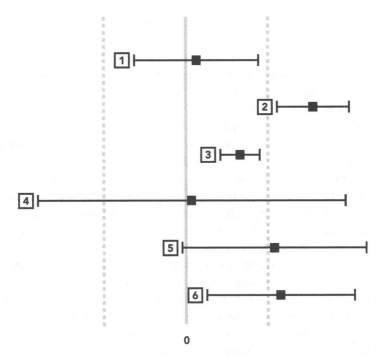

Figure 2.4 Examples for understanding statistical and practical significance when making launch decisions. The practical significance boundary is drawn as two dashed lines. The estimated difference for each example result is the black box, together with its confidence interval

only stay up for a few days. In that case, the downside of making the wrong decision is low because the change has a short lifespan. In this case, you may be willing to lower the bar for both statistical and practical significance.

You need to take these contexts into consideration as you construct your statistical and practical significance thresholds. These thresholds are critical as we move from the results of the experiment to a decision or action. Assuming we have updated the thresholds prior to the start of the experiment to reflect the broader context, let us walk through the examples in Figure 2.4 to illustrate how to use these thresholds to guide our decisions.

1. The result is not statistically significant. It is also clear that there is no practical significance. This leads to an easy conclusion that the change does not do much. You may either decide to iterate or abandon this idea.

2. The result is statistically and practically significant. Again, an easy decision: launch!
3. The result is statistically significant but not practically significant. In this case, you are confident about the magnitude of change, but that magnitude may not be sufficient to outweigh other factors such as cost. This change may not be worth launching.
4. Consider this example neutral, like our first example; however, the confidence intervals are outside of what is practically significant. If you run an experiment and find out it could either increase or decrease revenue by 10%, would you really accept that experiment and say that change is neutral? It's better to say you do not have enough power to draw a strong conclusion, and it is also such that we do not have enough data to make any launch decision. For this result, we recommend running a follow-up test with more units, providing greater statistical power.
5. The result is likely practically significant but not statistically significant. So even though your best guess is that this change has an impact you care about, there is also a good chance that there is no impact at all. From a measurement perspective, the best recommendation would be to repeat this test but with greater power to gain more precision in the result.
6. The result is statistically significant, and likely practically significant. Like 5, it is possible that the change is not practically significant. Thus here, like the prior example, we suggest repeating the test with more power. From a launch/no-launch decision, however, choosing to launch is a reasonable decision.

The key thing to remember is that there will be times you might have to decide even though there may not be clear answer from the results. In those situations, you need to be explicit about what factors you are considering, especially how they would translate into practical and statistical significance boundaries. This will serve as the basis for future decisions versus simply a local decision.

# 3

# Twyman's Law and Experimentation Trustworthiness

Twyman's law, perhaps the most important single law in the whole of data analysis... The more unusual or interesting the data, the more likely they are to have been the result of an error of one kind or another
– *Catherine Marsh and Jane Elliott (2009)*

Twyman's Law: "Any figure that looks interesting or different is usually wrong"
– *A.S.C. Ehrenberg (1975)*

Twyman's Law: "Any statistic that appears interesting is almost certainly a mistake"
– *Paul Dickson (1999)*

William Anthony Twyman was a UK radio and television audience measurement veteran (MR Web 2014) credited with formulating Twyman's law, although he apparently never explicitly put it in writing, and multiple variants of it exist, as shown in the above quotations.

When we see a surprisingly positive result, such as a significant improvement to a key metric, the inclination is to build a story around it, share it, and celebrate. When the result is surprisingly negative, the inclination is to find some limitation of the study or a minor flaw and dismiss it.

Experience tells us that many extreme results are more likely to be the result of an error in instrumentation (e.g., logging), loss of data (or duplication of data), or a computational error.

To increase trust in experiment results, we recommend a set of tests and practices to indicate that something may be wrong with the results. In databases, there are integrity constraints; in defensive programming, we are encouraged to write `assert()`s to validate that constraints hold. In experimentation, we can run tests that check for underlying issues, similar to asserts:

if every user should see either Control or Treatment from a certain time, then having many users in both variants is a red flag; if the experiment design calls for equal percentages in the two variants, then large deviations that are probabilistically unlikely should likewise raise questions. Next, we share some great examples of findings that fit Twyman's law, and then discuss what you can do to improve the trustworthiness of controlled experiments.

## Misinterpretation of the Statistical Results

Here are several common errors in interpreting the statistics behind controlled experiments.

### Lack of Statistical Power

In our framework of Null Hypothesis Significance Testing (NHST), we typically assume that there is no difference in metric value between Control and Treatment (the Null hypothesis) and reject the hypothesis if the data presents strong evidence against it. A common mistake is to assume that just because a metric is not statistically significant, there is no Treatment effect. It could very well be that the experiment is underpowered to detect the effect size we are seeing, that is, there are not enough users in the test. For example, an evaluation of 115 A/B tests at GoodUI.org suggests that most were underpowered (Georgiev 2018). This is one reason that it is important to define what is practically significant in your setting (see Chapter 2) and ensure that you have sufficient power to detect a change of that magnitude or smaller.

If an experiment impacts only a small subset of the population, it is important to analyze just the impacted subset; even a large effect on a small set of users could be diluted and not be detectable overall (see Chapter 20 and Lu and Liu (2014)).

### Misinterpreting p-values

P-value is often misinterpreted. The most common interpretation error is the belief that the p-value represents the probability that the average metric value in Control is different from the average metric value in Treatment, based on data in a single experiment.

The p-value is the probability of obtaining a result equal to or more extreme than what was observed, assuming that the Null hypothesis is true. The conditioning on the Null hypothesis is critical.

Here are some incorrect statements and explanations from *A Dirty Dozen: Twelve P-Value Misconceptions* (Goodman 2008):

1. *If the p-value = .05, the Null hypothesis has only a 5% chance of being true.*
The p-value is calculated assuming that the Null hypothesis is true.
2. *A non-significant difference (e.g., p-value >.05) means there is no difference between groups.*

    The observed results are consistent with the Null hypothesis of zero Treatment effect and a range of other values. When confidence intervals are shown for a typical controlled experiment, then it includes zero. This does not mean that zero is more likely than other values in the confidence interval. It could very well be that the experiment is under-powered.
3. *P-value = .05 means that we observed data that would occur only 5% of the time under the Null hypothesis.*

    This is incorrect by the definition of p-value above, which includes equal or more extreme values than what was observed.
4. *p-value = .05 means that if you reject the Null hypothesis, the probability of a false positive is only 5%.*

    This is like the first example, but harder to see. The following example might help: Suppose you are trying to transmute lead to gold by subjecting the lead to heat and pressure and pouring elixirs on it. You measure the amount of "goldliness" in the resulting concoction, a noisy measurement. Since we know that chemical Treatments can't change the atomic number of lead from 82 to 79, any rejection of the Null hypothesis (of no change) would be false, so 100% of rejections are false positives, regardless of the p-value. To compute the false positive rate, that is, when the p-value is < 0.05 and yet the Null Hypothesis is true (note, conjunction, not conditioned on the Null hypothesis being true), we could use Bayes Theorem and would require some prior probability.

Even the above common definition of p-value, which assumes that the Null hypothesis is true, is not explicitly stating other assumptions explicitly, such as how the data was collected (e.g., randomly sampled) and what assumptions the statistical tests make. If an intermediate analysis was done, which impacted the choice of analysis to present, or if a p-value was selected for presentation because of its small size, then these assumptions are clearly violated (Greenland et al. 2016).

## Peeking at p-values

When running an online controlled experiment, you could continuously monitor the p-values. In fact, early versions of the commercial product Optimizely encouraged this (Johari et al. 2017). Such multiple hypothesis testing results in significant bias (by $5-10x$) in declaring results to be statistically significant. Here are two alternatives:

1. Use sequential tests with always valid p-values, as suggested by Johari et al. (2017), or a Bayesian testing framework (Deng, Lu and Chen 2016).
2. Use a predetermined experiment duration, such as a week, for the determining statistical significance.

Optimizely implemented a solution based on the first method, whereas the experimentation platforms being used at Google, LinkedIn, and Microsoft use the second.

## Multiple Hypothesis Tests

The following story comes from the fun book, *What is a p-value anyway?* (Vickers 2009):

**Statistician:**  Oh, so you have already calculated the p-value?
**Surgeon:**  Yes, I used multinomial logistic regression.
**Statistician:**  Really? How did you come up with that?
**Surgeon:**  I tried each analysis on the statistical software drop-down menus, and that was the one that gave the smallest p-value.

The multiple comparisons problem (Wikipedia contributors, Multiple Comparisons problem 2019) is a generalization of peeking described above. When there are multiple tests, and we choose the lowest p-value, our estimates of the p-value and the effect size are likely to be biased. This is manifested in the following:

1. Looking at multiple metrics.
2. Looking at p-values across time (peeking as noted above).
3. Looking at segments of the population (e.g., countries, browser type, heavy/light, new/tenured).
4. Looking at multiple iterations of an experiment. For example, if the experiment truly does nothing (an A/A), running it 20 times may result in a p-value smaller than 0.05 by chance.

False Discovery Rate (Hochberg and Benjamini 1995) is a key concept to deal with multiple tests (see also Chapter 17).

## Confidence Intervals

Confidence intervals, loosely speaking, quantify the degree of uncertainty in the Treatment effect. The confidence level represents how often the confidence interval should contain the true Treatment effect. There is a duality between p-values and confidence intervals. For the Null hypothesis of no-difference commonly used in controlled experiments, a 95% confidence interval of the Treatment effect that does not cross zero implies that the p-value is $< 0.05$.

A common mistake is to look at the confidence intervals separately for the Control and Treatment, and assume that if they overlap, the Treatment effect is not statistically different. That is incorrect, as shown in Statistical Rules of Thumb (van Belle 2008, section 2.6). Confidence intervals can overlap as much as 29% and yet the delta will be statistically significant. The opposite, however, is true: if the 95% confidence intervals do not overlap, then the Treatment effect is statistically significant with p-value $< 0.05$.

Another common misunderstanding about confidence intervals is the belief that the presented 95% confidence interval has a 95% chance of containing the true Treatment effect. For a specific confidence interval, the true Treatment effect is either 100% within it, or 0%. The 95% refers to how often the 95% confidence intervals computed from many studies would contain the true Treatment effect (Greenland et al. 2016); see Chapter 17 for more details.

## Threats to Internal Validity

Internal validity refers to the correctness of the experimental results without attempting to generalize to other populations or time periods. Here are some common threats:

### Violations of SUTVA

In the analysis of controlled experiments, it is common to apply the Stable Unit Treatment Value Assumption (SUTVA) (Imbens and Rubin 2015), which states that experiment units (e.g., users) do not interfere with one another. Their behavior is impacted by their own variant assignment, and not by the assignment of others. The assumption could clearly be violated in settings, including the following:

- Social networks, where a feature might spillover to a user's network.
- Skype (a communication tool), where peer-to-peer calls can violate SUTVA.

- Document authoring tools (e.g., Microsoft Office and Google Docs) with co-authoring support.
- Two-sided marketplaces (such as ad auctions, Airbnb, eBay, Lift, or Uber) can violate SUTVA through the "other" side. For example, lowering prices for Treatment has impact on Controls during auctions.
- Shared resources (such as CPU, storage, and caches) can impact SUTVA (Kohavi and Longbotham 2010). If the Treatment leaks memory and causes processes to slow down due to garbage collection and possibly swapping of resources to disk, all variants suffer. In an experiment we ran, the Treatment crashed the machine in certain scenarios. Those crashes also took down users who were in Control, so the delta on key metrics was not different— both populations suffered similarly.

See Chapter 22 for ways to address some of these violations.

## Survivorship Bias

Analyzing users who have been active for some time (e.g., two months) introduces survivorship bias. A great example of this problem and the biases it introduces comes from World War II, when there was a decision to add armor to bombers. Recordings were made about where the planes took the most damage, and the military naturally wanted to add armor where the planes were hit the most. Abraham Wald pointed out that these were the **worst** places to add armor. Bullet holes were almost uniformly distributed, so armor should be added to the places where there were no bullet holes because bombers that were hit in those places... never made it back to be inspected (Denrell 2005, Dmitriev, et al. 2016).

## Intention-to-Treat

In some experiments, there is non-random attrition from the variants. For example, in medical settings, patients in a Treatment may stop taking a medication if it has side effects. In the online world, you may offer all advertisers the opportunity to optimize their ad campaign, but only some advertisers choose to do the suggested optimization. Analyzing only those who participate, results in selection bias and commonly overstates the Treatment effect. Intention-to-treat uses the initial assignment, whether it was executed or not. The Treatment effect we are measuring is therefore based on the offer, or intention to treat, not whether it was actually applied.

In display advertising and e-mail marketing, we do not observe the Control group exposure and there are techniques proposed to address this motivated by intent-to-treat (Barajas et al. 2016).

## Sample Ratio Mismatch (SRM)

If the ratio of users (or any randomization unit) between the variants is not close to the designed ratio, the experiment suffers from a Sample Ratio Mismatch (SRM). For example, if the experiment design is for a ratio of one-to-one (equally sized Control and Treatment), then deviations in the actual ratio of users in an experiment likely indicate a problem (see Chapter 21) that requires debugging. We share some examples below.

With large numbers, a ratio smaller than 0.99 or larger than 1.01 for a design that called for 1.0 more than likely indicates a serious issue. The experimentation system should generate a strong warning and hide any scorecards and reports, if the p-value for the ratio is low (e.g., below 0.001).

As defined earlier, the p-value is the probability of obtaining a result equal to or more extreme than what was observed, assuming that the Null hypothesis is true. If the experiment design was for equal allocations to both variants, then by design you should get a ratio close to 1.0, that is, the Null hypothesis *should be* true. The p-value thus represents the probability that the ratio we observed, or more extreme, is consistent with our experimentation system's design. This simple test has identified numerous issues in experiments, many that looked either great or terrible initially and invoked Twyman's law. Here are some other examples:

- **Browser redirects** (Kohavi and Longbotham 2010).
  A very common and practical mechanism to implement an A/B test is to redirect the Treatment to another page. Like many ideas, it is simple, elegant, and wrong; several different attempts have shown that this consistently causes an SRM. There are several reasons:
  a. **Performance differences.** Users in the Treatment group suffer an extra redirect, which may appear fast in the lab, but delays for users may be significant, on the order of hundreds of milliseconds, which has significant impact on key metrics (see Chapter 5).
  b. **Bots.** Robots handle redirects differently: some may not redirect on the http-equiv="REFRESH" meta tag; some will tag this as a new page worthy of deep crawling and crawl it more often.
  c. **Redirects are asymmetric.** When users are redirected to the Treatment page, they may bookmark it or pass a link to their friends. In most

implementations, the Treatment page does not check that the user should really have been randomized into the Treatment, so this causes contamination.

The lesson here is to avoid redirects in implementations and prefer a server-side mechanism. When that is not possible, make sure that both Control and Treatment have the same "penalty," that is, redirect both the Control and Treatment.

- **Lossy instrumentation** (Kohavi and Longbotham 2010, Kohavi, Messner et al. 2010, Kohavi et al. 2012, Zhao et al. 2016)

  Click tracking is typically done using web beacons (typically a 1x1 GIF sent to the server to signal a click), which is known to be lossy (i.e., not 100% of clicks are properly recorded). This is not normally an issue, as the loss is similar for all variants, but sometimes the Treatment can impact the loss rate, making low-activity users (e.g., those who only had a single click) appear at a different rate and cause an SRM. When the web beacon is placed in a different area of the page, timing differences will skew the instrumentation.

- **Residual or carryover effects**

  New experiments usually involve new code and the bug rate tends to be higher. It is common for a new experiment to cause some unexpected egregious issue and be aborted or kept running for a quick bug fix. After the bug is fixed, the experiment continues, but some users were already impacted. In some cases, that residual effect could be severe and last for months (Kohavi et al. 2012, Lu and Liu 2014). This is why it is important to run pre-experiment A/A tests (see Chapter 19) and proactively re-randomize users, recognizing that in some cases the re-randomization breaks the user consistency, as some users bounce from one variant to another.

  The opposite could also be true. At LinkedIn, a new version of the People You May Know algorithm was evaluated and turned out to be highly beneficial, increasing user visits. When the experiment was stopped and restarted, there was a significant carryover effect from the prior experiment, enough to create an SRM and invalidate the results (Chen, Liu and Xu 2019).

  Residual information in browser cookies can impact experiments. Take, for example, an educational campaign that shows a message to users in Treatment, but in order to avoid bothering users, the message is shown only three times. The implementation uses a browser cookie that counts the number of times the message was shown. If the experiment is restarted, some Treatment users will have the cookie with a count $> 0$, and thus will either see fewer impressions or none at all, diluting the Treatment effect or creating an SRM (Chen et al. 2019).

- **Bad hash function for randomization**
  Zhao et al. (2016) describe how Treatment assignment was done at Yahoo! using the Fowler-Noll-Vo hash function, which sufficed for single-layer randomization, but which failed to properly distribute users in multiple concurrent experiments when the system was generalized to overlapping experiments. Cryptographic hash functions like MD5 are good (Kohavi et al. 2009) but slow; a non-cryptographic function used at Microsoft is Jenkins SpookyHash (www.burtleburtle.net/bob/hash/spooky.html).

- **Triggering impacted by Treatment**
  It is common to only trigger a segment of users into an experiment. For example, you may only trigger users in a certain country, say the US. These users are then randomly split into the variants.

  If triggering is done based on attributes that are changing over time, then you must ensure that no attributes used for triggering could be impacted by the Treatment. For example, assume you run an e-mail campaign that triggers for users who have been inactive for three months. If the campaign is effective, those users become active and the next iteration of the campaign could have an SRM.

- **Time-of-Day Effects**
  Let's demonstrate this again using an e-mail campaign setup as an A/B test with different e-mail body text for each variant. In the real example, users were properly randomized into equally sized Control and Treatment groups, yet the e-mail open rates, which should be approximately the same, showed up as an SRM.

  A long investigation found that the open times clustered around different time periods, which led to the conjecture, later confirmed, that due to ease of implementation, the e-mails were first sent to Control users and then to Treatment users—the first group received the e-mails during work hours, whereas the second group received them after work.

- **Data pipeline impacted by Treatment.**
  The MSN portal (www.msn.com) has an Info Pane area on the page with multiple "slides" that rotate and a dot that indicates each slide (see arrow on Figure 3.1) (Kohavi 2016).

  A key component of the MSN OEC is clicks-per-user, which represents user engagement. The team ran an experiment where the Treatment increased the number of slides in the Info Pane from 12 to 16.

  Initial results showed a significant reduction in user engagement for the Treatment, but the experiment had an SRM: the ratio was 0.992 instead of 1.0. With over 800,000 users in each variant, the p-value of such a split was 0.0000007, which meant that the probability of such a split happening by

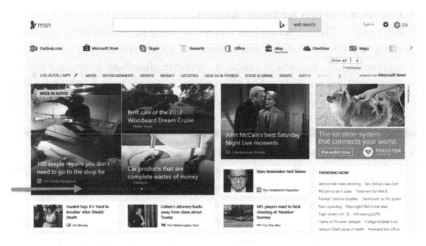

Figure 3.1 MSN portal example

chance, given that the design was for an equal split, was extremely unlikely. The investigation discovered that because user engagement increased in the Treatment, some of the most heavily engaged users were classified as bots and removed from analysis. After correcting this bot filtering, the results showed the reverse Treatment effect: user engagement increased by 3.3% in the Treatment!

Bot filtering is a serious problem, especially for search engines. For Bing, over 50% of US traffic is from bots, and that number is higher than 90% in China and Russia.

An SRM check is critical. Even a small imbalance can cause a reversal in the Treatment effect, as the last example shows. SRMs are commonly due to missing users (generally, experiment units) that are either extremely good, such as heavy users, or extremely bad, those users with no click count. This demonstrates that even though the population difference appears small, it can significantly skew the results. A paper on diagnosing SRMs was recently published (Fabijan et al. 2019).

## Threats to External Validity

External validity refers to the extent to which the results of a controlled experiment can be generalized along axes such as different populations (e.g., other countries, other websites) and over time (e.g., will the 2% revenue increase continue for a long time or diminish?).

Generalizations across populations are usually questionable; features that work on one site may not work on another, but the solution is usually easy: rerun the experiment. For example, successful experiments in the United States are typically tested in other markets instead of assuming the results will generalize.

Generalizations across time are harder. Sometimes a holdout experiment is left running for months to assess the long-term effects (Hohnhold, O'Brien and Tang 2015). Chapter 19 discusses how to address long-term effects. Two key threats to external validity on a time-basis are *primacy* effects and *novelty* effects.

## Primacy Effects

When a change is introduced, users may need time to adopt, as they are *primed* in the old feature, that is, used to the way it works. Machine-learning algorithms may also learn better models and depending on the update cycle, this may take time.

## Novelty Effects

Novelty effect, or newness effect, is an un-sustained effect. When you introduce a new feature, especially one that's easily noticed, initially it attracts users to try it. If users don't find the feature useful, repeat usage will be small. A Treatment may appear to perform well at first, but the Treatment effect will quickly decline over time.

An example of something that we are *not* looking for is one told in *Yes!: 50 Scientifically proven ways to be Persuasive* (Goldstein, Martin and Cialdini 2008). In that book, the authors discuss how Colleen Szot authored a television program that shattered a nearly 20-year sales record for a home-shopping channel. Szot changed three words in a standard infomercial line that caused a huge increase in the number of people who purchased her product: instead of the all-too-familiar "Operators are waiting, please call now," it was "If operators are busy, please call again." The authors explain that this is social proof: viewers think "If the phone lines are busy, then other people, like me, who are also watching this infomercial are calling, too."

Ploys, such as the above, have a short shelf life if users recognize that it is used regularly. In a controlled experiment, the analysis will show an effect that quickly diminishes.

Another example is shown in Figure 3.2. The MSN website had a stripe at the top that looked like this (Dmitriev et al. 2017):

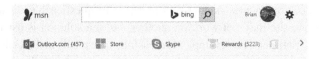

Figure 3.2 MSN page with Outlook.com link

Figure 3.3 MSN page changed to use link to Outlook application

Figure 3.4 Phone ad with fake hair, hoping you'll swipe it off and click-through
by mistake

Microsoft changed the Outlook.com link and icon to directly open the
Outlook Mail application (Figure 3.3), which gives users a richer, better
e-mail experience.

As expected, the experiment showed that more users in Treatment used the
Mail app relative to Control, but there was no expectation that the click-
through rate would increase. Surprisingly though, there was an extremely large
increase of 28% in the number of clicks on that link in Treatment relative to
Control. Were users liking the Mail app more and using it more frequently?
No. The investigation showed that users were confused that Outlook.com did
not open and clicked the link multiple times.

Finally, Chinese sneaker manufacturer Kaiwei Ni had an Instagram ad that
showed up on phones with a fake stray hair as shown in Figure 3.4. Users were
tricked into swiping on the ad to remove the hair, and many of them clicked

through. The novelty effect was likely significant here. More than that, the ad was not only removed from Instagram, but the account was disabled (Tiffany 2017).

## Detecting Primacy and Novelty Effects

An important check for primacy and novelty effects is to plot usage over time and see whether it's increasing or decreasing. Take the above MSN example, the percentage of users clicking the Mail link clearly decreased over time, as shown in the graph in Figure 3.5.

The standard analysis of experiments assumes that the Treatment effect is constant over time. This kind of trend is a red flag that indicates a violation of the assumptions. Such experiments need to run longer to determine when the Treatment effect stabilizes. In many cases, and stressed in this example, the insight is enough to declare the idea bad. This approach is simple and effective in most cases, but we must warn you that there are some caveats to watch out for, especially if you do run the experiment a long time (See Chapter 23).

One additional option to highlight possible novelty/primacy effects is to take the users who appeared in the first day or two (as opposed to all users over time) and plot the treatment effect for them over time.

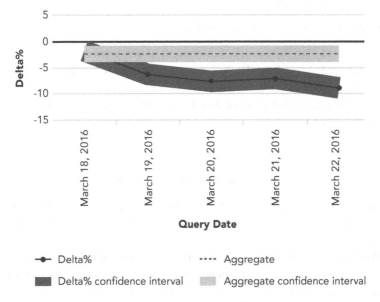

Figure 3.5  MSN user engagement decreasing over time

## Segment Differences

Analyzing a metric by different segments can provide interesting insights and lead to discoveries, for which we sometimes invoke Twyman's law and discover a flaw or new insight to help with future iterations of an idea. These are advanced tests with an example that you can address in the later maturity phases of your experimentation system.

What are good segments? Here are several:

- Market or country: some features work better in some countries; sometimes an underperforming feature is the result of poor translation to another language, that is, localization.
- Device or platform: is the user interface on a browser, desktop, or mobile phone? Which mobile platform are they using: iOS or Android? Sometimes the browser version can help identify JavaScript bugs and incompatibilities. On mobile phones, the manufacturers (e.g., Samsung, Motorola) provide add-ons that can cause features to fail.
- Time of day and day of week: plotting effects over time can show interesting patterns. Users on weekends can be different in many characteristics.
- User type: new or existing, where new users are ones that joined after a date (e.g., experiment start, or perhaps a month prior).
- User account characteristics: single or shared account at Netflix, or single vs. family traveler on Airbnb.

Segmented views are commonly used two ways:

1. Segmented view of a metric, independent of any experiment.
2. Segmented view of the Treatment effect for a metric, in the context of an experiment, referred to in Statistics as *heterogeneous* Treatment effects, indicating that the Treatment effect is not homogenous or uniform across different segments.

## Segmented View of a Metric

When the click-through rates on Bing mobile ads were segmented by different mobile operating systems, they were very different as shown in the graph in Figure 3.6.

While the initial inclination was to form stories about the loyalty of the users and how the populations differ, an investigation uncovered that this was due to different click tracking methodologies used for different operating systems. There are several ways of tracking clicks, and they differ in fidelity (Kohavi,

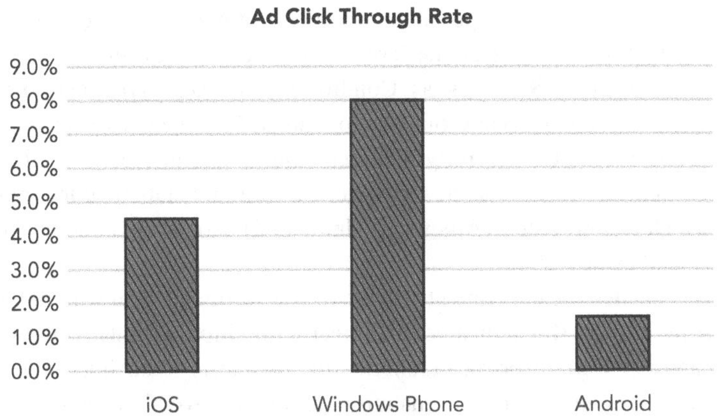

**Ad Click Through Rate**

Figure 3.6 CTRs for different mobile Operating Systems

Messner et al. 2010), which leads to different loss rates. On iOS and Windows Phone, a redirect was used to track the clicks, that is, the click always goes to a server, is logged, and is then redirected to the destination. This methodology has high fidelity, but the user experience is slower. On Android, click tracking was done using a web beacon to indicate a click and then redirected the browser to the destination page. This methodology is faster for the user, but lossy; some web beacons will not make it and the link will not be recorded. This can explain the click-through rate (CTR) difference between iOS and Android, but why was the Windows Phone click-through rate so high? The investigation discovered that along with the redirect, there was a bug where user swipes were incorrectly recorded as a click. Bugs happen. When you see anomalous data, think of Twyman's law and investigate the issue.

## Segmented View of the Treatment Effect (Heterogeneous Treatment Effect)

In one experiment, a user interface change was made, which resulted in a very strong difference between browser segments. For almost all browser segments, the Treatment effect was a small positive improvement on key metrics, but for the Internet Explorer 7 segment, there was a strongly negative Treatment effect on key metrics. As with any strong effect (positive or negative), you should invoke Twyman's law and drill into the cause. An investigation revealed that the JavaScript used was incompatible with Internet Explorer 7, causing an error that prevented users from clicking links in certain scenarios.

Such insight is only possible when drilldowns into segments are enabled, that is, looking at the Treatment effect for different segments, also referred to in Statistics as Conditional Average Treatment Effects (CATEs). A good overview on Heterogenous Treatment Effects is available at EGAP (2018). Identifying interesting segments, or searching for interactions, can be done using machine learning and statistical techniques, such as Decision Trees (Athey and Imbens 2016) and Random Forests (Wager and Athey 2018).

If you can alert the experimenter to interesting segments, you will find many interesting insights (but remember to correct for multiple hypothesis testing, as noted above). Getting organizations to run A/B tests is an important step; providing them with more information than just the overall Treatment effect gives new insights that help accelerate innovation.

## Analysis by Segments Impacted by Treatment Can Mislead

It is possible to evaluate the Treatment effect of two mutually exhaustive and exclusive segments, and see that the OEC increases for both, yet declines overall. Unlike Simpson's paradox (described in the next section), this is due to migration of users from one segment to another.

For example, assume you have a metric, sessions-per-user, that you care about. You are working on a new product feature F, which few users use, so you focus on users of F and the complement (those not using F). You see that in your experiment, sessions-per-user goes up for users of F. Now you look at the complement and see that their sessions-per-user go up. Can you celebrate? NO! It is possible that sessions-per-user overall decreased or stayed flat.

As an example, users of F average 20 sessions-per-user, while those not using F average 10 sessions-per-user. If the Treatment causes users with 15 sessions-per-user to stop using F, the average sessions-per-user will rise for the segment using F (we removed users with lower than average sessions-per-user), and it will rise for the complement (we added users with higher average sessions-per-user), but the aggregate could move in any direction: up, down, or flat (Dmitriev et al. 2016, section 5.8).

When users move from one segment to another, interpreting metric movements at the segment level may be misleading, so the Treatment effect of the non-segmented metric (aggregate) should be used. Ideally, segmenting should be done only by values that are determined prior to the experiment, so that the Treatment could not cause users to change segments, though in practice restricting segments this way may be hard for some use cases.

# Simpson's Paradox

The following is based on Crook et al. (2009). If an experiment goes through ramp-up (see Chapter 15) that is, two or more periods with different percentages assigned to the variants, combining the results can result in directionally incorrect estimates of the Treatment effects, that is, Treatment may be better than Control in the first phase and in the second phase, but worse overall when the two periods are combined. This phenomenon is called Simpson's paradox because it is unintuitive (Simpson 1951, Malinas and Bigelow 2004, Wikipedia contributors, Simpson's paradox 2019, Pearl 2009).

Table 3.1 shows a simple example, where a website has 1 million visitors per day on two days: Friday and Saturday. On Friday, the experiment runs with 1% of traffic assigned to the Treatment. On Saturday that percentage is raised to 50%. Even though the Treatment has a conversion rate that is better on Friday (2.30% vs. 2.02%) and a conversion rate that is better on Saturday (1.2% vs. 1.00%), if the data is simply combined over the two days, it appears that the Treatment is performing worse (1.20% vs. 1.68%).

There is nothing wrong with the above math. It is mathematically possible that $\frac{a}{b} < \frac{A}{B}$ and that $\frac{c}{d} < \frac{C}{D}$ while $\frac{a+c}{b+d} > \frac{A+C}{B+D}$. The reason this seems unintuitive is that we are dealing with weighted averages, and the impact of Saturday, which was a day with an overall worse conversion rate, impacted the average Treatment effect more because it had more Treatment users.

Here are other examples from controlled experiments where Simpson's paradox may arise:

- Users are sampled. Because there is concern about getting a representative sample from all browser types, the sampling is not uniform, and users in some browsers (such as, Opera or Firefox) are sampled at higher rates. It is

Table 3.1 *Conversion Rate for two days. Each day has 1M customers, and the Treatment (T) is better than Control (C) on each day, yet worse overall*

|   | Friday | Saturday | Total |
|---|--------|----------|-------|
|   | C/T split: 99% / 1% | C/T split: 50% / 50% | |
| C | $\frac{20,000}{990,000} = 2.02\%$ | $\frac{5,000}{500,000} = 1.00\%$ | $\frac{25,000}{1,490,000} = 1.68\%$ |
| T | $\frac{230}{10,000} = 2.30\%$ | $\frac{6,000}{500,000} = 1.20\%$ | $\frac{6,230}{510,000} = 1.20\%$ |

possible that the overall results will show that the Treatment is better, but once the users are segmented into the browser types, the Treatment is worse for all browser types.

- An experiment runs on a website that is implemented in multiple countries, say the United States and Canada. The proportions assigned to the Control and Treatment vary by country (e.g., the United States runs at 1% for the Treatment, while the Canadians do power calculations and determine they need 50% for the Treatment). If the results are combined, the Treatment may seem superior, even though the results were segmented by country, the Treatment will be inferior. This example directly mirrors our previous ramp-up example.

- An experiment is run at 50/50% for Control/Treatment, but an advocate for the most valuable customers (say top 1% in spending) is concerned and convinces the business that this customer segment be kept stable and only 1% participate in the experiment. Similar to the example above, it is possible that the experiment will be positive overall, yet it will be worse for both the most valuable customers and for "less-valuable" customers.

- An upgrade of the website is done for customers in data center DC1 and customer satisfaction improves. A second upgrade is done for customers in data center DC2, and customer satisfaction there also improves. It is possible that the auditors looking at the combined data from the upgrade will see that overall customer satisfaction decreased.

While occurrences of Simpson's paradox are unintuitive, they are not uncommon. We have seen them happen multiple times in real experiments (Xu, Chen and Fernandez et al. 2015, Kohavi and Longbotham 2010). One must be careful when aggregating data collected at different percentages.

Simpson's reversal seems to imply that it is mathematically possible for a drug to increase the probability of recovery in the aggregate population yet decrease the probability (so it is harmful) in every subpopulation, say males and females. This would seem to imply that one should take the drug if gender is unknown yet avoid it if gender is either male or female, which is clearly absurd. Pearl (2009) shows that observational data alone cannot help us resolve this paradox, as the causal model will determine which data to use (the aggregate or the subpopulation). The "Sure-Thing Principal" Theorem (6.1.1) states that if an action increases the probability of an event E in each subpopulation, it must also increase the probability of E in the population as a whole.

## Encourage Healthy Skepticism

It had been six months since we started concerted A/B testing efforts at SumAll, and we had come to an uncomfortable conclusion: most of our winning results were not translating into improved user acquisition. If anything, we were going sideways...
— *Peter Borden (2014)*

Trustworthy experimentation is sometimes tough for organizations to invest in, as it involves investing in the unknown—building tests that would invalidate results if the tests fired. Good data scientists are skeptics: they look at anomalies, they question results, and they invoke Twyman's law when the results look too good.

# 4

# Experimentation Platform and Culture

If you have to kiss a lot of frogs to find a prince, find more frogs and kiss them faster and faster
– *Mike Moran, Do It Wrong Quickly (2007)*

As discussed in Chapter 1, running trustworthy controlled experiments is the scientific gold standard in evaluating many (but not all) ideas and making data-informed decisions. What may be less clear is that making controlled experiments easy to run also accelerates innovation by decreasing the cost of trying new ideas, as the quotation from Moran shows above, and learning from them in a virtuous feedback loop. In this chapter, we focus on what it takes to build a robust and trustworthy experiment platform. We start by introducing experimentation maturity models that show the various phases an organization generally goes through when starting to do experiments, and then we dive into the technical details of building an experimentation platform.

Important organizational considerations include leadership, process, and training, whether the work should be done in-house or outsourced, and how the results are ultimately used. The technical tools will support experiment design, deployment, scaling, and analysis to accelerate insight.

## Experimentation Maturity Models

Experimentation maturity models (Fabijan, Dmitriev and Olsson et al. 2017, Fabijan, Dmitriev and McFarland et al. 2018, Optimizely 2018c, Wider Funnel 2018, Brooks Bell 2015) consist of the phases that organizations are likely to go through on the way to being data-driven and running every change through A/B experiments.

We use these four phases of maturity, following Fabijan et al. (2017):

1. **Crawl**: The goal is building the foundational prerequisites, specifically instrumentation and basic data science capabilities, to compute the summary statistics needed for hypothesis testing so that you can design, run, and analyze a few experiments. Having a few successful experiments, where success means that the results meaningfully guide forward progress, is critical to generating momentum to progress to the next stage.
2. **Walk**: The goal shifts from prerequisites and running a few experiments to a focus on defining standard metrics and getting the organization to run more experiments. In this phase, you improve trust by validating instrumentation, running A/A tests, and sample ratio mismatch (SRM) tests (see Chapter 21).
3. **Run**: The goal shifts to running experiments at scale. Metrics are comprehensive and the goal is to achieve an agreed upon set of metrics or going all the way to codifying an OEC that captures tradeoffs between multiple metrics. The organization uses experimentation to evaluate most new features and changes.
4. **Fly**: Now you are running A/B experiments as the norm for every change. Feature teams should be adept at analyzing most experiments—especially the straightforward ones—without the help of data scientists. The focus shifts to automation to support this scale, as well as establishing institutional memory, which is a record of all experiments and changes made, enabling learning from past experiments (see Chapter 17) to sharing surprising results and best practices, with a goal of improving the culture of experimentation.

As a rough rule of thumb, in the Crawl phase, an organization is running experiments approximately once a month (~10/year), and it increases by 4−5x for each phase: organizations in the Walk phase will run experiments approximately once a week (~50/year), Run is daily (~250/year), and Fly is when you reach thousand(s)/year.

As an organization progresses through these phases, the technical focus, the OEC, and even the team set-ups will shift. Before we dig into the technical aspects of building an experiment platform in the Walk, Run, and Fly phases, let's highlight several areas for organizations to focus on regardless of phase, including leadership and processes.

## Leadership

Leadership buy-in is critical for establishing a strong culture around experimentation and embedding A/B testing as an integral part of the product development process. Our experience is that organizations and cultures go through stages in learning to experiment as well (Kohavi 2010). The first stage, which precedes any experimentation, is hubris, where measurement and experimentation are not necessary because of confidence in the HiPPO (Highest Paid Person's Opinion). Next is measurement and control, where an organization starts measuring key metrics and controlling for unexplained differences. As Thomas Kuhn notes, paradigm shifts happen "only through something's first going wrong with normal research" (Kuhn 1996). However, there is still a strong dependence on the HiPPO and entrenched norms, beliefs, and paradigms, as an organization may reject new knowledge that is contradictory per the Semmelweis Reflex (Wikipedia contributors, Semmelweis reflex 2019). It is only through persistent measurement, experimentation, and knowledge gathering that an organization can reach a fundamental understanding, where causes are understood, and models actually work.

To reach this last stage, in our experience, buy-in from executives and managers must happen at multiple different levels and include:

- Engaging in the process of establishing shared goals and agreeing on the high-level goal metrics and guardrail metrics (see Chapter 18) and ideally codifying tradeoffs as steps to establishing an OEC (see Chapter 7)
- Setting goals in terms of improvements to metrics instead of goals to ship features X and Y. There is a fundamental shift that happens when teams change from shipping a feature when it does not hurt key metrics, to NOT SHIPPING a feature unless it improves key metrics. Using experiments as a guardrail is a difficult cultural change, especially for large, established teams to make as they shift towards a data-informed culture.
- Empowering teams to innovate and improve key metrics within the organizational guardrails (see Chapter 21). Expecting ideas to be evaluated and for many of them to fail and showing humility when their ideas fail to move the metrics they were designed to improve. Establishing a culture of failing fast.
- Expecting proper instrumentation and high data quality.
- Reviewing experiment results, knowing how to interpret them, enforcing standards on interpretation (e.g., to minimize p-hacking (Wikipedia contributors, Data dredging 2019)), and giving transparency to how those results affect decision making.
- As discussed in Chapter 1, many of the decisions that experiments can best help inform are optimization; a long sequence of experiments can also inform overall strategy as well. For example, Bing's integration with social networks, such as Facebook and Twitter, was abandoned after experiments showed no value for two years. As another example, evaluating an idea like

whether including videos in promotional e-mails results in higher conversion rates would require testing multiple implementations.

- Ensuring a portfolio of high-risk/high-rewards projects relative to more incremental gain projects, understanding that some will work, and many —even most—will fail. Learning from the failures is important for continued innovation.
- Supporting long-term learning from experiments, like running experiments just to collect data or establish return-on-investment (ROI). Experimentation is not just useful for making ship/no-ship decisions on individual changes, but also holds an important role in measuring impact and assessing ROI for various initiatives. For example, see Chapter 5 and long-term experiments (Hohnhold, O'Brien and Tang 2015).
- Improving agility with short release cycles to create a healthy, quick feedback loop for experimentation, requiring establishing sensitive surrogate metrics (see Chapter 7).

Leaders cannot just provide the organization with an experimentation platform and tools. They must provide the right incentives, processes, and empowerment for the organization to make data-driven decisions. Leadership engaging in these activities is especially crucial in the Crawl and Walk maturity phases to align the organization on goals.

## Process

As an organization moves through the phases of experimentation maturity, establishing educational processes and cultural norms is necessary to ensure trustworthy results. Education ensures that everyone has the basic understanding to do a good job at designing and executing trustworthy experiments and interpreting the results correctly. The cultural norms help set an expectation of innovation, celebrating surprising failures and always wanting to learn. Note that this is an ongoing challenge, as at a summit in 2019 with 13 online companies on experiments, establishing cultures and process that encourage experimentation and innovation continues to be a challenge (Gupta, Kohavi et al. 2019).

For education, establishing just-in-time processes during experiment design and experiment analysis can really up-level an organization. Let's consider this example from Google: When experimenters working on search wanted to run an experiment, they had to complete a checklist that was reviewed by experts. The checklist included basic questions like, "What is your hypothesis?" and "How big of a change do you care about?" and went all the way through to power analysis questions. Because trying to teach everyone to do a proper power analysis was unrealistic, the checklist also helped ensure that experiments were sufficiently powered by linking to a power calculator tool. Once the organization was sufficiently up-leveled, the search organization no longer needed such an explicit checklist process.

Generally, experimenters only require hand-holding the first few times they run an experiment. They get faster and more independent with every subsequent experiment. The more experienced the experimenter, the better they explain concepts to teammates and, over time, serve as expert reviewers. That said, even experienced experimenters typically still need help for experiments requiring unique designs or new metrics.

Both LinkedIn and Microsoft (Google too, although not regularly) hold classes to keep employees aware of experimental concepts (Kohavi, Crook and Longbotham 2009). The classes have grown in popularity as the culture grows more accepting of experiments over time.

Analogous to the checklist at experiment design time, regular experiment review meetings for analysis results provide similar just-in-time education benefits. In these meetings, experts examine the results, first for trustworthiness − oftentimes finding instrumentation issues, especially for first-time experimenters − before diving into useful discussions resulting in launch/no-launch recommendations that experimenters could take to their leaders. These discussions broadened the understanding of goal, guardrail, quality, and debug metrics (see Chapter 6) and developers were more likely to anticipate those issues during the development lifecycle. These discussions also established metric tradeoffs that can be codified and captured in an OEC (see Chapter 7). These experiment reviews are also where failed experiments are discussed and learned from: many high-risk/high-reward ideas do not succeed on the first iteration, and learning from failures is critical for the refinement needed to nurture these ideas to success, as well as to decide when to move on (see Chapter 1).

Over time, the experts see patterns in changes, such as seeing how the impact of an experiment relates to similar prior experiments, and how this can be further examined in a meta-analysis (see Chapter 8) that can lead to user experience improvements and updates to key metric definitions. The other unintended, but positive, outcome we noticed about this experiment analysis review forum is that it brought together different teams in a single meeting so that they could learn from each other. Note that we have observed that the teams do need to be working on the same product and share the same metrics and OEC so that there is enough shared context for learning. If the teams are too diverse or if there is insufficient maturity in the tooling, then this meeting can be unproductive. We suspect that this type of review starts being effective in the late Walk or in the Run phases of maturity.

Through the platform or processes, we can share learnings from experiments broadly, be it the meta-learning from experts observing many experiments or the learning gained from a single experiment. This can happen via regular newsletters, Twitter-feed, a curated homepage, a "social network" attached to the experiment platform to encourage discussion (as is done at Booking.com) or other channels. Institutional memory (see Chapter 8) becomes increasingly useful in the Fly phase.

For experimentation to succeed and scale, there must also be a culture around intellectual integrity—the learning matters most, not the results or whether we ship the change. From that perspective, full transparency on the experiment impact is critical. Here are some ways we found to achieve this:

- Compute many metrics, ensure that the important metrics, such as the OEC, guardrail, and other related metrics, are highly visible on the experiment dashboard, so that teams cannot cherry-pick when sharing results.
- Send out newsletters or e-mails about surprising results (failures and successes), meta-analyses over many prior experiments to build intuition, how teams incorporate experiments, and more (see Chapter 8). The goal is to emphasize the learning and the needed cultural support.
- Make it hard for experimenters to launch a Treatment if it impacts important metrics negatively. This can go from a warning to the experimenter, a notification to people who care about those metrics, all the way to even potentially blocking a launch (this last extreme can be counterproductive as it is better to have a culture where metrics are looked at and controversial decisions can be openly discussed).
- Embrace learning from failed ideas. Most ideas will fail, so the key is to learn from that failure to improve on subsequent experiments.

## Build vs. Buy

Figure 4.1 shows how Google, LinkedIn, and Microsoft scaled experimentation over the years, with year-1 being a year where experimentation scaled to over an experiment per day (over 365/year). The graph shows an order of magnitude growth over the next four years for Bing, Google, and LinkedIn. In the early years, growth was slowed by the experimentation platform capabilities itself. In the case of Microsoft Office, which just started to use controlled experiments as a safe deployment mechanism for feature rollouts at scale in 2017, the platform was not a limiting factor because of its prior use in Bing, and experiments grew

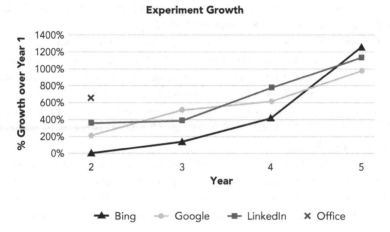

Figure 4.1 Experimentation Growth over the years for Bing, Google, LinkedIn, and Office. Today, Google, LinkedIn, and Microsoft are at a run rate of over 20,000 controlled experiments/year, although counting methodologies differ (e.g., ramping up the exposure from 1% of users to 5% to 10% can be counted as one or three experiments; an experiment consisting of a Control plus two Treatments can count as either one or two experiments)

by over 600% in 2018. Growth slows when the organization reaches a culture of "test everything" and the limiting factor becomes its ability to convert ideas into code that can be deployed in controlled experiments.

While we all have been heavily involved in building in-house experimentation platforms at our respective companies, we are not necessarily recommending that every company should build their own. Especially in the Walk phase, building or buying is an ROI decision (statistics on building versus buying available in Fabijian et al. (2018)). Here are several questions to consider when making that decision.

### Can an External Platform Provide the Functionality You Need?

- Consider the types of experiments you want to run, such as frontend vs. backend, server vs. client, or mobile vs. web. Many third-party solutions are not versatile enough to cover all types. For example, solutions based on JavaScript would not work for backend experiments or scale well for many concurrent experiments. Some vendors are strong in one channel, but not others (e.g., great softwar development kit (SDK) for mobile, but weak ability to handle web; or great WYSIWYG editor for web, but a mobile SDK that crashes too often).

- Consider website speed. Several external solutions require additional Java-Script, which is known to slow down page loads (Optimizely 2018, Kingston 2015, Neumann 2017, Kesar 2018, Abrahamse 2016). As shown in Chapter 5, increased latency impacts user engagement.
- Consider the dimensions and metrics you may want to use. For example, some external platforms are limited on what metrics you can compute on experiments. Complex metrics that require sessionization are not possible in external solutions. Even metrics like percentiles, which are commonly used to measure latency where the tail rather than average tends to be more sensitive, are not often supported. Since broad business reporting might have to be built separately, it could also be harder to establish a common language of dimensions and metrics, so ensuring consistency may be more difficult if you buy.
- Consider what randomization unit you want to use and what data sharing is acceptable (e.g., to ensure that user privacy is respected). There are usually restrictions on what information (especially about users, see Chapter 9) can be passed on to external parties, which may be limiting or induce additional costs.
- Is data logged to the external party easily accessible? Do clients need to log to two places (dual-logging)? What happens when summary statistics diverge? Are there tools to reconcile? These are often under-estimated complexities that have reduced trust and raised valid questions about the reliability of different systems.
- Can you integrate additional sources of data? Do you want to integrate purchase data, returns, demographics? Some external systems do not allow you to join such external data.
- Do you need near real-time (NRT) results? These are often useful for quickly detecting and stopping bad experiments.
- Are you running enough experiments that you want to establish your own institutional memory? Many third-party experiment systems do not have institutional memory features.
- Can you implement your feature in its final version? Many WYSIWYG systems require you to re-implement your feature for real post-experiment. At scale, this can be limiting, with a queue of features that need re-implementation.

### What Would the Cost Be to Build Your Own?

Building a scalable system is both hard and expensive, as you will see in our discussion on the technical platform issues later in this chapter.

**What's the Trajectory of Your Experimentation Needs?**

This type of infrastructure investment is about anticipation, that is, how many experiments your organization will run if it truly embraces experimentation, not how many are currently running. If the momentum and demand is there, and the volume may grow beyond what an external solution can accommodate, build. It takes longer to build an internal solution, but integrating an external solution takes effort too, especially if you need to switch to a different solution as the company scales.

**Do You Need to Integrate into Your System's Configuration and Deployment Methods?**

Experimentation can be an integral part of a continuous deployment process. There is a lot of synergy between experimentation and how the engineering system handles configuration and deployment (see Chapter 15). If the integration is necessary, such as for more complicated debugging situations, it may be harder with a third-party solution.

Your organization may not be ready for the investment and commitment of building your own platform, so it may make sense to leverage an external solution to demonstrate the impact from more experimentation before determining if and when to make a case for building your own experiment platform.

# Infrastructure and Tools

In Chapter 3, we showed that there are many ways an experiment can go wrong. Creating an experiment platform is not just about accelerating innovation with experimentation, it is also critical to ensuring the trustworthiness of the results for decision making. Scaling experimentation at a company not only involves building the infrastructure for the experiment platform but also the tools and processes to embed experimentation deeply into the company's culture, development, and decision-making processes. The goal of an experiment platform is to make experimentation self-service and minimize the incremental costs of running a trustworthy experiment.

An experimentation platform must encompass every step of the process, from designing and deploying experiments to analyzing them (Gupta et al. 2018). If you look at the components of an experiment platform from Bing

(Kohavi, Longbotham et al. 2009), LinkedIn (Xu et al. 2015), or Google (Tang et al. 2010), there are four high-level components:

- Experiment definition, setup, and management via a user interface (UI) or application programming interface (API) and stored in the experiment system configuration
- Experiment deployment, both server- and client-side, that covers variant assignment and parameterization
- Experiment instrumentation
- Experiment analysis, which includes definition and computation of metrics and statistical tests like p-values.

You can see how these components fit together in Figure 4.2. In this section, we dive into each of these components.

## Experiment Definition, Set-up, and Management

To run many experiments, experimenters need a way to easily define, setup, and manage the experiment lifecycle. To define, or specify, an experiment, we need an owner, a name, a description, start and end dates, and several other fields (see Chapter 12). The platform also needs to allow experiments to have multiple *iterations* for the following reasons:

- To evolve the feature based on experiment results, which may also involve fixing bugs discovered during the experiment.
- To progressively roll out the experiment to a broader audience. This could either be via pre-defined rings (e.g., developers on the team, all employees within the company) or larger percentages of the outside population (Xia et al. 2019).

All iterations should be managed under the same experiment. In general, one iteration per experiment should be active at any time, although different platforms may need different iterations.

The platform needs some interface and/or tools to easily manage many experiments and their multiple iterations. Functionalities should include:

- Writing, editing, and saving draft experiment specifications.
- Comparing the draft iteration of an experiment with the current (running) iteration.
- Viewing the history or timeline of an experiment (even if it is no longer running).

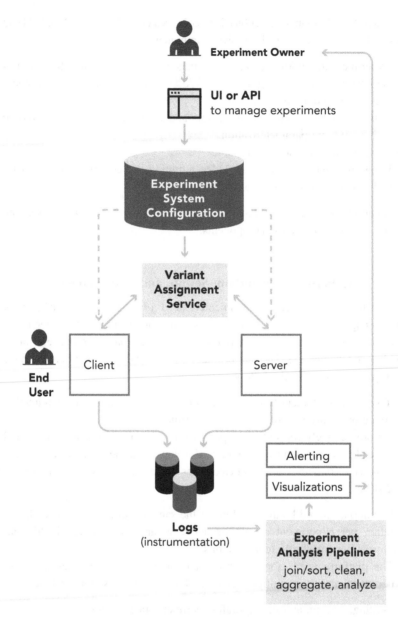

Figure 4.2 Possible experiment platform architecture. The client and/or the server can call the Variant Assignment Service. The Variant Assignment Service may be a separate server, or a library embedded in the client and/or server (in which case the configurations would be pushed directly to the client and/or server). See the discussion later on in this chapter for a discussion of the different architecture options

- Automatically assigning generated experiment IDs, variants, and iterations and adding them to the experiment specification. These IDs are needed in the experiment instrumentation (discussed later in this chapter).
- Validating that there are no obvious errors in the specifications, such as configuration conflicts, invalid targeting audience, and so on.
- Checking the status of an experiment as well as starting/stopping an experiment. To guard against human error, usually only experiment owners or individuals with special permission can start an experiment. However, due to the asymmetry of harming users, anyone can stop an experiment, although alerts are generated to ensure that experiment owners are informed.

Also, since the experiment is impacting real users, additional tools or workflows are needed to check the experiment variants before they go live. Options range from test code that must be run before deployment or a permission control system where experiments must get approval from trusted experts.

Beyond these basic checks, especially in the Fly phase when experiments are being run at scale, the platform also needs to support:

- Automation of how experiments are released and ramped up (see Chapter 15 for more detail)
- Near-real-time monitoring and alerting, to catch bad experiments early
- Automated detection and shutdown of bad experiments.

These increase the safety of the experiments.

## Experiment Deployment

After creating an experiment specification, the specification needs to be deployed to affect a user's experience. Deployment usually involves two components:

1. An experimentation infrastructure that provides experiment definitions, variant assignments, and other information
2. Production code changes that implement variant behavior according to the experiment assignment.

The experimentation infrastructure must provide:

- **Variant assignment**: Given a user request and its attributes (e.g., country, language, OS, platform), which experiment and variant combinations is that request assigned to? This assignment is based on the experiment specification and a pseudo-random hash of an ID, that is, $f(ID)$. In most cases, to ensure the assignment is consistent for a user, a user ID is used. Variant assignment must also be independent, in that knowing the variant assignment of one user should not tell us anything about variant assignment for a different user. We discuss this in more depth in Chapter 14. In this chapter, we assume *user* is the randomization unit.

- **Production code, system parameters and values**: Now that you have variant assignment and definitions, how do you ensure that the user receives the appropriate experience: how do you manage different production code and which system parameters should change to what values?

This interface (or interfaces) is represented as the Variant Assignment Service in Figure 4.2, and can return either just the variant assignment or a full configuration with the parameter values for performance reasons. In either case, the variant assignment service does not need to be a distinct server. Instead, it can be incorporated directly into the client or server via a shared library. Regardless of interface, a single implementation is critical to prevent inadvertent divergence and bugs.

There are important subtleties to consider when implementing the infrastructure, especially when operating at scale. For example, is *atomicity* required, and if so, at what granularity? Atomicity means whether all servers simultaneously switch over to the next iteration of an experiment. One example of where atomicity is important is in a web service, where a single request can call hundreds of servers, and inconsistent assignment leads to an inconsistent user experience (e.g., imagine a search query that requires multiple servers, each handling a disjoint part of the search index; if the ranking algorithm has changed, the same algorithm must be used by all servers). To fix this example, the parent service can perform variant assignment and pass it down to the child services. There are also differences in experiment deployment between client-based and server-based experiments, discussed further in Chapter 12.

Another consideration is where in the flow variant assignment happens (i.e., when the variant assignment interface is called). As discussed in Kohavi, Longbottom et al. (2009), variant assignment can happen in several places: outside of production code entirely using traffic splitting (e.g., traffic front door), client side (e.g., mobile app), or server side. To be better informed while making this decision, consider these key questions:

- **At what point in the flow do you have all the required information to do variant assignment?** For example, if you only have a user request, you may have information, such as user ID, language, and device. To use additional information, such as the age of the account, the time of their last visit, or frequency of visits, you may need to do a look-up before you can use that criteria for variant assignment. This could push variant assignment to later in the flow.

- **Do you allow experiment assignment to happen only at one point in the flow or at multiple points?** If you are in the early stages of building your experiment platform (Walk or early Run phases), we recommend having only one point where experiment assignment happens to keep it simple. If you have multiple assignment points, you will need orthogonality guarantees (e.g., overlapping experiments, as discussed in *Concurrent Experiments* later in this chapter) to ensure that experiment assignment that happens earlier does not bias experiment assignment that happens later in the flow.

Now that you have assigned variants, it is time to ensure that the system provides the appropriate Treatment to the user. There are three main choices for architecture.

- The first architecture creates a code fork based on variant assignment:
  ```
  variant = getVariant(userId)
  If (variant == Treatment) then
    buttonColor = red
  Else
    buttonColor = blue
  ```
- The second architecture moves to a parameterized system, where any possible change that you want to test in an experiment must be controlled by an experiment parameter. You can either choose to continue to use code forks:
  ```
  variant = getVariant(userId)
  If (variant == Treatment) then
    buttonColor = variant.getParam("buttonColor")
  Else
    buttonColor = blue
  ```
  Or move to:
  ```
  variant = getVariant(userId)
  ...
  buttonColor = variant.getParam("buttonColor")
  ```
- The third architecture removes even the getVariant() call. Instead, early in the flow, variant assignment is done, and a configuration with the variant and all parameter values for that variant and for that user are passed down through the remaining flow.
  ```
  buttonColor = config.getParam("buttonColor")
  ```
  Each system parameter has a default setting (e.g., the default button-Color is blue), and for Treatment, you only need to specify which system

parameters change and their values. The config that is passed contains all parameters and the appropriate values.

There are advantages and disadvantages to each architecture. The main advantage of the first architecture is that variant assignment happens close to the actual code change, so handling triggering is easier. The Control and Treatment populations in the first architecture both contain only the affected users (see Chapter 20); however, the disadvantage can be escalating technical debt, as managing forked code paths can become quite challenging. The second architecture, especially with the second option, reduces the code debt while maintaining the advantage of handling triggering more easily. The third architecture moves variant assignment early, so handling triggering is more challenging. However, it can also be more performant: as a system grows to have hundreds to thousands of parameters, even if an experiment likely affects only a few parameters, then optimizing parameter handling, perhaps with caches, becomes critical from a performance perspective.

Google shifted from the first architecture to the third based on a combination of performance reasons as well as the technical debt and the challenges of reconciling code paths when it came time to merge back into a single path to make future changes easier. Bing also uses the third architecture. Microsoft Office uses the first option in the second architecture but implemented a system where a bug ID is passed as an experiment parameter, triggering an alert after three months to remind engineers to remove experimental code paths.

Regardless of which architecture you choose, you must measure the cost and impact of running experiments. An experiment platform can also have performance implications, so running some traffic outside of the experimentation platform is itself an experiment to measure the impact of the platform, be that in site speed latency, CPU utilization and machine cost, or any other factor.

## Experiment Instrumentation

We assume you already log basic instrumentation, such as user actions and system performance (see Chapter 13 for what to instrument). Especially when testing new features, you must update your basic instrumentation to reflect these new features, as these updates to your instrumentation allow you to perform proper analysis. The focus during the Crawl phase is on this level of instrumentation, and leadership must ensure that instrumentation is constantly being reviewed and improved.

For experiments, you should also instrument every user request and interaction with which variant and iteration is run. The iteration is important especially when an experiment starts or ramps up, because not all servers or clients will simultaneously change the user Treatment (Chapter 12).

In many cases, especially as you get to the Run and Fly phases, we want to log the counterfactual, or what would have happened. For example, for a Treatment user, we may want to log what search results would have returned if they were the Control variant. In the system parameterized architecture described above, where variant assignment happens early, you may find counterfactual logging quite challenging but necessary (see Chapter 20). Counterfactual logging can be expensive from a performance perspective, in which case you may need to establish guidelines about when it is needed. If your product has a place for users to enter feedback, that feedback and the variant IDs must be logged. This is helpful when feedback is specific to the variant.

## Scaling Experimentation: Digging into Variant Assignment

As companies move from the Walk to Run phase, to provide enough statistical power to experiments, a sufficient percentage of users must be assigned to each variant. Where maximal power is desired, an experiment will run at 50%/50% and include all users. To scale the number of experiments, users must be in multiple experiments. How does that work?

### Single-Layer Method

Variant assignment is the process by which users are consistently assigned to an experiment variant. In the Walk phase, the number of experiments is usually small and it is common to divide all traffic with each experiment variant receiving a specified fraction of the total traffic. You might have one experiment with one Control and two Treatment variants taking up 60% of traffic, and another experiment with just one Control and one Treatment taking up the other 40% of traffic (Figure 4.3). This assignment is typically done using a

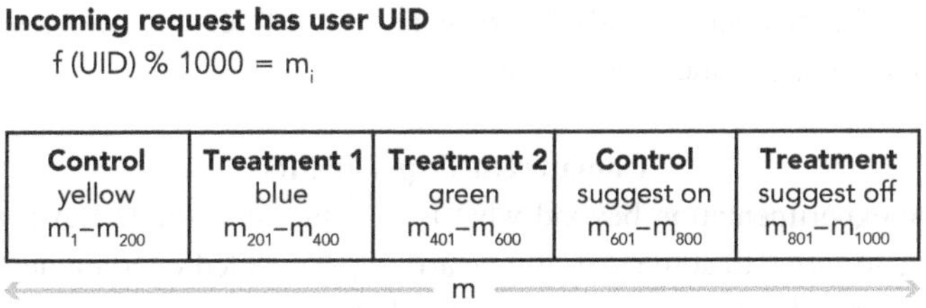

**Incoming request has user UID**
$f(UID) \% 1000 = m_i$

| Control<br>yellow<br>$m_1-m_{200}$ | Treatment 1<br>blue<br>$m_{201}-m_{400}$ | Treatment 2<br>green<br>$m_{401}-m_{600}$ | Control<br>suggest on<br>$m_{601}-m_{800}$ | Treatment<br>suggest off<br>$m_{801}-m_{1000}$ |
|---|---|---|---|---|

$$\longleftarrow \qquad\qquad\qquad m \qquad\qquad\qquad \longrightarrow$$

Figure 4.3 Example Control-Treatment assignment in the Single-Layer Method

hash function to consistently assign the users to buckets. In this example, we use 1,000 disjoint buckets and specify which variant gets which buckets. In this example, a variant with 200 buckets has a 20% traffic allocation.

The assignment of users to buckets must be random but deterministic. If you compare any two buckets running the same Treatment, they are assumed to be statistically similar (see Chapter 19):

- There should be roughly the same number of users in each bucket (see Chapter 3). If you broke it down by key dimensions, such as country, platform, or language, comparing slices across buckets will also be roughly the same.
- Your key metrics (goal, guardrail, quality), should have roughly the same values (within normal variability).

Monitoring assignments are key! Google, Microsoft, and many other companies found errors in the randomization code by monitoring bucket characteristics. Another common issue are carry-over effects (see Chapter 23), where prior experiments can taint buckets for the current experiment. Re-randomization, or shuffling, the buckets with every experiment so that they are no longer contiguous is a common solution (Kohavi, et al. 2012).

The Single-Layer (also called a numberline) method is simple and allows multiple experiments to run simultaneously (each user is only in a single experiment). It is a plausible choice in early maturity phases when few experiments run concurrently; however, the main drawback is the limitation on the number of concurrent experiments, as you must ensure that each experiment has enough traffic for adequate power. Operationally, managing experimental traffic in a Single-Layer system can be challenging, as even in this early phase, experiments are running concurrently—just not on a single user. To manage the concurrency, LinkedIn, Bing, and Google all started with manual methods (at LinkedIn, teams would negotiate traffic "ranges" using e-mails; at Bing, it was managed by a program manager, whose office was usually packed with people begging for experimental traffic; while at Google, it started with e-mail and instant messaging negotiation, before moving to a program manager). However, the manual methods do not scale, so all three companies shifted to programmatic assignment over time.

### Concurrent Experiments

To scale experimentation beyond what is possible in a Single-Layer method, you need to move to some sort of concurrent (also called overlapping) experiment system, where each user can be in multiple experiments at the same time. One way to achieve this is to have multiple experiment layers where each layer

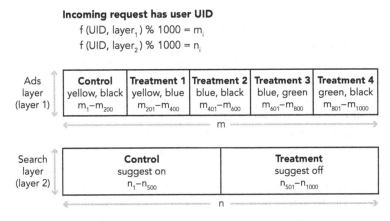

**Incoming request has user UID**

$$f(\text{UID}, \text{layer}_1) \% 1000 = m_i$$
$$f(\text{UID}, \text{layer}_2) \% 1000 = n_i$$

Figure 4.4  Control-Treatment assignment example in an overlapping methodology

behaves like the Single-Layer method. To ensure orthogonality of experiments across layers, in the assignment of users to buckets, add the layer ID. This is also where you would add, as in the experiment specification discussed above, the layer ID (or some other way of specifying constraints).

When a request comes in, variant assignment is done once for each layer (see Figure 4.4 for an example with two layers). This implies that both production code and instrumentation must handle a vector of variant IDs. The main question with a concurrent experiment system is how to determine the layers, and there are several options.

One possibility is to extend a full factorial experiment design into a full factorial platform design. In a full factorial experiment design, every possible combination of factors is tested as a variant. If we extend that to a platform, then a user is in all experiments simultaneously: the user is assigned to a variant (Control or any of the Treatments) for every experiment running. Each experiment is associated with a unique layer ID, so all experiments are orthogonal to each other. Iterations of the same experiment usually share the same hash ID to ensure a consistent experience for a user. This simple parallel experimentation structure allows you to scale the number of experiments easily in a decentralized manner.

The main drawback of this platform design is that it does not avoid potential collisions, where certain Treatments from two different experiments give users a poor experience if they coexist. For example, we could be testing blue text in Experiment One and blue background in Experiment Two. It would have been a horrible experience for any users who happen to fall into both Treatments.

In statistical terms, these two experiments "interact" with each other. It is not only a poor user experience, the results measured for each experiment independently may also be incorrect without considering any interactions between the two experiments. Note that not all interactions are antagonistic—sometimes being in both Treatments helps more than the sum.

That said, a factorial platform design might be preferred if the reduction on statistical power when splitting up traffic outweighs the potential concern of interaction. Moreover, if we set up these experiments independently, we can analyze to see which experiments interact what their effects would be without interaction. Of course, if there is no significant interaction, each experiment can be analyzed separately, and each gets to enjoy the full amount of traffic available for maximum power. Microsoft's experimentation platform has a robust system that automates the detection of interactions (Kohavi et al. 2013).

To prevent poor user experiences, we can either use a *nested* platform design (Tang et al. 2010) or a *constraints-based* platform design (Kohavi et al. 2013). For scalability, Google, LinkedIn, Microsoft, and Facebook use some variation of these designs (Xu 2015, Bakshy, Eckles and Bernstein 2014).

In a nested design, system parameters are partitioned into layers so that experiments that in combination may produce a poor user experience must be in the same layer and be prevented by design from running for the same user. For example, there might be one layer for the common UI elements (e.g., the header of the page and all information in the header), another layer for the body, a third layer for back-end systems, a fourth layer for ranking parameters, and so on.

A constraints-based design has experimenters specify the constraints and the system uses a graph-coloring algorithm to ensure that no two experiments that share a concern are exposed to the user. Automated systems for detecting interactions (Kohavi et al. 2013) can be a useful extension.

## Experimentation Analytics

To move to the later phases of experimentation maturity, we also need automated analysis, which is crucial both for saving teams from needing to do time-consuming ad hoc analysis, and ensuring that the methodology behind the reports is solid, consistent, and scientifically founded. We assume that the work of choosing the goal, guardrail, and quality metrics is already done, as well as any codification of tradeoffs into an OEC.

Automating analysis first requires *data processing*, where the goal is to get data into a usable state to compute and visualize the experiment results. Since instrumentation about a user request may happen in multiple systems, data processing typically involves sorting and joining the different logs and cleansing, sessionizing and enriching them. This process is sometimes referred to as *cooking* the data.

When you have the processed data, the goal is to summarize and highlight the key metrics to help guide decision makers to a launch/no-launch decision. This requires *data computation* of metrics (e.g. OEC, guardrail metrics, quality metrics) by segments (e.g., country, language, device/platform), computations of p-values/confidence intervals, also trustworthiness checks, such as the SRM check. It can also include analysis to automatically find which segments are most interesting (see Chapter 3). Note that while the data computation may compute all of these in a single step, when you actually look at the experiment data, you must look at the trustworthiness checks first, before checking the OEC, doing any segmentation, and so on. However, before you look at the experiment data, all of the data cooking and computation must also be thoroughly tested and checked to ensure the trustworthiness of these processes.

Given the computation, we can finally create the *data visualization* to highlight key metrics and interesting metrics and segments in an easy-to-understand way. This visualization can be as simple as an Excel-like spreadsheet. Metrics are presented as a relative change, with clear indication if results are statistically significant, often using color-coding to make significant changes stand out. To foster a culture of intellectual integrity, ensure that results use common definitions that are tracked and accessible, as well as frequently reviewed, agreed upon and updated.

As an organization moves into the Run and Fly phase, there can be many metrics –even thousands! This is when you group metrics by tier (company-wide, product-specific, feature-specific (Xu et al. 2015, Dmitriev and Wu 2016)) or by function (OEC, goal, guardrail, quality, debug; see Chapter 7). Multiple testing becomes more important as the number of metrics grow, and we found that one common question arose from experimenters: Why did this metric move significantly when it seems irrelevant?

While education can help, options in the tool to use p-value thresholds smaller than the standard 0.05 value are effective. Lower thresholds allow experimenters to quickly filter to the most significant metrics (Xu et al. 2015).

Use visualization tools to generate per-metric views of all experiment results, which allows stakeholders to closely monitor the global health of key metrics and see which experiments are most impactful. This transparency encourages conversations between experiment owners and metric owners, which in turn increases the overall knowledge of experimentation in your company.

Visualization tools are a great gateway for accessing *institutional memory* to capture what was experimented, why the decision was made, and successes and failures that lead to knowledge discovery and learning. For example, through mining historical experiments, you can run a meta-analysis on which kind of experiments tend to move certain metrics, and which metrics tend to move together (beyond their natural correlation). We discuss this more in Chapter 8. When new employees join the company, visuals help them quickly form intuition, get a feel for corporate goals, and learn your hypothesis process. As your ecosystem evolves, having historical results and refined parameters allows you to rerun experiments that failed.

# PART II

## Selected Topics for Everyone

Part II provides details on five topics relevant for everyone involved with experiments, especially leaders and executives.

We start with *Speed Matters: An End-to-End Case Study*, which is an end-to-end example of using careful experiment design and analysis to establish the importance of latency and site speed as a sensitive surrogate metric for user engagement and revenue. It is also a good example of the type of result that is likely applicable across sites and domains.

Next, because metrics are crucial for data-informed decisions in every company, we introduce *Organizational Metrics* that leaders should understand, discuss, and establish for their organization regardless of whether they are running experiments. We discuss the desiderata for those metrics, as well as how to create, validate, and iterate on them.

Especially as an organization evolves their experimentation practices, leaders need to discuss – and ideally agree – on *Metrics for Experimentation and the Overall Evaluation Criterion (OEC)*. An OEC combines one or more organizational metrics that meet specific criteria needed for experimentation. The combination is used to encode tradeoffs between these metrics to make online controlled experiments and driving innovation at scale easier.

As an organization begins to scale experimentation in the *Run and Fly* maturity phases (see Chapter 4), establishing *Institutional Memory and Meta-Analysis* becomes increasingly useful. Institutional memory captures past experiments and changes, and drives innovation, to help encourage a culture of data-informed decision making and facilitate continuous learning.

Finally, online controlled experiments are run on real people, so *Ethics in Controlled Experiments* and end-user considerations are very important. We motivate the importance of ethics for online controlled experimentation, summarize key important considerations, and give pointers to other resources in the field.

# 5

# Speed Matters

## *An End-to-End Case Study*

The dangers of a slow web site: frustrated users, negative brand perception, increased operating expenses, and loss of revenue
*– Steve Souders (2009)*

An engineer that improves server performance by 10 msec (that's 1/30 of the speed that our eyes blink) more than pays for his (or her) fully-loaded annual costs. Every millisecond counts
*– Kohavi, Deng, Frasca, Walker, Xu and Pohlmann (2013)*

Fast is my favorite Feature
*– Google shirt circa 2009*

***Why you care:*** *We begin with an end-to-end example of the design (with explicit assumptions), execution, and interpretation of an experiment to assess the importance of speed. Many examples of experiments focus on the User Interface (UI) because it is easy to show examples, but there are many breakthroughs on the back-end side, and as multiple companies discovered: speed matters a lot! Of course, faster is better, but how important is it to improve performance by a tenth of a second? Should you have a person focused on performance? Maybe a team of five? The return-on-investment (ROI) of such efforts can be quantified by running a simple slowdown experiment. In 2017, every tenth of a second improvement for Bing was worth $18 million in incremental annual revenue, enough to fund a sizable team. Based on these results and multiple replications at several companies through the years, we recommend using latency as a guardrail metric.*

How important is product performance? Where in the product is reducing latency important? Controlled experiments provide clear answers to these questions through a simple yet powerful technique: slowdown experiments. By slowing down the product, we can assess the impact of increased latency on key metrics, including declines in revenue and user satisfaction metrics. Under mild assumptions that we can verify, we can show that an improvement to performance that is, reducing latency, improves these metrics: revenue and satisfaction increase.

At Amazon, a 100 msec slowdown experiment decreased sales by 1% (Linden 2006, 10). A rare joint talk by speakers from Bing and Google (Schurman and Brutlag 2009) showed the significant impact of performance on key metrics, including distinct queries, revenue, clicks, satisfaction, and time-to-click. A 2012 detailed study at Bing (Kohavi et al.2013) showed that every 100 msec speedup improves revenue by 0.6%. In 2015, as Bing's performance improved, there were questions about whether there is still value to performance improvements when the server was returning results in under a second at the 95th percentile. A follow-on study was conducted and while the impact on revenue was somewhat reduced, Bing's revenue improved so much that each millisecond in improved performance was worth more than in the past: every four milliseconds improvement funded an engineer for a year!

Multiple performance-related results were shared in *Why Performance Matters* (Wagner 2019), showing improvements to conversions and user engagement, although many of the results are not from controlled experiments, so their results are confounded with other changes.

One decision you might face is whether to use a third-party product for personalization or optimization. Some of these products require that you insert a JavaScript snippet at the top of the HTML page. These are blocking snippets that slow the page significantly because they require a roundtrip to the snippet provider and transfer the JavaScript, which is typically tens of kilobytes (Schrijvers 2017, Optimizely 2018b). Putting the snippet lower on the page results in page *flashing*. Based on latency experiment results, any increase in goal metrics might be offset by the cost of the latency increase. Thus, we recommend using server-side personalization and optimization whenever possible, that is, have the server side do the variant assignment (see Chapter 12) and generate the HTML code for that variant.

Our goal is to show how to measure the impact of performance on key metrics, not the specific techniques for improving performance. There are several excellent resources available for improving performance (Sullivan 2008, Souders 2007, 2009).

Another benefit of running this type of experiment is that you can generate a mapping from performance delta to the delta impact on key metrics to answer such questions as:

- What is the immediate revenue impact of performance improvements?
- Is there a long-term impact (e.g., reduced churn) from performance improvements?

- What is the impact to a metric X? It is often the case that the initial implementation of a new feature is inefficient. If the A/B test shows a degradation to metric X, would speeding the implementation be enough to address the degradation? In many cases, a new feature slightly slows down the web site or application, so there is a tradeoff to make, and this mapping helps.
- Where are the performance improvements more critical? For example, increased latency for elements that users must scroll to see (also known as "below the fold") may be less critical. Similarly, right-pane elements have been found to be less critical.

To conduct a controlled experiment, you want to isolate latency as the *only* factor changed. It is very hard to improve performance or else developers would have already made those changes, so we resort to a simple technique: slowing down the web site or product. By slowing the Treatment relative to Control it is easy to measure the impact on any metric, but you need to make some assumptions.

## Key Assumption: Local Linear Approximation

The key assumption for slowdown experiments is that the metric (e.g., revenue) graph vs. performance is well approximated by a linear line around the point matching today's performance. This is a first-order Taylor-series approximation, or linear approximation.

Figure 5.1 shows a graph depicting a common relationship between time (performance) and a metric of interest (e.g., click-throughrate (CTR) or revenue-per-user). Typically, the faster the site, the better (higher in this example) the metric value.

When we slow down the Treatment, we move from the point where the vertical line intersects the graph to the right, and we can measure the change to the metric. The assumption we make is that if we were to move left of the vertical line (improving performance), the vertical delta on the left would be approximately the same as the one we measured on the right.

Is the assumption realistic? Two things make this a good assumption:

1. From our own experience as users, faster is better in search. It is hard to think about reasons why there would be discontinuities or dramatic changes in the graph, especially around today's performance point. If we delayed by three seconds, one can imagine a significant cliff, but for adding or subtracting a tenth of a second, this is less likely.

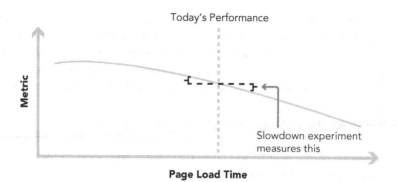

Figure 5.1 Typical relationship between performance (time) and a metric of interest

2. We can sample the graph at two points to see whether a linear approximation is reasonable. Specifically, Bing ran the slowdown experiment with a 100 msec and a 250 msec slowdown. The delta for the 250 msec experiment was ~2.5 times that of the 100 msec study (within the confidence intervals) for several key metrics, which supports the linearity assumption.

## How to Measure Website Performance

Measuring website performance is not obvious. This section shares some of the complexity involved and some of the assumptions made. These significant details impact your experiment design. We go into details here to give a taste of real-life complexity for something that appears simple; feel free to skim this section.

To reliably measure latency, servers must be synchronized as requests are typically handled by different servers and we have seen clock skew between servers contribute to data quality issues (e.g., negative durations). It is very important that servers sync their clocks often. Our examples do not mix client and server times, because they can be in different time zones (see Chapter 13), and client clocks are usually less reliable, sometimes years off (e.g., when their batteries die).

Figure 5.2 shows a request for a highly optimized website, such as a search engine. The steps are as follows:

1. The user makes a request at time T0, say typing a query into the browser address bar or search box and hitting return or clicking on the magnifying glass.

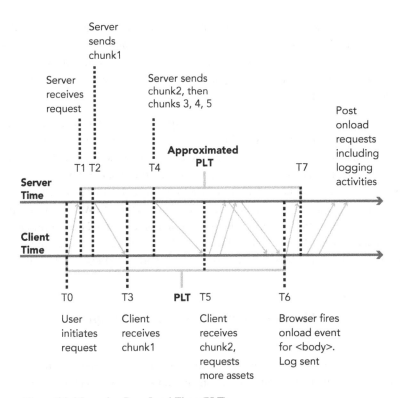

Figure 5.2 Measuring Page Load Time (PLT)

2. The request takes time to reach the server, and it arrives at time T1. T1−T0 seems extremely hard to estimate, but there is a nice trick we can deploy that we explain after this numbered list.

3. On receiving the request, the server typically sends the first chunk of HTML to the client, time T2.

   This first chunk is independent of the request (e.g., query or URL parameters), so can be served quickly. It typically contains the basic page elements, such as the header, navigation elements, and JavaScript functions. Providing the user with visible feedback that the request was received is beneficial: the page typically clears, and a header displays with some page decorations, sometimes called the chrome or frame. Since the server takes time (to time T4) to compute the URL-dependent part of the page (e.g., query, or URL parameters), the more "code" that can be shipped, the faster the page will be, as the client and network are typically idle.

4. At time T4, the server starts sending the rest of the page, which can involve additional round trips for other assets (e.g., images).

5. At time T6, the browser fires the Onload event, indicating the page is ready. At this point, it makes a log request, typically a simple $1 \times 1$ image request (beacon) or equivalent. That request reaches the server at time T7. There may be other activities that happen after the Onload event and additional logging (e.g., user actions like scrolls, hovers, and clicks).

The Page Load Time (PLT) the user experiences is T6−T0, which we approximate by measuring T7−T1. Because the time the initial request takes to reach the server is likely to be very similar to the time it takes the Onload event beacon to reach the server (both are small requests), these two deltas will probably be very similar and allow us to approximate the user experience time.

In newer browsers that support new W3C (World Wide Web Consortium) standards, Navigation Timing calls provide multiple PLT-related information (see www.w3.org/TR/navigation-timing/). The above measurements are more generic, and the numbers from the W3C Navigation Timings match well.

## The Slowdown Experiment Design

What may seem like a trivial experiment turns out to be more complex. One question is where to insert the slowdown? Bing initially slowed down sending Chunk1 (see Figure 5.2), but had too big an impact and was deemed unreasonable because of the following:

1. Chunk1 is sent from the server quickly because there is nothing to compute. It is therefore unreasonable to say that we can improve the latency of Chunk1.
2. Chunk1 is what gives the user the feedback that the request was properly received by painting the page chrome or frame. Delaying that has multiple negative effects unrelated to overall site performance.

The right place to delay is when the server finishes computing Chunk2, which is the URL-dependent HTML. Instead of the server sending the HTML, we delay the response, *as if* the server took longer to generate the query-dependent part of the HTML.

How long should the delay be? There are several factors at play here:

• Every metric we compute has a confidence interval. We would like the Treatment effect to be large so that we can estimate the "slope" more accurately. Figure 5.3 shows two possible measurements at 100 msec and 250 msec the delay time axis. If both have a similar confidence interval size, then measuring at 250 msec provides us with much tighter bounds on the slope. This factor calls for making the delay larger.

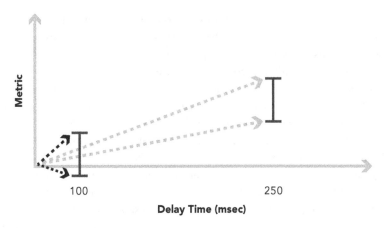

Figure 5.3  Confidence intervals around different delay times

- A longer delay implies that our first-order Taylor series approximation may be less accurate. This factor calls for a shorter delay.
- A long delay causes more harm to our users, as we strongly believe that faster is better and therefore slowing the experiences causes harm. This factor calls for a shorter delay.

Another question is whether the delay is constant or some percentage, to account for geographical network differences (e.g., Bing users in South Africa have very slow page load times, so 250 msec delay may not feel like much). Given that the experiment is modeling a back-end server-side delay, a constant delay was deemed a good choice. If we wanted to model what happens relative to network differences, then the experiment might be based on, for example, payload size instead of latency.

Finally, there is a question of whether speedup is more important on the first page or later pages in the session. Some speedup techniques (e.g., caching of JavaScript) can improve the performance of later pages in a session.

Given the above factors, slowdowns of 100 msec and 250 msec were determined to be reasonable choices by Bing.

## Impact of Different Page Elements Differs

Performance of different areas of the page differs. The speed of showing the algorithmic search results of Bing were critical and slowdowns had material impact on key metrics, such as revenue and key user metrics.

What about other areas of the page? It turns out they are much less critical. At Bing, some elements on the right pane are loaded late (technically, after the `window.onload` event). A slowdown-controlled experiment was run, like that described above, delaying when the right-pane elements display by 250 msec. No statistically significant impact was detected for key metrics, despite having almost 20 million users in the experiment.

PLT is often measured using the `window.onload` to mark the end of the useful browser activity rather than the sequence described above. However, this measurement has severe deficiencies with modern web pages. As Steve Souders showed (2013), an Amazon page can render in 2.0 seconds above the fold (Wikipedia contributors, Above the Fold 2014), that is, on the visible part of the page, but the `window.onload` event fires at 5.2 seconds. Schurman and Brutlag (2009) reported that being able to progressively render a page so that the header displays early helps. The opposite is also true with Gmail, as a good example: the `window.onload` fires at 3.3 seconds, at which point only the progress bar is visible and the above-the-fold content displays at 4.8 seconds.

The term "perceived performance" often denotes the intuitive idea that users start to interpret the page once enough of it is showing. The concept of perceived performance is easier to state abstractly than it is to measure in practice, and `perception.ready()` isn't on any browser's roadmap (Souders 2013). Multiple proposals have been developed to estimate perceived performance, including:

- **Time to first result**. When a list displays, such as on Twitter, the time to the first tweet is a possible metric.
- **Above the Fold Time (AFT)**. You can measure the time until pixels above the fold are painted (Brutlag, Abrams and Meenan 2011). Implementations must use heuristics to handle videos, animated GIFs, rotating galleries, and other dynamic content that changes the page above the fold. Thresholds can be set for "percent of pixels painted" to avoid trivial elements of little consequence from prolonging the measured time.
- **Speed Index**. This is a generalization of AFT (Meenan 2012) that averages the time when visible elements on the page display. This does not suffer from trivial elements showing late, but still suffers from dynamic content changing above the fold.
- **Page Phase Time and User Ready Time**. Page Phase Time requires identifying which rendering phase satisfies perceived performance, and phases are determined by pixel-changing velocity. User Ready Time measures the time until the essential elements of the page (defined for each context) are ready to use (Meenan, Feng and Petrovich 2013).

One way to avoid coming up with definitions for perceived performance is to measure the time-to-user action, such as a click. This technique works well when there's an expected action by the user. A more sophisticated variant of time-to-click is time-to-successful-click, where success can be defined as a click that does not result in the user coming back for 30 seconds, thus avoiding "bait" clicks. Such metrics do not suffer from the heuristics needed for many performance metrics and are robust to many changes. The main problem with such metrics is that they work only when an action is expected. If a user issues a query "time in Paris" and gets a good instant answer, there is nothing to click.

## Extreme Results

While speed matters a lot, we have also seen some results we believe are overstated. In a Web 2.0 talk by Marissa Mayer, then at Google, she described an experiment where Google increased the number of search results on the Search Engine Result Page (SERP) from ten to thirty (Linden 2006). She claimed that traffic and revenue from Google searchers in the experimental group dropped by 20%. Her explanation? The page took half a second more to generate. Performance is a critical factor, but multiple factors were changed, and we suspect that the performance only accounts for a small percentage of the loss. See Kohavi et al. (2014) for details.

Conversely, Dan McKinley (2012), then at Etsy, claimed that a 200 msec delay did not matter at all. It is possible that for Etsy users, performance is not critical, but we believe a more likely hypothesis is that the experiment did not have sufficient statistical power to detect the differences. Telling an organization that performance doesn't matter will make the site slower very quickly, to the point where users abandon it in droves.

Finally, in rare scenarios, too fast may reduce user trust that some activity was done, so some products add fake progress bars (Bodlewski 2017).

When reviewing results of experiments, ask yourself what trust level to apply, and remember that even if the idea worked for a specific site, it may not work as well for another. One thing you can do is report replications of prior experiments (successful or not). This is how science works best.

# 6

# Organizational Metrics

If you can't measure it, you can't improve it
— *Peter Drucker (longer version by Lord Kelvin)*

[Watermelon Metric:] . . .teams think they are doing a great job hitting green targets, their customers view it quite differently and only see red
— *Barclay Rae (2014)*

When optimizing for conversion, we often find clients trying to improve engine torque while ignoring a flat tire
— *Bryan Eisenberg and John Quarto-vonTivadar (2008)*

*Why you care?* Organizations that want to measure their progress and accountability need good metrics. For example, one popular way of running an organization is to use Objectives and Key Results (OKRs), where an Objective is a long-term goal, and the Key Results are shorter-term, measurable results that move towards the goal (Doerr 2018). When using the OKR system, good metrics are key to tracking progress towards those goals. Understanding the different types of organizational metrics, the important criteria that these metrics need to meet, how to create and evaluate these metrics, and the importance of iteration over time can help generate the insights needed to make data-informed decisions, regardless of whether you also run experiments.

## Metrics Taxonomy

In a data-driven organization, metrics and the accompanying data analyses can be used at every level, from top-level goal setting and accountability on down through the teams. The discussion of what the metrics should be for an organization or a team is useful for aligning on goals, and subsequently providing transparency and accountability on executing towards those goals (Doerr 2018). This section focuses on organizational metrics overall, whereas Chapter 7 discusses metrics specific for experimentation and Chapter 21 discusses the role of guardrail metrics for alerting in experiments.

In discussing organizational metrics, the taxonomy commonly used is goals, drivers, and guardrails. This taxonomy is useful regardless of whether we are talking about an organization that is an entire company or a specific team within a larger organization.

**Goal metrics**, also called *success metrics* or *true north metrics*, reflect what the organization ultimately cares about. When trying to come up with a goal metric, we recommend first articulating what you want in words. Why does your product exist? What does success look like for your organization? The leaders of the organization must engage in answering these questions, and the answers are often tied to a mission statement. For example, if Microsoft's mission is to empower every person and every organization on the planet to achieve more, or Google's mission is to organize the world's information, then their goals are often directly related to those missions.

Being able to articulate your goal in words is important, as the transformation of that goal into metrics is often imperfect, and your goal metrics may be proxies of what you really care about and require iteration over time. Having people understand the limitations and differences between the metrics and the articulation of the goal is critical to driving the business in the right direction.

Goal metrics are usually a single or a very small set of metrics that best captures the ultimate success you are striving towards. These metrics may not be easy to move in the short term because each initiative may have only a very small impact on the metric, or because impacts take a long time to materialize.

**Driver metrics,** also called *sign post metrics*, *surrogate metrics*, *indirect* or *predictive metrics*, tend to be shorter-term, faster-moving, and more-sensitive metrics than goal metrics. Driver metrics reflect a mental causal model of what it takes for the organization to succeed, that is, hypotheses on the drivers of success rather than just what success looks like.

There are several useful metrics frameworks for thinking about what drives success: The HEART framework (Happiness, Engagement, Adoption, Retention, and Task Success) (Rodden, Hutchinson and Fu 2010), Dave McClure's PIRATE framework (*AARRR! Acquisition, Activation, Retention, Referral, Revenue*) (McClure 2007), or user funnels in general. These frameworks can help break down the steps that lead to success. For example, before ultimately achieving revenue, a typical company must acquire users and ensure that their product is engaging enough to retain them.

A good driver metric indicates that we are moving in the right direction to move the goal metric(s).

**Guardrail metrics** guard against violated assumptions and come in two types: metrics that protect the business and metrics that assess the trustworthiness and internal validity of experiment results. Here, we focus on the first type of organizational guardrails, while trustworthiness guardrail metrics are discussed in Chapter 21.

While our eyes are usually on the goal and driver metrics, guardrail metrics are important to ensure we move towards success with the right balance and without violating important constraints. For example, our goal may be to get as many users as possible to register, but we don't want the per-user engagement level to drop drastically. Another example is a password management company. There might be a tradeoff between security (no hijackings or information stolen), ease-of-use, and accessibility (i.e, how often users are locked out). While security may be the goal, the ease-of-use and accessibility can be guardrails. Finally, while page-load-time may not be a goal metric, we still need to make sure that feature launches do not degrade load times (see Chapter 5). Guardrail metrics are frequently more sensitive than goal or driver metrics. See Chapter 21 for more examples of guardrail metrics.

While we find goal, driver, and guardrail metrics offer the right amount of granularity and comprehensiveness, there are other business metric taxonomies as well:

- **Asset vs. engagement metrics**: Asset metrics measure the accumulation of static assets, like the total number of Facebook users (accounts) or total number of connections. Engagement metrics measure the value a user receives as a result of an action or by others using the product, such as a session or a pageview.
- **Business vs. operational metrics:** Business metrics, such as revenue- per-user or daily active user (DAU), track the health of the business. Operational metrics, such as queries per second, track whether there are operational concerns.

While we discuss metrics for experiments further in Chapter 7, there are also other types of metrics commonly used in experimentation. **Data quality metrics** ensure the internal validity and trustworthiness of the underlying experiments (see also Chapter 3 and Chapter 21). **Diagnosis or debug metrics** are helpful when debugging a scenario where the goal, driver, or guardrail metrics indicate there is a problem. They might provide additional granularity or other information typically too detailed to track on an ongoing basis but useful when drilling down into a situation. For example, if click-through rate (CTR) is a key metric, you might have 20 metrics to indicate clicks on certain areas of the page. Or, if revenue is a key metric, you might want to decompose revenue into two metrics: a revenue indicator that is a Boolean (0/1) indicating whether the user purchased at all; and a Conditional Revenue metric that comprises the revenue if the user purchased and is null otherwise (when averaged, only the revenue from purchasing users is averaged). Average overall revenue is the product of these two metrics, but each tells a different story about revenue. Did it increase/decrease because more/less people purchased or because the average purchase price changed?

Regardless of the taxonomy used, having discussions on metrics is useful, as agreeing on metrics requires clear goal articulation and alignment. The metrics can subsequently be used for goal setting at the company level, team level, feature level or individual level, and be used for everything from executive reporting to engineering system monitoring. Iterating on metrics over time is also expected, both as the organization evolves and the understanding of the metrics evolves.

We often need to measure goals, drivers, and guardrails at both the company level and team level. Each team is likely to contribute differently to the overall success of the company. Some teams might be more focused on adoption, others on happiness, still others on retention or performance or latency. Each team must articulate their goal and hypothesis on how their metrics relate to the overall company metrics. The same metric may play a different role for different teams. Some teams may use latency or other performance metrics as a guardrail, while an infrastructure team may use those same latency or performance metrics as their goal metric and use the other business metrics as their guardrail metrics.

For example, let's say you are working on a product where the overall goal metric is long-term revenue, and driver metrics at a business level are user engagement and retention. Now, you have a team that is working on a support site for this product. This team tried to set "time-on-site" as the key driver metric to improve, but is more time on the site better or worse? This type of discussion is useful at every level of the company to understand and align on.

Parmenter in *Key Performance Indicators* (2015) uses the diagram shown in Figure 6.1 to emphasize the importance of aligning goal and driver metrics to your overall business strategy.

Depending on organization size and objectives, you may have multiple teams, each with their own goal, driver, and guardrail metrics, and all of which must align with your overall goal, driver, guardrail metrics.

Figure 6.1 It is important to align each team's metrics with the overall goal and strategic direction

## Formulating Metrics: Principles and Techniques

Now that you have it down in words what success looks like and possible drivers, let's start formulating metrics. This is when we take a qualitative concept to a concrete, quantifiable definition. In some cases, such as revenue, the answer may be obvious. However, a company may define success as long-term revenue, which is harder to measure than revenue realized today. Other difficult-to-measure concepts of success include user happiness and user trust.

Key principles when developing goal and driver metrics are:

1. Ensure that your goal metrics are:
   - **Simple**: easily understood and broadly accepted by stakeholders.
   - **Stable:** it should not be necessary to update goal metrics every time you launch a new feature.
2. Ensure that driver metrics are:
   - **Aligned with the goal**: It is important to validate that the driver metrics are in fact drivers of success. One common technique for this validation is to run experiments expressly for this purpose. We discuss this further below.
   - **Actionable and relevant**: Teams must feel that they can act on the levers (e.g., product features) to move these metrics.
   - **Sensitive**: Driver metrics are leading indicators for goal metrics. Ensure that they are sensitive enough to measure impact from most initiatives.
   - **Resistant to gaming**: Because driver metrics and your goal metrics measure success, don't make them easily gameable. Think through the incentives and what behavior a metric may drive and how it might be gamed. See *Sidebar: Gameability* later in this chapter.

With these principles in mind, here are some helpful techniques and considerations for developing metrics:

- Use hypotheses from less-scalable methods to generate ideas, and then validate them in scalable data analyses to determine a precise definition (see Chapter 10). For example, user happiness or user task success might only be directly measurable through user surveys, a methodology that is not scalable. However, we can conduct surveys or user experience research (UER) studies (see Chapter 10) to observe the types of behavior typically correlated with success and happiness. You can explore those behavior patterns using online logs data analysis at scale to determine whether those metrics work as a high-level metric. One concrete example is bounce rate, which is the proportion of users that stay only a short time on a website. We may notice that a short stay correlates with dissatisfaction. Combining that observation with a data analysis helps determine the exact threshold (should the threshold be 1 pageview? 20 seconds?) needed to precisely define the metric (Dmitriev and Wu 2016, Huang, White and Dumais 2012).

- Consider *quality* when defining goal or driver metrics. A click on a search result is a "bad" click if the user clicks the back button right away; a new user signup is a "good" signup if the user actively engages with the website; a LinkedIn profile is a "good" profile if it contains sufficient information to represent the user, such as education history or current and past positions. Building a quality concept, such as with human evaluation (see Chapter 10), into your goal and driver metrics makes it much more likely that movement from these metrics leads to a solid interpretation on which to base decisions.

- When incorporating statistical models in the definition of a metric, it is essential to keep the model interpretable and validated over time. For instance, to measure long-term revenue from a subscription, it is common to compute the lifetime value (LTV) based on predicted survival probability. However, if the survival function is too complicated, it may be hard to get buy-in from stakeholders, even harder if a sudden drop on the metric needs to be investigated. Another example is Netflix using bucketized watch hours as driver metrics because they are interpretable and indicative of long-term user retention (Xie and Aurisset 2016).

- Sometimes it may be easier to precisely measure what you do not want, such as user dissatisfaction or unhappiness, than it is to measure what you want. For example, how long does a user have to stay on a site to be considered "satisfied?" On sites with tasks, like search engines, a short visit to a site pointed to from a search result is more often correlated with a user being unhappy than a long visit. That said, a long visit can imply either that a user is finding what they need or that they are trying hard to do something and in fact getting frustrated. In this way, *negative* metrics are useful as guardrail or debug metrics.

- Always remember that metrics are themselves proxies; each has its own set of failure cases. For example, a search engine may want to use CTR to measure user engagement but driving just CTR may lead to increased clickbait. In such cases, you must create additional metrics to measure the edge cases. In this example, one possibility is to use human evaluation (see Chapter 10) as a metric to measure relevance and counterbalance a tendency towards rewarding clickbait.

## Evaluating Metrics

We have outlined several principles to follow when developing metrics. Most metrics evaluation and validation happen during the formulation phase, but there is work that needs to be done over time and continuously. For example, before adding a new metric, evaluate whether it provides additional information compared to your existing metrics. Lifetime value (LTV) metrics must be evaluated over time to ensure that prediction errors stay small. Metrics heavily relied on for experimentation must be evaluated periodically to determine whether they encouraged gaming (i.e., whether a threshold used in a metric definition cause disproportional focus on moving users across the threshold).

One of the most common and challenging evaluations is establishing the causal relationship of driver metrics to organizational goal metrics, that is, whether this driver metric really drives the goal metrics. In for-profit organizations, Kaplan and Norton wrote "Ultimately, causal paths from all the measures on a scorecard should be linked to financial objectives" (Kaplan and Norton 1996). Hauser and Katz (Hauser and Katz 1998) write, "the firm must identify metrics that the team can affect today, but which, ultimately, will affect the firm's long-term goals." Spitzer (Spitzer 2007) wrote that "measurement frameworks are initially composed of hypotheses (assumptions) of the key measures and their causal relationships. These hypotheses are then tested with actual data, and can be confirmed, disconfirmed, or modified." This characteristic is the hardest to satisfy, as we often don't know the underlying causal model, and merely have a hypothesized mental causal model.

Here are a few high-level approaches to tackle causal validation that you can also apply to other types of metrics evaluation:

- Utilize other data sources such as surveys, focus groups, or user experience research (UER) studies to check whether they all point in the same direction.
- Analyze observational data. While it is difficult to establish causal relationships with observational data (as we discuss in Chapter 11), a carefully conducted observational study can help invalidate hypotheses.

- Check whether similar validation is done at other companies. For instance, several companies have shared studies that show how site speed impacts revenue and user engagement (see Chapter 5). Another example is studies that show the impact of app size on app downloads (Reinhardt 2016, Tolomei 2017).
- Conduct an experiment with a primary goal of evaluating metrics. For example, to determine whether a customer loyalty program increases customer retention and therefore customer LTV, run experiments that slowly rollout the customer loyalty program, and measure retention and customer LTV. We caution that these experiments often test a relatively narrow hypothesis, so it still requires work to generalize the results.
- Use a corpus of historical experiments as "golden" samples for evaluating new metrics. It is important that these experiments are well understood and trustworthy. We can use these historical experiments to check for sensitivity and causal alignment (Dmitriev and Wu 2016).

Note that the challenge of relating driver metrics to goal metrics also applies for guardrail metrics. See our example in Chapter 5 of how to conduct an experiment to measure the impact of latency, a guardrail metric, on goal metrics.

## Evolving Metrics

Metric definitions evolve over time. Even if the concept stays the same, the exact definition may still change. Change can happen because:

- The business evolved: The business may have grown and created new business lines. This could lead to the business changing its focus, such as shifting from adoption to engagement and retention. One specific type of evolution to call out is a shift in user base. When calculating metrics or running experiments, note that all of that data is coming from the existing user base. Especially for early-stage products or start-ups, early adopters may not be representative of the user base that a business desires in the long-term (Forte 2019).
- The environment evolved: The competitive landscape may have changed, more users may be aware of privacy concerns, or new government policies may be in effect. All of these changes can shift the business focus or perspective, and therefore what you measure with metrics.
- Your understanding of the metrics evolved: Even metrics you carefully evaluated during the development phase, when observing its performance

in action (e.g., looking for gameability), you may discover areas of improvement that leads to more granularity or different metric formulations. Hubbard (Hubbard 2014) discusses Expected Value of Information (EVI), which is a concept that captures how additional information helps you make decisions. Taking the time and effort to investigate metrics and modify existing metrics has high EVI. It is not enough to be agile and to measure, you must make sure your metrics guide you in the right direction.

Certain metrics may evolve more quickly than others. For example, driver, guardrail, and data quality metrics may evolve more quickly than goal metrics, often because those are driven by methodology improvements rather than fundamental business or environmental evolutions.

Because metrics will evolve over time, you should become more structured in handling changes in metrics as your organization grows. Specifically, you will need infrastructure to support the evaluation of new metrics, the associated schema changes, backfilling of data needed, and more.

## Additional Resources

There are several great books about metrics, measurements, and performance indicators (Spitzer 2007, Parmenter 2015, McChesney, Covey and Huling 2012). Spitzer notes that "What makes measurement so potent is its capacity to instigate informed action—to provide the opportunity for people to engage in the right behavior at the right time." In the context of controlled experiments, because the Treatment is the *cause* of the impact to each metric (with high probability for highly statistically significant effects), formulating the key metrics is an assessment of the value of an idea (the Treatment) on some axis of interest.

## SIDEBAR: Guardrail Metrics

There are two types of guardrail metrics: trustworthiness-related guardrail metrics and organizational guardrail metrics. Trustworthiness-related guardrail metrics are discussed in detail in Chapter 21, as those are necessary to ensure that experimental results are trustworthy. Here we discuss organizational guardrail metrics.

As we discuss in Chapter 5, an increase in latency of even a few milliseconds can result in revenue loss and a reduction in user satisfaction. Thus, latency is often used as a guardrail metric because it is so sensitive, especially relative to revenue and user satisfaction metrics. Most teams are typically working on new features that are trying to move goal or driver metrics but, in doing so, they check latency and try to ensure that their feature does not increase latency. If it does, then that triggers a discussion about tradeoffs such as whether the impact of the new feature is worth the impact from the increase in latency, whether there are ways to mitigate the increase, or whether there are ways to offset the new feature with other features that improve (decrease) latency.

Many organizational guardrail metrics are similar to latency, sensitive metrics that measure phenomena known to impact the goal or driver metrics, but that most teams should not be affecting. Examples of such metrics include:

1. HTML response size per page. On a website, the server response size is an early indicator that a large amount of code (such as JavaScript) was introduced. Alerting on such a change is a great way to uncover a possibly sloppy piece of code that could be optimized.

2. JavaScript errors per page. Degrading (i.e., increasing) the average number of errors on the page is a ship blocker. Segmenting by browsers helps to identify whether the JavaScript issue is browser dependent.

3. Revenue-per-user. A team that works on one part of the product, such as relevance, may not realize that they are hurting revenue. Revenue-per-user usually has high statistical variance, so it is not sensitive as a guardrail; more sensitive variants can be great alternatives, such as revenue indicator-per-user (was there revenue for user: yes/no), capped revenue-per-user (anything over $X is capped to $X), and revenue-per-page (there are more page units, although care must be taken to correctly compute the variance, see Chapter 22).

4. Pageviews-per-user. Because many metrics are measured per page (such as, CTR), a change to pageviews-per-user could imply that many metrics changed. It is natural to focus on the numerator, but if pageviews-per-user changes, it is the denominator that changes, which requires thought. If the change is unexpected, it is worth reviewing the reasons carefully (Dmitriev et al. 2017). Note that pageviews-per-user may not work as a guardrail in all cases; for example, if you are testing an infinite scroll feature, then page-views-per-user will almost certainly change.

5. Client crashes. For client software (e.g., Office Word/PowerPoint/Excel, Adobe Reader) or phone applications (e.g., Facebook, LinkedIn, Minecraft, Netflix), crash rate is a critical guardrail metric. In addition to a count metric (crashes-per-user), an indicator is commonly used (Did the user crash

during the experiment?), which is averaged over all users, as indicators have lower variance and thus show statistical significance earlier.

Different teams may swap which metrics are their goal, driver, and guardrail metrics. For example, while most teams may use the canonical goal, driver, and guardrail metrics, an infrastructure team, for example, may use performance or organizational guardrail metrics as their goal (and use the product team's goal and driver metrics as their guardrails). Just like driver metrics, it is important to establish the causal relationship between guardrail metrics and goal metrics, as was done in Chapter 5.

## SIDEBAR: Gameability

Your goal and driver metrics need to be hard to game: when given a numerical target, humans can be quite ingenious, especially when the measures are tied to rewards. There are numerous examples throughout history:

- Vasili Alexeyev, a famous Russian super-heavyweight weightlifter, was offered an incentive for every world record he broke. The result of this contingent measurement was that he kept breaking world records a gram or two at a time to maximize his reward payout (Spitzer 2007).
- A manager of a fast-food restaurant strived to achieve an award for attaining a perfect 100 percent on the restaurant's "chicken efficiency" measure (the ratio of how many pieces of chicken sold to the number thrown away). He did so by waiting until the chicken was ordered before cooking it. He won the award but drove the restaurant out of business because of the long wait times (Spitzer 2007).
- A company paid bonuses to its central warehouse spare parts personnel for maintaining low inventory. As a result, necessary spare parts were not available in the warehouse, and operations had to be shut down until the parts could be ordered and delivered (Spitzer 2007).
- Managers at a hospital in the United Kingdom were concerned about the time it was taking to treat patients in the accident and emergency department. They decided to measure the time from patient registration to being seen by a house doctor. The nursing staff thus began asking the paramedics to leave their patients in the ambulance until a house doctor was ready to see them, thus improving the "average time it took to treat patients" (Parmenter 2015).
- In Hanoi, under French colonial rule, a program paying people a bounty for each rat tail handed in was intended to exterminate rats. Instead, it led to the

farming of rats (Vann 2003). A similar example, although likely anecdotal, is mentioned with regards to cobra snakes, where presumably the British government offered bounty for every dead cobra in Delhi and enterprising people began to breed cobras for the income (Wikipedia contributors, Cobra Effect 2019).

- Between 1945 and 1960, the federal Canadian government paid 70 cents a day per orphan to orphanages, and psychiatric hospitals received $2.25 per day, per patient. Allegedly, up to 20,000 orphaned children were falsely certified as mentally ill so the Catholic Church could get $2.25 per day, per patient (Wikipedia contributors, Data dredging 2019).
- Funding fire departments by the number of fire calls made is intended to reward the fire departments that do the most work. However, it may discourage them from fire-prevention activities that reduce the number of fires (Wikipedia contributors, Perverse Incentive 2019).

While these examples show the importance of choosing metrics carefully, how does this apply in the online domain? One common scenario is to use short-term revenue as a key metric. However, you could increase short-term revenues by raising prices or plastering a website with ads, and either of those would likely lead to users abandoning the site and customer LTV declining. Customer LTV is a useful guiding principle when considering metrics. More generally, many unconstrained metrics are gameable. A metric that measures ad revenue *constrained* to space on the page or to a measure of quality is a much better metric to ensure a high-quality user experience. How many queries return no results is gameable without some quality constraint because one can always return bad results.

Generally, we recommend using metrics that measure user value and actions. You should avoid vanity metrics that indicate a count of your actions, which users often ignore (the count of banner ads is a vanity metric, whereas clicks on ads indicates potential user interest). At Facebook, creating user "Likes" is an example where there is a UI feature that both captures user actions and is a fundamental part of the user experience.

# 7

# Metrics for Experimentation and the Overall Evaluation Criterion

Tell me how you measure me, and I will tell you how I will behave
— *Eliyahu M. Goldratt (1990)*

The first rule is that a measurement—any measurement—is better than none. But a genuinely effective indicator will cover the output of the work unit, and not simply the activity involved. Obviously, you measure a salesman by the orders he gets (output), not by the calls he makes (activity)
— *Andrew S. Grove in High Output Management (1995)*

***Why you care:*** *To design and run a good online controlled experiment, you need metrics that meet certain characteristics. They must be measurable in the short term (experiment duration) and computable, as well as sufficiently sensitive and timely to be useful for experimentation. If you use multiple metrics to measure success for an experiment, ideally you may want to combine them into an Overall Evaluation Criterion (OEC), which is believed to causally impact long-term objectives. It often requires multiple iterations to adjust and refine the OEC, but as the quotation above, by Eliyahu Goldratt, highlights, it provides a clear alignment mechanism to the organization.*

## From Business Metrics to Metrics Appropriate for Experimentation

As discussed in Chapter 6, data-driven organizations often use goal, driver, and guardrail metrics to align and execute on business goals with transparency and accountability. However, these business metrics may not be directly useful for online experimentation, as metrics for experimentation must be:

- **Measurable:** Even in an online world, not all effects are easily measurable. For example, post-purchase satisfaction can be challenging to measure.
- **Attributable:** To compute the metrics for experiment purposes, we must be able to attribute metric values to the experiment variant. For example, to analyze whether the Treatment is causing a higher app crash rate than the Control, we must be able to attribute an app crash to its variant. This attribution may not be available for metrics provided by other data providers, such as third parties.
- **Sensitive and timely:** Experiment metrics must be sensitive enough to detect changes that matter in a timely fashion. Sensitivity depends on the statistical variance of the underlying metric, the effect size (the delta between Treatment and Control in an experiment), and the number of randomization units (such as users). As an extreme example of an insensitive metric, you could run a controlled experiment and look at the stock price of the company. Because the ability of routine product changes to impact the stock price during the experiment period is practically zero, the stock-price metric will not be sufficiently sensitive. At the other extreme, you could measure the existence of the new feature (is it showing?), and that will be very sensitive, but not informative about its actual value to users. Between the two extremes, click-throughs on the new feature will be sensitive but highly localized: a click-through metric will not capture the impact on the rest of the page and possible cannibalization of other features. A whole-page click-through metric (especially if penalized for quick-backs where users come back quickly), a measure of "success" (like a purchase), and time-to-success are usually good key metrics sensitive enough for experimentation. See Dmitriev and Wu (2016) for an in-depth discussion on sensitivity. Here are a couple more common examples:
  - With ads revenue, it is common for a few outliers to have a disproportionally high influence on revenue, like clicks with very high cost-per-click. While a dollar is a dollar and these expensive clicks should be included in business reporting, these large outliers inflate variance and make it harder to detect Treatment effects. For this reason, you could consider a truncated version of revenue for experiments as an additional more sensitive metric (see Chapter 22).
  - Consider a subscription contract that has a yearly renewal cycle. Unless you are willing to run a year-long experiment, it will be hard to measure

the impact on the renewal rate. For this case, instead of using renewal rate in experiments, it is common to find surrogate metrics, such as usage, which are early indicators of satisfaction that will lead to renewals.

Based on these considerations, you can see that not all metrics that are used for business reporting purposes are appropriate for experimentation. We do agree with Andrew Grove's quotation above: when in doubt, measure more, but more importantly: think hard about what you are optimizing for. Declaring time-on-site as a metric to optimize without qualifiers like (good/successful session) will lead to interstitial pages and a slow site, which will increase the metric in the short term, but cause abandonment in the long term.

In general, for experimentation, you will be choosing the subset of business goal, driver, and organizational guardrail metrics that meet these measurability, computability, sensitivity, and timeliness characteristics. Then you may need to further augment that metric set with:

- Additional surrogate metrics for your business goals and drivers
- More granular metrics, such as feature-level metrics to help understand movements of specific features. For example, a page-click-through rate may be broken into click-through rate on the dozens of features on the page.
- Additional trustworthiness guardrails (see Chapter 21) and data quality metrics
- Diagnostic and debug metrics that provide information too detailed to track on an ongoing basis but useful when drilling into a situation where the goal, driver, or guardrail metrics indicate a problem.

Given all the different taxonomies and use cases for metrics, a typical experiment scorecard will have a few key metrics, and hundreds to thousands of other metrics, all of which can be segmented by dimensions, such as browsers and markets.

## Combining Key Metrics into an OEC

Given the common situation where you have multiple goal and driver metrics, what do you do? Do you need to choose just one metric, or do you keep more than one? Do you combine them all into single combination metric?

While some books advocate focusing on just one metric (*Lean Analytics* (Croll and Yoskovitz 2013) suggest the One Metric that Matters (OMTM) and *The 4 Disciplines of Execution* (McChesney, Covey and Huling 2012) suggest focusing on Wildly Important Goal (WIG)), we find that motivating but an oversimplification. Except for trivial scenarios, there is usually no single metric that captures what a business is optimizing for. Kaplan and Norton (1996) give a good example: imagine entering a modern jet airplane. Is there a single metric that you should put on the pilot's dashboard? Airspeed? Altitude? Remaining fuel? You know the pilot must have access to these metrics and more. When you have an online business, you will have several key goal and driver metrics, typically measuring user engagement (e.g., active days, sessions-per-user, clicks- per-user) and monetary value (e.g., revenue-per-user). There is usually no simple single metric to optimize for.

In practice, many organizations examine multiple key metrics, and have a mental model of the tradeoffs they are willing to accept when they see any particular combination. For example, they may have a good idea about how much they are willing to lose (churn) users if the remaining users increase their engagement and revenue to more than compensate. Other organizations that prioritize growth may not be willing to accept a similar tradeoff.

Oftentimes, there is a mental model of the tradeoffs, and devising a single metric – an OEC – that is a weighted combination of such objectives (Roy 2001, 50, 405–429) may be the more desired solution. And like metrics overall, ensuring that the metrics and the combination are not gameable is critical (see *Sidebar: Gameability* in Chapter 6). For example, basketball scoreboards don't keep track of shots beyond the two- and three-point lines, only the combined score for each team, which is the OEC. FICO credit scores combine multiple metrics into a single score ranging from 300 to 850. The ability to have a single summary score is typical in sports and critical for business. A single metric makes the exact definition of success clear and has a similar value to agreeing on metrics in the first place: it aligns people in an organization about the tradeoffs. Moreover, by having the discussion and making the tradeoffs explicit, there is more consistency in decision making and people can better understand the limitations of the combination to determine when the OEC itself needs to evolve. This approach empowers teams to make decisions without having to escalate to management and provides an opportunity for automated searches (parameter sweeps).

If you have multiple metrics, one possibility proposed by Roy (2001) is to normalize each metric to a predefined range, say 0–1, and assign each a weight. Your OEC is the weighted sum of the normalized metrics.

Coming up with a single weighted combination may be hard initially, but you can start with classifying your decisions into four groups:

1. If all key metrics are flat (not statistically significant) or positive (statistically significant), with at least one metrics positive, then ship the change.

2. If all key metrics are flat or negative, with at least one metric negative, then don't ship the change.
3. If all key metrics are flat, then don't ship the change and consider either increasing the experiment power, failing fast, or pivoting.
4. If some key metrics are positive and some key metrics are negative, then decide based on the tradeoffs. When you have accumulated enough of these decisions, you may be able to assign weights.

If you are unable to combine your key metrics into a single OEC, try to minimize the number of key metrics. Pfeffer and Sutton (1999) warn about the Otis Redding problem, named after the famous song "Sitting by the Dock of the Bay," which has this line: "Can't do what ten people tell me to do, so I guess I'll remain the same." Having too many metrics may cause cognitive overload and complexity, potentially leading the organization to ignore the key metrics. Reducing the number of metrics also helps with the multiple comparison problems in Statistics.

One rough rule of thumb is to try to limit your key metrics to five. While using a strong 0.05 p-value threshold by itself can be abused − p-hacked, if you will (Wikipedia contributors, Multiple Comparisons problem 2019)− we can still use the underlying statistical concept as a way to understand this heuristic. Specifically, if the Null hypothesis is true (no change), then the probability of a p-value $< 0.05$ for a single metric is 5%. When you have $k$ (independent) metrics, the probability of having at least one p-value $< 0.05$ is $1 - (1 - 0.05)^k$. For $k = 5$, you have a 23% probability of seeing something statistically significant. For $k = 10$, that probability rises to 40%. The more metrics you have, the higher the chance that one would be significant, causing potential conflicts or questions.

One final benefit of an OEC that is agreed upon: you can automatically ship changes (both simple experiments and parameter sweeps).

## Example: OEC for E-mail at Amazon

At Amazon, a system was built to send e-mails based on programmatic campaigns that targeted customers based on various conditions, such as (Kohavi and Longbotham 2010):

- Previously bought books by an author with a new release: A campaign e-mailed them about the new release.
- Purchase history: A program using Amazon's recommendation algorithm sent an e-mail like this: "Amazon.com has new recommendations for you based on items you purchased or told us you own."

- Cross-pollination: Many programs were very specific and defined by humans to e-mail product recommendations to customers who bought items from specific combinations of product categories.

The question is what OEC should be used for these programs? The initial OEC, or "fitness function," as it was called at Amazon, gave credit to a program based on the revenue it generated from users clicking-through on the e-mail.

The problem is that this metric is monotonically increasing with e-mail volume: more campaigns and more e-mails can only increase revenue, which led to spamming users. Note that this property of increasing revenue with e-mail volume is true even when comparing revenue from the Treatment users (those receiving the e-mail) to Control users (those who don't).

Red flags went up when users began complaining about receiving too many e-mails. Amazon's initial solution was to add a constraint: a user can only receive an e-mail every X days. They built an e-mail traffic cop, but the problem was that it became an optimization program: which e-mail should be sent every X days when multiple e-mail programs want to target the user? How could they determine which users might be open to receiving more e-mails if they found them truly useful?

Their key insight was that the click-through revenue OEC is optimizing for short-term revenue instead of user lifetime value. Annoyed users unsubscribe and Amazon then loses the opportunity to target them in the future. They built a simple model to construct a lower bound on the user lifetime opportunity loss when a user unsubscribes. Their OEC was:

$$\text{OEC} = \left( \sum_i Rev_i - s * unsubscribe\_lifetime\_loss \right) \Big/ n$$

where:

- $i$ ranges over e-mail recipients for the variant
- $s$ is the number of unsubscribes in the variant
- unsubscribe_lifetime_loss is the estimated revenue loss of not being able to e-mail a person for "life"
- $n$ is the number of users in the variant.

When they implemented this OEC with just a few dollars assigned to unsubscribe lifetime loss, more than half of the programmatic campaigns were showing a negative OEC!

More interestingly, the realization that unsubscribes have such a big loss led to a different unsubscribe page, where the default was to unsubscribe from this "campaign family," not from all Amazon e-mails, drastically diminishing the cost of an unsubscribe.

## Example: OEC for Bing's Search Engine

Bing uses two key organizational metrics to measure progress: query share and revenue, as described in *Trustworthy online controlled experiments: Five puzzling outcomes explained* (Kohavi et al. 2012). The example shows how short-term and long-term objectives can diverge diametrically. This problem is also included in *Data Science Interviews Exposed* (Huang et al. 2015).

When Bing had a ranker bug that resulted in very poor results being shown to users in a Treatment, two key organizational metrics improved significantly: distinct queries per user went up over 10%, and revenue-per-user went up over 30%. What should the OEC for a search engine be? Clearly, the search engine's long-term goals do not align with these two key metrics in experiments. If they did, search engines would intentionally degrade quality to raise query share and revenue!

The degraded algorithmic results (the main search engine results shown to users, also known as the 10 blue links) forced people to issue more queries (increasing queries-per-user) and click more on ads (increasing revenue). To understand the problem, let's decompose query share:

Monthly *query share* is defined as distinct queries for the search engine divided by distinct queries for all search engines over one month. Distinct queries per month decomposes to the product of these three terms as shown in Equation 7.1:

$$n \; \frac{Users}{Month} \times \frac{Sessions}{User} \times \frac{Distinct \; queries}{Session}, \qquad (7.1)$$

where the second and third terms in the product are computed over the month, and a session is defined as user activity that begins with a query and ends with 30 minutes of inactivity on the search engine.

If the goal of a search engine is to allow users to find their answer or complete their task quickly, then reducing the distinct queries per task is a clear goal, which conflicts with the business objective of increasing query share. As this metric correlates highly with distinct queries per session (more easily measurable than tasks), distinct queries alone should not be used as an OEC for search experiments.

Given the decomposition of distinct queries shown in Equation 7.1, let's look at the three terms:

1. Users per month. In a controlled experiment, the number of unique users is determined by the design. For example, in an A/B test with 50/50 split, the number of users that fall in each variant will be approximately the same, so you cannot use this term as part of the OEC for controlled experiments.
2. Distinct queries per task should be minimized, but it is hard to measure. You can use the metric distinct queries per session as a surrogate; however, this is a subtle metric because increasing it may indicate that users have to issue more queries to complete the task but decreasing it may indicate abandonment. Thus, you can aim to decrease this metric as long as you also check that the task is successfully completed (i.e., abandonment does not increase).
3. Sessions-per-user is the key metric to optimize (increase) in controlled experiments. Satisfied users visit more often.

Revenue per user should likewise not be used as an OEC for search and ad experiments without adding other constraints. When looking at revenue metrics, we want to increase them without negatively impacting engagements metrics. A common constraint is to restrict the average number of pixels that ads can use over multiple queries. Increasing revenue per search given this constraint is a constraint optimization problem.

## Goodhart's Law, Campbell's Law, and the Lucas Critique

The OEC must be measurable in the short term (the duration of an experiment) yet believed to causally drive long-term strategic objectives. Goodhart's law, Campbell's law, and the Lucas Critique all highlight that correlation does not imply causation and that in many situations organizations that pick an OEC are fooled by correlations.

Charles Goodhart, a British economist, originally wrote the law: "Any observed statistical regularity will tend to collapse once pressure is placed upon it for control purposes" (Goodhart 1975, Chrystal and Mizen 2001). Today it's more common to reference Goodhart's law as: "When a measure becomes a target, it ceases to be a good measure" (Goodhart's law 2018, Strathern 1997).

Campbell's law, named after Donald Campbell, states that "The more any quantitative social indicator is used for social decision-making, the more subject it will be to corruption pressures and the more apt it will be to distort and corrupt the social processes it is intended to monitor" (Campbell's law 2018, Campbell 1979).

Lucas critique (Lucas critique 2018, Lucas 1976) observes that relationships observed in historical data cannot be considered structural, or causal. Policy decisions can alter the structure of economic models and the correlations that held historically will no longer hold. The Phillips Curve, for example, showed a historical negative correlation between inflation and unemployment; over the study period of 1861–1957 in the United Kingdom: when inflation was high, unemployment was low and vice versa (Phillips 1958). Raising inflation in the hope that it would lower unemployment assumes an incorrect causal relationship. As a point in fact, in the 1973–1975 US recession, both inflation and unemployment increased. In the long run, the current belief is that the rate of inflation has no causal effect on unemployment (Hoover 2008).

Tim Harford addresses the fallacy of using historical data by using the following example (Harford 2014, 147): "Fort Knox has never been robbed, so we can save money by sacking the guards." You can't look just at the empirical data; you need also to think about incentives. Obviously, such a change in policy would cause robbers to re-evaluate their probability of success.

Finding correlations in historical data does not imply that you can pick a point on a correlational curve by modifying one of the variables and expecting the other to change. For that to happen, the relationship must be causal, which makes picking metrics for the OEC a challenge.

# 8

# Institutional Memory and Meta-Analysis

Individuals sometimes forgive, but bodies and societies never do
– *Lord Chesterfield (1694–1773)*

*Why you care: As your organization moves into the "Fly" maturity phase, institutional memory, which contains a history of all experiments and changes made, becomes increasingly important. It can be used to identify patterns that generalize across experiments, to foster a culture of experimentation, to improve future innovations, and more.*

## What Is Institutional Memory?

After fully embracing controlled experiments as a default step in the innovation process, your company can effectively have a digital journal of all changes through experimentation, including descriptions, screen shots, and key results. Each of the hundreds or even thousands of experiments run in the past is a page in the journal, with precious and rich data on each change (launched or not). This digital journal is what we refer to as *Institutional Memory*. This section is about how to utilize the institutional memory through meta-analysis, and mining data from all these historical experiments.

It goes without saying that you need to capture and organize data as part of institutional memory. Having a centralized experimentation platform, where all changes are tested, certainly makes it easier. It is highly recommended that you capture meta information on each experiment, such as who the owners are; when the experiment started; how long it ran; descriptions and screen shots if the change was visual. You should also have results summarizing how much impact the experiment had on various metrics, including a definitive scorecard with triggered and overall impact (see Chapter 20). Lastly, you should capture the hypothesis the experiment is based on; what decision was made and why.

## Why Is Institutional Memory Useful?

What can you get from mining data from all these experiments? This is what we refer to here as meta-analysis. We organize the use cases into these five categories:

1. **Experiment culture.** Having a summary view of past experiments can really highlight the importance of experimentation and help solidify the culture. Here are a few concrete examples of meta-analysis to do:
   - **How has experimentation been contributing to the growth of the broader organizational goals?** For example, if the company's goal is to improve sessions-per-user, how much session-per-user improvement over the past year is attributable to changes launched through experiments? This can be many inch-by-inch wins added together. Bing Ads shared a powerful plot that shows how their revenue gains between 2013 and 2015 were attributable to incremental improvements from hundreds of experiments (see Chapter 1).
   - **What are the experiments with big or surprising impact?** While numbers are great at helping organizations gain insights at-scale, people relate to concrete examples. We find it helpful to regularly share experiments that are big wins or that have surprising results (see Chapter 1). As we mentioned in Chapter 4, we can also share a regular report on experiments that have a big impact on the metrics people care about.
   - **How many experiments positively or negatively impacted metrics?** At well-optimized domains such as Bing and Google, by some measures success rate is only 10–20% (Manzi 2012) (Kohavi et al. 2012). Microsoft shared that a third of their experiments moved key metrics positively, a third moved negatively, and a third didn't have significant impact (Kohavi, Longbotham et al. 2009). LinkedIn observed similar statistics. It's always humbling to realize that without experimentation to offer an objective true assessment, we could end up shipping both positive and negative experiments, canceling impact from each other.
   - **What percentage of features launch through experiments? Which teams have run the most experiments?** What is the growth quarter over quarter or year over year? Which team is the most effective at moving your OEC? Which outages are associated with changes that were not

experimented with? When postmortems on outages must answer such questions, the culture changes because people realize that experiments indeed provide a safety net. For bigger companies where there are many teams involved in running many experiments, it helps to create the breakdown and encourages better accountability.

2. **Experiment best practices.** Not necessarily every experimenter follows the best practices. This is especially common when more and more people start to experiment. For example, does the experiment go through the internal beta ramp period that is recommended? Is the experiment powered enough to detect movement of key metrics? Once you have enough experiments, you can conduct meta-analysis and report summary statistics to show teams and leadership where they can improve. You can break down the statistics by teams to further raise accountability. These insights help you decide whether you should invest in the automation to address the biggest gaps. For instance, by examining experiment ramp schedules, LinkedIn realized many experiments spent too much time on early ramp phases, while others did not even go through the internal beta ramp phase (see Chapter 14). To address this, LinkedIn built an auto-ramp feature that helps experimenters follow best ramping practices (Xu, Duan and Huang 2018).

3. **Future innovations.** For someone new to your company or new to a team, having a catalog of what worked and what didn't in the past is highly valuable. This helps avoid repeating mistakes and inspires effective innovation. Changes that did not work in the past, perhaps because of macro environment changes may be worth trying again. As you conduct meta-analysis on many experiments, patterns emerge that can guide you to better ideas. For example, which type of experiments are most effective for moving key metrics? Which kind of UI patterns are more likely to engage users? GoodUI.org summarizes many UI patterns that win repeatedly (Linowski 2018).

    After running many experiments that optimize a particular page, such as the Search Engine Results Page (SERP), you could predict the impact that changes to spacing, bolding, line length, thumbnails, and so on has on the metrics. Therefore, when you add a new element to the SERP, you can narrow the space of experiments to run. Another example is looking at experiment heterogeneity across countries (see Chapter 3), you can uncover hidden insights on how countries react differently for features, which allows you to build a better user experience customized for these users.

4. **Metrics.** Metrics are inseparable from experimentation (see Chapter 7). You can look across your experiments and how various metrics are

performing to develop a deeper understanding of how to better leverage them. Here are some example use cases of meta-analysis for metrics:

- **Metric sensitivity.** While developing metrics, one key criterion is whether they can be meaningfully measured during experiments. A metric that no experiment can move statistically significantly is not a good metric (see Chapter 7). While variance is a key factor influencing sensitivity, how likely an exogenous change can impact a metric is also a consideration. For example, daily active users (DAU) is a metric that is hard to move in short-term experiments. Studying existing metrics by comparing their performance in past experiments allows you to identify potential long-term vs. short-term metrics (Azevedo et al. 2019). You can also construct a corpus of trusted experiments to evaluate new metrics and compare different definition options (Dmitriev and Wu 2016).

- **Related metrics**. You can use the movement of metrics in experiments to identify how they relate to each other. Note that this is different from metric-to-metric correlation. For example, a user who visits LinkedIn more often tends to also send a lot more messages. However, sessions and messages don't necessarily move together in experiments. One example of related metrics in experiments is early indicators, which are metrics that tend to show leading signals for other metrics that take time to show impact. This is especially useful if those slow-moving metrics are critical for decision making (see Chapter 7). By studying a lot of experiments, you can uncover these relationships. See Chen, Liu and Xu (2019) for how such insights are uncovered and utilized at LinkedIn.

- **Probabilistic priors for Bayesian approaches**. As the Bayesian view of evaluating experiments gains popularity, one key concern is whether you can construct reasonable priors. For more matured products, it is reasonable to assume metric movement in historical experiments can offer reasonable prior distribution. See Deng (2015). For product areas evolving rapidly, it is not clear whether empirical distributions from the past can reasonably represent the future.

5. **Empirical research.** The vast amount of experiment data also offers researchers empirical evidence to evaluate and study their theories through meta-analysis. For example, Azevedo et al. (2019) studied how a company can best utilize experimentation to improve innovation productivity. They proposed an optimal implementation and experimentation strategy based on thousands of experiments that ran on Microsoft's experimentation platform. Experiment randomization can also act as a great instrumental variable.

By looking at 700 experiments conducted on the "People You May Know" algorithm at LinkedIn between 2014 and 2016, Saint-Jacques et al. (2018) found causal evidence that it is not the strongest connections that help people land a job, but those that strike a compromise between strength and diversity. Lee and Shen (2018) looked at how to aggregate impact from many launched experiments. When a group of experiments is conducted, usually those with significant successful results are chosen to be launched into the product. They investigate the statistical selection bias in this process and propose a correction method based on studying the experiments run on Airbnb's experimentation platform.

# 9

# Ethics in Controlled Experiments

The progress of science is far ahead of man's ethical behavior
– *Charlie Chaplin (1964)*

...testing where changes in program CODE induce user
DECEPTION... [we] call this new approach C/D experimentation to
distinguish it from...A/B testing
– *Raquel Benbunan-Fich (2017)*

***Why you care:*** *Understanding the ethics of experiments is critical for every-one, from leadership to engineers to product managers to data scientists; all should be informed and mindful of the ethical considerations. Controlled experiments, whether in technology, anthropology, psychology, sociology, or medicine, are conducted on actual people. Here are questions and concerns to consider when determining when to seek expert counsel regarding the ethics of your experiments.*

## Background

A broad definition of ethics is the set of rules or morals that govern what we should or should not do. Ethics, as applied to research, govern the rules of conduct that ensure the integrity of the results, the values essential for collab-orative work, public accountability, as well as moral and social values, includ-ing both public safety and the protection of human subjects (Resnick 2015). The application of ethics to research can change over time, reflecting the changing world, culture, and human responses to the unexpected ramifications of research studies over time. As Charlie Chaplin wrote in the quotation above, rules and regulations for ethical behavior are developing and lagging the science.

This subject is too deep to delve into fully here, so we only give an overview of the research ethics of controlled experiments. For a deeper study, we recommend several references (Loukides, Mason and Patil 2018, FAT/ML 2019, ACM 2018, King, Churchill and Tan 2017, Benbunan-Fich 2017, Meyer 2015, 2018), which present key principles, checklists, and practical guides. While experimenters are often not experts, we should ask ourselves questions, critically examine our practices, and consider the long-term best interests of our users and the business. Note that we are writing this in our capacity as individuals and not as representatives of Google, LinkedIn, or Microsoft.

Two recent examples from technology illustrate the need for these questions.

1. Facebook and Cornell researchers studied emotional contagion via social media (Kramer, Guillory and Hancock 2014) to determine whether randomly selected participants exposed to slightly more negative posts posted more negative content a week later and, conversely, whether other randomly selected participants exposed to slightly more positive posts had more positive posts themselves a week later.
2. OKCupid ran an experiment where they enrolled pairs of customers whom the algorithm said were 30%, 60%, and 90% matches, and, for each of these three groups, told a third of them that they were 30% matches, a third of them that they were 60% matches, and a third of them that they were 90% matches (The Guardian 2014, Meyer 2018).

Given these examples, and many others, how do we assess and evaluate which A/B experiments to run?

We can first turn to the Belmont Report, released in 1979 (The National Commission for the Protection of Human Subjects of Biomedical and Behavioral Research 1979) that establishes principles for biomedical and behavioral studies, and to the Common Rule (Office for Human Research Protections 1991) that establishes actionable review criteria based on these principles (Meyer 2012). These were established after several examples, including the Tuskegee Syphilis study from the 1930s (CDC 2015) and the Milgram experiment in the 1960s (Milgram 2009) in the medical domain, where the risk of substantial harm is commonly much higher than that in online experiments. Based on these guidelines, we now ask questions about whether this clinical trial is justified (Hemkens, Contopoulos-Ioannidis and Ioannidis 2016), and there are situations where conducting randomized controlled trials (RCTs) is unrealistic or perceived as unethical (Djulbegovic and Hozo 2002).

The Belmont report and the Common Rule provide three key principles in the context of biomedical and behavioral human subjects research:

- **Respect for persons:** Treat them with respect, that is, treat people as autonomous agents when they are and protect them when they are not. This translates to a focus on transparency, truthfulness, and voluntariness (choice and consent).
- **Beneficence:** Protect people from harm. While the Belmont Report states that beneficence means minimizing risks and maximizing benefits to participants, the Common Rule recognizes the challenge in doing so and focuses instead on properly assessing the risks and benefits, and balancing those appropriately when reviewing proposed studies.
- **Justice:** Ensure that participants are not exploited and that there is a fair distribution of risks and benefits.

Because of the complexity, the Common Rule lays out provisions that balance not just the benefits and risks of the study itself but also informs the necessity of transparency, truthfulness, and voluntariness for participants in the study, including waivers.

While these questions are a useful framework from a discipline – medicine – in which substantial harms could occur, there are rarely unambiguous right or wrong answers, so assessing these principles with regards to specific online A/B experiments requires judgment, thought, care, and experience. Here are key areas to consider.

## Risk

In your study, what **risk** does a participant face? Does the risk exceed that of minimal risk, defined by the Common Rule as "the probability and magnitude of harm or discomfort anticipated in the research are not greater in and of themselves than those ordinarily encountered in daily life or during the performance of routine physical or psychological examinations or tests." The harm could be physical, psychological, emotional, social, or economic.

One useful concept is *equipoise* (Freedman 1987): whether the relevant expert community is in equipoise – genuine uncertainty – with respect to two treatments.

In evaluating online controlled experiments, one useful litmus test is whether you could ship a feature to all users without a controlled experiment, given the organizational standards. If you could make the change to an algorithm, or to the look-and-feel of a product without an experiment, surely you should be able to run an experiment and scientifically evaluate the change first; perhaps you will uncover unexpected effects. Shipping code is, in fact, an experiment. It may not be a controlled experiment, but rather an inefficient sequential test where one looks at the time series; if key metrics (e.g., revenue, user feedback) are negative, the feature is rolled back.

The resistance to an online controlled experiment when giving everyone either Control or Treatment would each be acceptable is sometimes referred to as the "A/B illusion" (Meyer 2015, Meyer et al. 2019). When you decide to ship something, you are assuming what effect will result, and that assumption may or may not hold. If you are willing to ship something to 100% of users, shipping to 50% with the intent of going to 100% as an experiment should also be fine. In an example Meyer wrote (Meyer 2015):

> ...the head of a company is concerned some of her employees are failing to save enough for retirement... She decides that from now on, when she sends out 401(k) mailings, she will include a statement about how many co-workers within five years of the employee's age have signed up for automatic enrollment. She hypothesizes that the minority of employees who haven't enrolled may be influenced to do so by knowledge of the majority's contrary behavior.

While the head of company is well-intentioned, and studies have shown the benefits of peer effects, when the controlled experiment was run, it resulted in oppositional reaction and decrease in savings (Beshears et al. 2011).

## Benefits

The other side of risk is to understand the benefits of the study. Oftentimes for online controlled experiments, benefits are considered in terms of improving the product, which can be directly for users in the Treatment, for all users who benefit from the results, or even indirectly in terms of building a sustainable business so that users can continue benefitting from the service. Improvements to user productivity might fall in the first two buckets, while improvements to ads revenue might fall in the last bucket of indirect benefit.

One situation where assessing the benefits may be trickier is when running experiments that knowingly provide participants a worse experience with a goal of ultimately improving the experience for all users, often by being able to quantify tradeoffs. Examples include running experiments that slow user experience (see Chapter 5), showing more ads to understand long-term effects (see Chapter 23) or disabling features such as recommendations to assess their value. These cases violate equipoise in that there is general agreement that the Treatment is not beneficial but has minimal risk to users. The benefit of running these experiments involves establishing tradeoffs that can be used for more informed decision making and ultimately help improve the user experience for all. Importantly, there is no deception of users in these cases. While there is a higher risk profile with a greater potential for harm than most online controlled experiments, there is a medical analogy for these types of experiments in drug toxicity studies: at some point, too much of a drug can be bad, but without running the studies, we could not know how much or how bad the effects are.

One point to emphasize is the major difference between running experiments to try out new features, new text, new algorithms and infrastructure, even to establish tradeoffs, versus running *deception* or *power-of-suggestion* experiments that focus on behavioral experimentation and relationships between people (Benbunan-Fich 2017). Deception experiments carry higher ethical risk and raise questions about whether participants are respected.

When thinking about respect for participants, the first questions we should ask are around transparency and expectation. Products set user expectations about what they provide by both what is in the UI and what is broadly communicated. Experiments should follow those expectations.

Alongside several other ways of ensuring transparency, informed consent is a key ethical concept where participants agree to participate in the study after they are fully informed about risks and benefits, the process, any alternative options, and what data is being gathered and how it is handled. Note that here, we are discussing consent in terms of its general meaning rather than specific to any legal definition, such as under Europe's General Data Protection Regulation (European Commission 2018). Most medical experiments have informed consent for each participant, and those that do not are typically minimal risk and meet other conditions, thus qualifying for a waiver of consent under the Common Rule. In contrast, experiments by online service providers usually involve a far lower level of risk to the participants, although as online services start impacting offline experiences, such as with shipping physical packages, ride sharing, and so on, the risk and consequentiality can increase. In addition, given the scale of experiments, obtaining informed consent is both prohibitively expensive and annoying to users. Instead, consider the range of possibility from experiments where consent is needed to those where the risk and potential harm to users is very low and consent is not needed. One alternative towards the middle of that spectrum is *presumptive consent*, where a smaller but representative group of people are asked how they would feel about participating in a study (or class of studies) and, if they agree, assuming that this sentiment would generalize to all participants (King et al. 2017).

## Provide Choices

Another consideration is what **choices** do participants have? For example, if you are testing changes to a search engine, participants always have the choice to use another search engine. Switching costs for other online services may be higher in terms of time, money, information sharing, and so on. These factors should be considered when assessing the choice offered to participants and the risks and benefits to be balanced. For example, in medical clinical trials testing new drugs for cancer, the main choice most participants face is death, making it allowable for the risk to be quite high, given informed consent.

# Data Collection

One prerequisite for running A/B experiments is that data instrumentation is present for experiment analysis and for making decisions. Often, this data must be collected to measure and provide a high quality of service to users. As a result, data collection consent is often included in the Terms of Service for online services. While other references discuss data collection in more detail (Loukides et al. 2018), and while it is of course a pre-requisite that any experiments comply with all applicable privacy and data protection laws, experimenters or engineers should be able to answer these key questions about data collection:

- What data is being collected and what do users understand about that collection, with privacy by design being one useful framework in this area (Wikipedia contributors, Privacy by Design 2019).
  - Do users understand what data is being collected about them?
  - How sensitive is the data? Does it include financial or health data? Could the data be used to discriminate against users in ways that infringe human rights?
  - Can the data be tied to the individual, that is, is it considered personally identifiable (see Sidebar later in this chapter)?
  - For what purpose is the data collected and how can the data be used, and by whom?
  - Is it necessary to collect the data for the purpose? How soon can the data be aggregated or deleted to protect individual users?
- What could go wrong with the data collection?
  - What harm would befall users if that data or some subset be made public?
  - Consider harm to their health, psychological or emotional state, social status, or financials.

- What are user's expectations of privacy and confidentiality, and how are those expectations being guaranteed?

  For example, if participants are being observed in a public setting (such as, a football stadium), there is a lower expectation of privacy. If the study is on existing public data, then there is also no expectation of further confidentiality. If the data is not personally identifiable (see Side bar on page 103), then privacy and confidentiality are not necessarily a concern (NSF 2018). Otherwise:

  ○ What level of confidentiality can participants expect?
  ○ What are the internal safeguards for handling that data? Can anyone at the company access the data, especially if it's personally identifiable, or is the data secure with access logged and audited? How are breaches to that security caught, communicated, and managed?
  ○ What redress will happen (will participants be informed) if these guarantees are not met?

## Culture and Processes

Many issues we address are complex and nuanced. It can be tempting to just rely on experts to make all judgments and set principles. However, to ensure that the ethical considerations are met, it is important that your corporate culture, everyone from your leadership down, understands and considers these questions and implications. Introspection is critical.

Companies – leaders – should implement processes to ensure that this level of understanding reaches across the board to:

- Establish cultural norms and education processes to keep employees familiar with the issues and ensure that these questions are asked at product and engineering reviews.
- Create a process that fulfills the purpose of Institutional Review Boards (IRBs). IRBs review possible human subjects research, assess the risks and benefits, ensure transparency, provide processes, and more to ensure the integrity and respect for participants. The IRB approves, requires alternatives, or denies studies. They provide questions for experimenters to consider that ensure thorough review and adequate introspection and establish just-in-time processes for educational purposes.
- Build tools, infrastructure, and processes so that all data, identified or not, is stored securely, with access time limited to those who need it to complete their job. There should be a clear set of principles and policies for what data

usage is acceptable and what is not acceptable. You should ensure that all
data use is logged and regularly audited for violations.

- Create a clear escalation path for how to handle cases that have more than
  minimal risk or data sensitivity issues.

These questions and processes around the ethics of experiments are not an item
to check off, but rather discussions that improve the design of the product and
experiments for end users.

## SIDEBAR: User Identifiers

One frequently asked question is what is the difference between identified,
pseudonymous, and anonymous data? While the precise definitions may shift
based on context or applicable laws and are still being discussed, an overview
of the high-level concepts associated with these concepts are:

- **Identified** data is stored and collected with personally identifiable information (PII). This can be names, IDs (such as a social security number or
  driver's license), phone numbers, and so on. A common standard is HIPAA
  (Health and Human Services 2018b, Health and Human Services 2018c),
  which has 18 identifiers (HIPAA Journal 2018, Health and Human Services
  2018a) that are considered personally identifiable. Device ID (such as, a
  smartphone's device ID) is also considered personally identifiable in many
  instances. In Europe, GDPR (General Data Protection Regulation) holds an
  even higher standard, and considers any data to be personal data if it can be
  linked to an individual (European Commission 2018).
- **Anonymous** data is stored and collected without any personally identifiable
  information. This data is considered **pseudonymous** if it is stored with a
  randomly generated ID, such as a cookie, that is assigned to some event, such
  as the first time a user opens an app or visits website and does not have an ID
  stored. However, simply stating that data is pseudonymous or anonymous
  does not mean that re-identification cannot happen (McCullagh 2006). Why?
  We must distinguish between anonymous data and anonymized data. Anonymized data is identified or anonymous data that has been looked at and
  guaranteed in some way that the re-identification risk is low-to-nonexistent,
  that is, given the data it almost impossible for someone to determine which
  individual this data refers to. Often, this guarantee is done via the Safe Harbor
  method or other methods such as k-anonymity (Samarati and Sweeney 1998)
  or differential privacy (Dwork and Roth 2014). Note that many of these
  methods do not guarantee that anonymous data will not have re-identification

risk, but rather try to quantify the risk and the constraints, such as limiting queries or adding noise with additional queries (Abadi et al. 2016).

In EU-based privacy literature, the current high bar globally with respect to privacy, they no longer discuss anonymous data as a separate category, but instead simply talk about personal data and anonymized data.

So, for the data being gathered, collected, stored, and used in the experiment, the questions are:

- How sensitive is the data?
- What is the re-identification risk of individuals from the data?

As the sensitivity and risk increases, you must increase the level of data protection, confidentiality, access control, security, monitoring and auditing, and so on.

# PART III

# Complementary and Alternative Techniques to Controlled Experiments

Part III introduces methods that complement online controlled experiments. This content is especially useful for data scientists and others who are likely to use the techniques, and for leaders to understand how to allocate resources to areas and to establish experiments to make data-informed decisions.

We start with *Complementary Techniques,* which is an overview of several techniques − user experience research studies, surveys, focus groups, and human evaluation − used in conjunction with online controlled experiments. Use these techniques as part of generating and evaluating ideas in an "ideas funnel" before investing in an online controlled experiment, and for generating and validating metrics for use either for the organization broadly, or as surrogate metrics in online controlled experiments.

We then focus on *Observational Causal Studies.* While online controlled experiments are considered the gold standard for establishing causal impact for a change to your product or service, they are not always possible. In the chapter, we discuss several common scenarios in which online controlled experiments may not be possible and give a brief overview of common methods for such situations.

# PART III

## Complementary and Alternative Techniques to Controlled Experiments

# 10

# Complementary Techniques

If all you have is a hammer, everything looks like a nail
– *Abraham Maslow*

*Why you care: When running experiments, you also need to generate ideas to test, create, and validate metrics, and establish evidence to support broader conclusions. For these needs, there are techniques such as user experience research, focus groups, surveys, human evaluation, and observational studies that are useful to complement and augment a healthy A/B testing culture.*

## The Space of Complementary Techniques

To have successful A/B experiments, we not only need the care and rigor in analysis and in creating the experimentation platform and tools, but we also need:

- Ideas for experiments, that is, an *ideas funnel* (Kohavi et al. 2013).
- Validated metrics to measure the effects we care about.
- Evidence supporting or refuting hypotheses, when running a controlled experiment is either not possible or insufficient.
- Optionally, metrics that are complementary to the metrics computed from controlled experiments.

For an idea funnel, you want to use every method at your disposal to generate ideas, including methods like observing users in a user experience study. For ideas that are easy to implement, we recommend testing them directly by running a controlled experiment; however, for ideas that are expensive to implement, you can use one of these complementary techniques for early evaluation and idea pruning to reduce implementation cost.

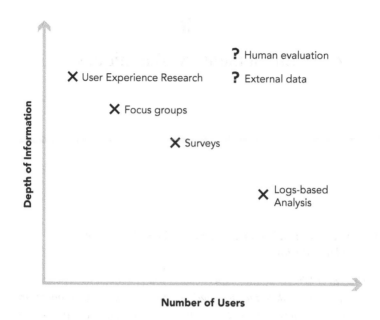

Figure 10.1  Number of users versus depth of information per user

As another example for using complementary techniques, what if you want a reliable proxy metric for user satisfaction, a concept that is quite difficult to measure. You can run a survey and gather self-reported user satisfaction data, and then analyze instrumented logs data to see what large-scale observational metrics correlate with the survey results. You can extend this further by running controlled experiments to validate the proposed proxy metrics.

The methods we discuss in this chapter vary along two axes: scale (i.e., number of users) vs. depth of information per user, as summarized in Figure 10.1, and as we discuss each in turn, we will see the tradeoff in terms of the generalizability that comes from the scale relative to the details we can get from lower-scale methods.

## Logs-based Analysis

One pre-requisite for running trustworthy A/B experiments is having proper instrumentation of user views, actions, and interactions to compute metrics for evaluating controlled experiments. The same is true for logs-based analyses, also called *retrospective* analyses. These help with:

- **Building intuition**: You can answer questions, such as the following, to define metrics and build intuition:
  - What is the distribution of sessions-per-user or click-through rate?
  - What is the difference by key segments, such as by country or platform (see Chapter 3)?
  - How do these distributions shift over time?
  - How are users growing over time?

  Building this intuition helps you understand your product and system baseline, what the variance is, what is happening organically independent of experimentation, what size change might be practically significant, and more.
- **Characterizing potential metrics**: Building intuition is the precursor for characterizing potential metrics. Characterization helps you understand the variance and distributions, how new metrics correlate with existing metrics. Log-based analyses establish understanding of how a potential metric might perform on past experiments. For example, is it useful for making decisions? Does it provide new/better information than existing metrics?
- **Generating ideas for A/B experiments based on exploring the underlying data:** You can examine the conversion rate at each step of the purchase funnel to identify large drop offs (McClure 2007). Analyzing sessionized data can uncover that a particular action sequence took longer than expected. This discovery path leads to ideas of how to make your product better, whether you're introducing new features or UI design changes.
- You can explore whether ideas generated using these complementary techniques happen at-scale and are worth investing time implementing and evaluating using an A/B experiment. For example, before investing in making an e-mail attachment easier to use, get an upper-bound sizing of the impact by analyzing the number of attachments sent.
- **Natural experiments**: These occur occasionally, either due to exogenous circumstances (e.g., an external company changing a default) or bugs (e.g., a bug that logs all users out). In those cases, run an observational analysis (see Chapter 11) to measure the effect.
- **Observational causal studies** (see Chapter 11): You can run these studies when experiments are not possible, for example, you can use quasi-experimental designs. When you use quasi-experimental designs in combination with experiments, they can lead to an improved inference of a more general result.

Logs-based analyses can serve many purposes complementary to A/B experiments. One limitation is that these analyses can only infer what will happen in the future based on what happened in the past. For example, you may decide not to further invest in the e-mail attachment feature because current usage is small; however, the current low usage might have been caused by the fact that it is difficult to use, which logs-based analysis may not reveal. Combining logs-based analysis with user and market research, as we discuss later in this chapter, gives a more comprehensive picture.

## Human Evaluation

Human evaluation is where a company pays a human judge, also called a *rater*, to complete some task. The results are then used in subsequent analysis. This is a common evaluation method in search and recommendation systems. Simple ratings can be questions such as, "Do you prefer side A or side B," or "Is this image pornographic?" and can get progressively more complicated, such as, "Please label this image," or "How relevant is this result for this query." The more complicated rating tasks may have detailed instructions to ensure more calibrated ratings. Typically, multiple raters are assigned the same task, as raters may disagree; you can use various voting or other disagreement resolution mechanisms to obtain high-quality aggregate labeling. For example, the quality of data from pay-systems, such as Mechanical Turk (Mechanical Turk 2019), varies depending on the incentives and payment amount, increasing the importance of quality-control and disagreement resolution (Buhrmester, Kwang and Gosling 2011).

One limitation of human evaluation is that raters are generally not your end users. Raters are doing tasks assigned to them – often in bulk, whereas your product is something your end users come by organically to their lives. In addition, raters can miss the local context of real users. For example, the search query "5/3" to many raters is an arithmetic query and will expect the result 1.667, yet users living near the "Fifth Third Bank," whose logo is "5/3," are looking for the bank information. This is an example of how hard it is to evaluate personalized recommendation algorithms. However, this limitation can also be an advantage, as raters can be trained to detect spam or other harmful experiences that users may not be able to perceive or detect. It is best to think that your human evaluation provides calibrated labeled data to complement data gathered from real users.

You can use metrics based on human evaluation as additional metrics for evaluating A/B experiments (Huffman 2008). Again, let's use search ranking changes. You can ask raters to rate results from either Control or Treatment for a given query and aggregate the ratings to see which variant is preferred; or use a side-by-side experiment, where Control and Treatment search results are shown side by side, and raters asked which side is "better." For example, Bing and Google's scaled-out human evaluation programs are fast enough for use alongside the online controlled experiment results to determine whether to launch the change.

Human evaluation results are also useful for debugging: you can examine the results in detail to understand where changes perform well and poorly. In our search query example, results rated a poor match for a query can be examined to help determine why the algorithm returned the result. You can also pair human evaluation with log-based analysis to understand what observed user actions correlate with highly relevant results for a query.

## User Experience Research (UER)

While user experience research (UER) uses a variety of methods, we focus here on a subset of field and lab studies that typically go deep with a few users, often by observing them doing tasks of interest and answering questions in either a lab setting or in situ (Alvarez 2017). This type of research is in-depth and intensive typically with at most tens of users, and is useful for generating ideas, spotting problems, and gaining insights from direct observation and timely questions. For example, if your website is trying to sell something, you can observe users trying to complete a purchase, and develop ideas for metrics based on observing where they struggle: Do we observe the purchase taking a long time? Are users struggling and going down a rabbit hole, such as looking for coupon codes?

These type of field and lab studies can include:

- Special equipment to gather data, such as eye-tracking that you cannot gather from your instrumentation
- Diary studies, where users self-document their behavior longitudinally, are useful for gathering data analogous to online instrumentation but augmented with data you cannot gather via instrumentation, such as user intent or offline activities.

These techniques can be useful for generating metric ideas based on correlating "true" user intent with what we observe via instrumentation. You must validate these ideas using methods that scale to more users, such as observational analyses and controlled experiments.

## Focus Groups

Focus groups are guided group discussions with recruited users or potential users. You can guide discussion to any range of topics, ranging from open-ended questions about user attitudes, "What is commonly done or discussed amongst their peers," to more specific questions, maybe using screenshots or a demo walk-through to elicit feedback.

Focus groups are more scalable than a UER study and can handle a similar level of ambiguous, open-ended questions that can guide product development and hypotheses. However, given the group nature and discussion format, less ground can be covered than in a UER study, and can fall prey to group-think and convergence on fewer opinions. What customers say in a focus group setting or a survey may not match their true preferences. A well-known example of this phenomenon occurred when Philips Electronics ran a focus group to gain insight into teenagers' preferences for boom box features. The focus group attendees expressed a strong preference for yellow boom boxes during the focus group, characterizing black boom boxes as "conservative." Yet when the attendees exited the room and were given the chance to take home a boom box as a reward for their participation, most chose black (Cross and Dixit 2005).

Focus groups can be useful for getting feedback on ill-formed hypotheses in the early stages of designing changes that become future experiments, or for trying to understand underlying emotional reactions, often for branding or marketing changes. Again, the goal is to gather information that cannot be measured via instrumentation and to get feedback on not-yet-fully-formed changes to help further the design process.

## Surveys

To run a survey, you recruit a population to answer a series of questions (Marsden and Wright 2010). The number of questions can vary, as can the type of questions. You can have multiple-choice answers, or open-ended questions where users give a free-form response. These can be done in-person, over the phone, or online directly on your app or site or via other methods of reaching and targeting users (such as Google Surveys (Google 2018)). You can also run surveys from within products, potentially pairing them with controlled experiments. For example, the Windows operating system prompts users with one or two short questions about the operating system and about other Microsoft products; Google has a method to ask a quick question tied to a user's in-product experience and satisfaction (Mueller and Sedley 2014).

While surveys may seem simple, they are actually quite challenging to design and analyze (Marsden and Wright 2010, Groves et al. 2009):

- Questions must be carefully worded, as they may be misinterpreted or unintentionally prime the respondents to give certain answers, or uncalibrated answers. The order of questions may change how respondents answer. And if you want to get data over time, you need to be careful about changes to the survey, as the changes may invalidate comparisons over time.
- Answers are self-reported: Users may not give full or truthful answers, even in anonymous surveys.
- The population can easily be biased and may not be representative of the true user population. This is exacerbated by "response bias," that is, which users respond may be biased (e.g., only people who are unhappy respond). Because of this bias, relative survey results (e.g., time period over time period) may be more useful than absolute results.

These pitfalls suggest that surveys are almost never directly comparable to any results observed from instrumentation. You can use surveys to reach larger numbers of users than UERs or focus groups, but they are primarily useful for getting answers to questions you cannot observe from your instrumented data, such as what happens when a user is offline or a user's opinion or trust and satisfaction levels. Questions might include what other information a user used when making a purchase decision, including offline actions such as talking to a friend, or asking about a user's satisfaction level three months post-purchase.

Surveys are also useful for observing trends over time on less-directly-measurable issues, such as trust or reputation, and are sometimes used to correlate with trends on highly aggregate business metrics, such as overall usage or growth. This correlation can then drive investment in a broad area such as how to improve user trust, but not necessarily generate specific ideas. You can use targeted UER studies for idea generation once you define the broad area.

Depending on the consent of survey participants, you may be able to pair survey results with observational analysis to see which survey responses correlate with observed user behavior, but the bias of the survey respondents will impact the believability and generalizability of the results.

## External Data

External data is data relevant to you and what you are looking at that a party external to your company has collected data and analyzed. There are several sources of external data:

- Companies providing per-site granular data (such as, the number of users to a website or detailed information about user online habits) based on data gathered from recruiting a large panel of users who agreed to have all online behavior tracked. One question has been around the representativeness of these users – while they are sampled from clear demographic buckets, there may be other differences in the users who agree to be tracked at this level of detail.
- Companies providing per-user granular data, such as user segments, that can be potentially joined with logs-based data.
- Companies running surveys and questionnaires either to publish themselves or who you can hire to run custom surveys. These companies use a variety of methods to answer questions you might be interested in, such as how many devices users have or their perspective on how trustworthy a brand is.
- Published academic papers. Researchers often publish studies of something of interest. There are a lot of papers out there, for example, papers comparing eye tracking – what the user looked at in a lab, with how they clicked on a search engine (Joachims et al. 2005) give you a good sense of how representative your click data is.
- Companies and websites providing lessons learned, often crowd-sourcing results to validate the lessons. This can be UI design patterns (Linowski 2018b)

External data can help validate simple business metrics if your site or industry appears in one of these lists. For example, if you want to look at total visitors to your site, you can compare your number computed from an internal observational analysis with the numbers provided by comScore or Hitwise, or you could compare the fraction of shopping traffic in each "vertical" category to what you see on your site. Rarely will these numbers exactly match. A better way to do validation is to look at a time series of both internal and external data to see whether the time series aligns in terms of the trend or seasonal variability. You can also provide supporting evidence for your business metrics, either directly measurable quantities or to get ideas for which measurable metrics make good proxies for other harder-to-measure quantities.

Publicly available academic papers, such as those pertaining to User Experience, often establish a general equivalence between different types of metrics. One example compares user-reported satisfaction with a search task to the measured task duration (Russell and Grimes 2007), that gives a good general correlation for satisfaction with duration, though with caveats. This study helped validate a metric, *duration*, that can be computed at scale and correlates with a metric that cannot be computed at scale, user-reported satisfaction.

External data can also add to the hierarchy of evidence. For example, companies could use the published work from Microsoft, Google, and others to establish that latency and performance is important without necessarily needing to run their own online controlled experiments (see Chapter 5). Companies would need to run their own experiments to understand specific tradeoffs for their product, but the general direction and investment could be based on external data for a smaller company without those resources.

External data can also provide competitive studies about how your company compares with your competitors, which can help provide benchmarking on your internal business metrics and give you a sense of what is attainable.

One caveat: because you do not control the sampling or know the exact methods used to do the analysis, the absolute numbers may not always be useful, but trends, correlations, and metric generation and validation are all good use cases.

## Putting It All Together

There are many ways to gather data about users, so the question is how to choose which one(s) to use. In large part, this depends on your goal. Do you want to figure out how to measure a particular user experience? Do you want to validate metrics? If you have no idea about what metrics to gather in the first place, more detailed, qualitative, brainstorming type of interactions, such as UER studies or focus groups work well. If you have no way of getting the data, because the interactions aren't on your site, a survey may work well. For validating metrics, external data and observational analyses work well since the data is usually collected over a large enough population that there are fewer sampling biases or other measurement issues.

All these techniques have different tradeoffs. You should consider how many people you are able to collect data from. This affects the generalizability of the results; in other words, whether you can establish external validity. The number of users is often a tradeoff against what type of detail you can get. For example, logs usually have user actions at-scale but not "why" a user acts a particular way that you might get in a UER field study. Where you are in a product cycle may also be a consideration. Early on, when you have too many ideas to test, more qualitative methods such as focus groups and user experience research may make more sense. And as you move towards having quantitative data, then observational studies and experiments make more sense.

Finally, remember that using multiple methods to triangulate towards a more accurate measurement − establishing a hierarchy of evidence − can lead to more robust results (Grimes, Tang and Russell 2007). Since no method can fully replicate the results from another method, use multiple methods to establish bounds for the answer. For example, to see whether users are happy with your personalized product recommendations, you must define signs of "happiness." To do that, you might observe users in an UER study, see whether they use the personalized recommendations, and ask them questions about whether they found the recommendations useful. Based on that feedback, you can look at the observational data for those users and see what behavioral signals you might see, such as a longer time reading the screen or certain click orders. You can then run a large observational analysis to validate the metric ideas generated from the small-scale UER study, see the interplay with the overall business metrics, and then potentially bolster that with an onscreen survey to reach a larger set of users with simple questions about whether they liked the recommendations. Accompanying this with learning experiments that change the recommendations, will allow you to better understand how user happiness metrics relate to the overall business metrics and improve your OEC.

# 11

# Observational Causal Studies

Shallow men believe in luck. Strong men believe in cause and effect
— *Ralph Waldo Emerson*

*Why you care: Randomized controlled experiments are the gold standard for establishing causality, but sometimes running such an experiment is not possible. Given that organizations are collecting massive amounts of data, there are observational causal studies that can be used to assess causality, although with lower levels of trust. Understanding the space of possible designs and common pitfalls can be useful if an online controlled experiment is not possible.*

## When Controlled Experiments Are Not Possible

What is the impact on product engagement if a user switches their phone from an iPhone to a Samsung? How many users come back if we forcibly sign them out? What happens to revenue if coupon codes are introduced as part of the business model? For all these questions, the goal is to measure the causal impact for a change, which requires comparing the outcome of a treated population to the outcome for an untreated population. The "basic identity of causal inference" (Varian 2016) is:

Outcome for treated $-$ Outcome for untreated
$=$ [Outcome for treated $-$ Outcome for treated if not treated]
$\quad+$[Outcome for treated if not treated $-$ Outcome for untreated]
$=$ Impact of Treatment on treated $+$ Selection bias

and shows that the comparison of the actual impact (what happens to the treated population) compared to the counterfactual (what would have happened if they had not been treated) is the critical concept for establishing causality (Angrist and Pischke 2009, Neyman 1923, Rubin 1974, Varian 2016, Shadish, Cook and Campbell 2001).

Controlled experiments are the gold standard for assessing causality because, with random assignment of units to variants, the first term is the observed difference between Treatment and Control and the second term has an expected value of zero.

However, sometimes you cannot run a properly controlled experiment. These situations include:

- When the causal action to be tested is not under the control of the organization. For example, you may want to understand how a user's behavior changes when they change their phone from an iPhone to a Samsung Galaxy phone. Even if you are Samsung with some levers to incent users to switch that can be randomized, generally you are not in control of users' choices here and paying people to switch biases the results.
- When there are too few units. For example, in a Merger and Acquisition (M&A) scenario, there is a single event that happens (or not) and estimating the counter-factual is extremely hard.
- When establishing a Control may incur too large an opportunity cost since they do not receive the Treatment (Varian 2016). For example, randomized experiments can be costly for rare events, such as establishing the impact of running ads during the Superbowl (Stephens-Davidowitz, Varian and Smith 2017), or when the desired OEC takes too long to measure, such as returning to a website to purchase a new car five years after the current car purchase.
- When the change is expensive relative to the perceived value. Some experiments are run to try to better understand relationships. For example, how many users will churn if you forcibly sign out all users after some time period? Or, what if you don't display ads on a search engine such as Bing or Google?
- When the desired unit of randomization cannot be properly randomized. When assessing the value of TV ads, it is practically impossible to randomize by viewers. The alternative of using Designated Market Areas (DMAs) (Wikipedia contributors, Multiple Comparisons problem 2019), results in far fewer units (e.g., about 210 in the US) and hence low statistical power, even when using techniques such as pairing.
- When what is being tested is unethical or illegal, such as withholding medical treatments that are believed to be beneficial.

In the above situations, often the best approach is to estimate the effects using multiple methods that are lower in the hierarchy of evidence, that is, answering the question using multiple methods, including small-scale user experience studies, surveys, and observational studies. See Chapter 10 for an introduction to several other techniques.

Our focus in this chapter is on estimating the causal effect from observational studies, which we will call *observational causal studies*. Some books, such as Shadish et al. (2001), use the term *observational (causal) studies* to refer to studies where there is no unit manipulation, and the term *quasi-experimental designs* to studies where units are assigned to variants, but the assignment is not random. For additional information, please see Varian (2016) and Angrist and Pischke (2009, 2014). Note that we differentiate an observational causal study from the more general observational, or retrospective, data analyses. While both are run on historical log data, the goal in an observational causal study is to try to get as close to a causal result as possible, while retrospective data analyses, as discussed in Chapter 10, have different goals, ranging from summarizing distributions, seeing how common certain behavioral patterns are, analyzing possible metrics, and looking for interesting patterns that may suggest hypotheses to be tested in controlled experiments.

## Designs for Observational Causal Studies

In observational causal studies, the challenges are:

- How to construct Control and Treatment groups for comparison.
- How to model the impact given those Control and Treatment groups.

### Interrupted Time Series

Interrupted Time Series (ITS) is a quasi-experimental design, where you can control the change within your system, but you cannot randomize the Treatment to have a proper Control and Treatment. Instead, you use the same population for Control and Treatment, and you vary what the population experiences over time.

Specifically, it uses multiple measurements over time, before an intervention, to create a model that can provide an estimate for the metric of interest after the intervention – a counterfactual. After the intervention, multiple measurements are taken, and the Treatment effect is estimated as the average difference between the actual values for the metric of interest and those predicted by the model (Charles and Melvin 2004, 130). One extension to the simple ITS is to introduce a Treatment and then reverse it, optionally repeating this procedure multiple times. For example, the effect of police helicopter surveillance on home *burglaries* was estimated using multiple Treatment interventions because over several months, surveillance was implemented and withdrawn several times. Each time that helicopter surveillance was implemented, the number of burglaries decreased; each time surveillance was removed, the number of burglaries increased (Charles and Melvin 2004). In an online setting, a similar example is to understand the impact of online advertising on search-related site visits. Note that sophisticated modeling may be necessary to infer the impact, with an online example of ITS being Bayesian Structural Time Series analysis (Charles and Melvin 2004).

One common issue with observational causal studies is ensuring that you are not attributing an effect to a change when in fact there is some confounding effect. The most common confounds for ITS are time-based effects as the comparisons are made across different points of time. Seasonality is the obvious example, but other underlying system changes can also confound. Changing back and forth multiple times will help reduce the likelihood of that. The other concern when using ITS is on the user experience: Will the user notice their experience flipping back and forth? If so, then that lack of consistency may irritate or frustrate the user in a way that the effect may not be due to the change but rather the inconsistency.

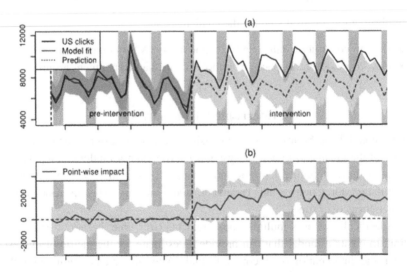

Figure 11.1 Interrupted Time Series using Bayesian Structural Time Series (Charles and Melvin 2004). (a) shows the model fit in the pre-intervention period and the actual observed metric in the solid line, with the dashed line the predicted counterfactual. The x-axis is days with shaded vertical bars indicating weekends. (b) shows the delta between the actual and the prediction; if the model is good, then it is an estimate of the Treatment effect. Weekends are shaded in grey

### Interleaved Experiments

Interleaved experiment design is a common design used to evaluate ranking algorithm changes, such as in search engines or search at a website (Chapelle et al. 2012, Radlinski and Craswell 2013). In an interleaved experiment, you have two ranking algorithms, X and Y. Algorithm X would show results $x_1$, $x_2$, ...$x_n$ in that order, and algorithm Y would show $y_1$, $y_2$, ...$y_n$ . An interleaved experiment would intersperse results mixed together, e.g. $x_1$, $y_1$, $x_2$, $y_2$, ...$x_n$, $y_n$ with duplicate results removed. One way to evaluate the algorithms would be to compare the click-through rate on results from the two algorithms. While this design is a powerful experiment design, it is limited in its applicability because the results must be homogenous. If, as is common, the first result takes up more space, or impacts the other areas of the page, then complexities arise.

### Regression Discontinuity Design

Regression Discontinuity Design (RDD) is a methodology that can be used whenever there is a clear threshold that identifies the Treatment population. Based on that threshold, we can reduce selection bias by identifying the population that is just below the threshold as Control and compared to the population that is just above the threshold as Treatment.

For example, when a scholarship is given, the near-winners are easily identified (Thistlewaite and Campbell 1960). If a scholarship is given for an 80% grade, then the Treatment group that received grades just above 80% is assumed to be similar to the Control group that received grades just below 80%. The assumption is violated when participants can impact their Treatment; for example, if the Treatment is applied to a passing grade, but students are able to convince their teachers to "mercy pass" them (McCrary 2008). An example using RDD is in assessing the impact of drinking on deaths: Americans over 21 can drink legally, so we can look at deaths by birthday, shown in Figure 11.2. The "Mortality risk shoots up on and immediately following a twenty-first birthday ... about 100 deaths to a baseline level of about 150 per day. The age-21 spike doesn't seem to be a generic party-hardy birthday effect. If this spike reflects birthday partying alone, we should expect to see deaths shoot up after the twentieth and twenty-second birthdays as well, but that doesn't happen" (Angrist and Pischke 2014).

As in the above example, one key issue is again confounding factors. In RDD, the threshold discontinuity may be contaminated by other factors that share the same threshold. For example, a study of the impact of alcohol that chooses the legal age of 21 as the threshold may be contaminated by the fact that this is also the threshold for legal gambling.

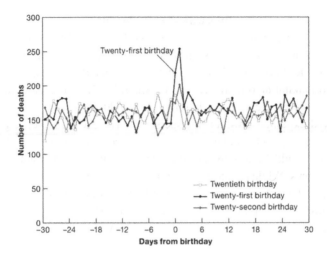

Figure 11.2 Deaths vs. Days from birthday for 20th, 21st, and 22nd birthday (Angrist and Pischke 2014)

RDD most commonly applies when there is an algorithm that generates a score, and something happens based on a threshold of that score. Note that when this happens in software, while one option is to use RDD, this is also a scenario that also easily lends itself to randomized controlled experiments, or some hybrid of the two (Owen and Varian 2018).

## Instrumented Variables (IV) and Natural Experiments

Instrumental Variables (IV) is a technique that tries to approximate random assignment. Specifically, the goal is to identify an Instrument that allows us to approximate random assignment (this happens organically in a natural experiment) (Angrist and Pischke 2014, Pearl 2009).

For example, to analyze difference in earnings between veterans and non-veterans, the Vietnam war draft lottery resembles random assignment of individuals into the military; charter school seats are allocated by lottery and can thus be a good IV for some studies. In both examples, the lottery does not guarantee attendance but has a large impact on attendance. A two-stage least-squares regression model is then commonly used to estimate the effect.

Sometimes, natural experiments that are "as good as random" can occur. In medicine, monozygotic twins allow running twin studies as natural experiments (Harden et al. 2008, McGue 2014). Online, when studying social or peer networks, running controlled experiments on members can be challenging as the effect may not be constrained to the Treatment population due to member-to-member communications. However, notification queues and the message delivery order are types of natural experiments that can be leveraged to understand the impact of notifications on engagement, for example Tutterow and Saint-Jacques (2019).

## Propensity Score Matching

Another class of approaches here is to construct comparable Control and Treatment populations, often by segmenting the users by common confounds, in something akin to stratified sampling. The idea is to ensure that the comparison between Control and Treatment population is not due to population mix changes. For example, if we are examining an exogenous change of the impact of users changing from Windows to iOS, we want to ensure that we are not measuring a demographic difference in the population.

We can take this approach further by moving to propensity score matching (PSM) that, instead of matching units on covariates, matches on a single number: a constructed propensity score (Rosenbaum and Rubin 1983, Imbens and Rubin 2015). This approach has been used in the online space, for example for evaluating the impact of online ad campaigns (Chan et al. 2010). The key concern about PSM is that only observed covariates are accounted for; unaccounted factors may result in hidden biases. Judea Pearl (2009, 352) wrote "Rosenbaum and Rubin ... were very clear in warning practitioners that propensity scores work only under 'strong ignorability' conditions. However, what they failed to realize is that it is not enough to warn people against dangers they cannot recognize." King and Nielsen (2018) claim that PSM "often accomplishes the opposite of its intended goal—thus increasing imbalance, inefficiency, model dependence, and bias."

For all of these methods, the key concern is confounding factors.

## Difference in Differences

Many of the methods above focus on how to identify a Control group that is as similar to a Treatment group as possible. Given that identification, one method to measure the effect of the Treatment is difference in differences (DD or DID) that, assuming common trends, assigns the difference in difference to the Treatment. In particular, the groups "may differ in the absence of Treatment yet move in parallel" (Angrist and Pischke 2014).

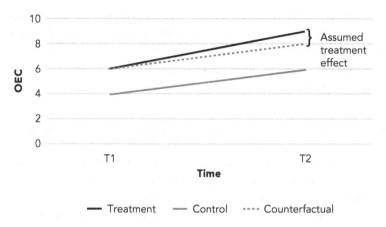

Figure 11.3 Difference in differences

Geographically based experiments commonly use this technique. You want to understand the impact of TV advertising on driving user acquisition, engagement, and retention. You run TV ads in one DMA and compare it to another DMA. For example, as shown in Figure 11.3, a change is made at time $T_1$ to the Treatment group. Measurements are taken for both the Treatment and Control just before $T_1$, and at a later point $T_2$. The difference in the metrics of interest, such as the OEC, between the two periods in the Control group are assumed to capture the external factors (e.g., seasonality, economic strength, inflation) and thus present the counterfactual of what would have happened to the Treatment group. The Treatment effect is estimated as the difference in a metric of interest minus the difference in Control for that metric over the same period.

Note that this method can also be applied even when you do not make the change, and the change happens exogenously. For example, when a change was made to the minimum wage in New Jersey, researchers who wanted to study its impact on employment levels in fast-food restaurants, compared it to eastern Pennsylvania, which matched on many characteristics (Card and Krueger 1994).

## Pitfalls

Although observational causal studies are sometimes your best option, they have many pitfalls that you should be aware of (see also Newcomer et al. (2015) for a more exhaustive list). As mentioned above, the main pitfall,

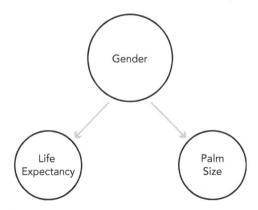

Figure 11.4 Instead of Palm Size predicting Life Expectancy, Gender is the common cause that predicts both

regardless of method, in conducting observational causal studies is unantici-pated confounds that can impact both the measured effect, as well as the attribution of causality to the change of interest. Because of these confounds, observational causal studies require a great deal of care to yield trustworthy results, with many examples of refuted observational causal studies (see *Side-bar: Refuted Observational Causal Studies* later in this chapter and Chapter 17 for a few).

One common type of confound is an unrecognized **common cause**. For example, in humans, palm size has a strong correlation with life expectancy: on average the smaller your palm, the longer you will live. However, the common cause of smaller palms and longer life expectancy is gender: women have smaller palms and live longer on average (about six years in the US).

As another example, for many products, including Microsoft Office 365, users that see more errors typically churn *less*! But do not try to show more errors expecting to reduce churn, as this correlation is due to a common cause: usage. Your heaviest users see more errors *and* churn at lower rates. It is not uncommon for feature owners to discover that users of their new feature churn at a lower rate, which implies that it is their feature that is reducing churn. Is it really the feature or (more likely) simply that heavy users churn less and are more likely to use more features? In these cases, to evaluate whether the new feature indeed reduces churn, run a controlled experiment (and analyze new and heavy users separately).

Another pitfall to be aware of are **spurious or deceptive correlations**. Deceptive correlations can be caused by strong outliers, for example as in

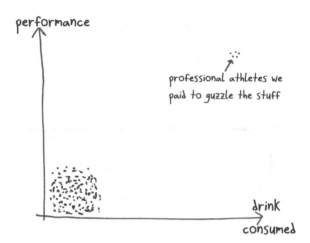

Figure 11.5 Deceptive correlation of athletic performance and amount of energy drink consumed. Correlation does not imply causation!

Figure 11.5, where a marketing company can claim that their energy drink is highly correlated with athletic performance and imply a causal relationship: drink our energy product and your athletic performance will improve (Orlin 2016).

Spurious correlations can almost always be found (Vigen 2018). When we test many hypotheses and when we do not have the intuition to reject a causal claim as we have in the above example, we may believe it. For example, if someone told you that they found a factor that had a strong correlation ($r=0.86$) with people killed by venomous spiders, you might be tempted to act on this information. Yet when you realize that the deaths are correlated with word length in the National Spelling Bee test, as shown in Figure 11.6, you quickly reject the request to shorten the word length in the National Spelling Bee as irrational.

Even when care is taken, there is never a guarantee that there is not some other factor not included in the observational causal study that may impact the results. Quasi-experimental methods, which attempt to derive a counterfactual to compare to and therefore establish causality, simply require making many assumptions, any of which can be wrong, and some assumptions are implicit. Incorrect assumptions can lead to a lack of internal validity but depending on the assumptions and how limiting they are, they can also impact the external validity of the study. While building intuition, as discussed in Chapter 1, can help improve the quality of assumptions, intuition will not mitigate all possible problems. Thus, the scientific gold standard for establishing causality is still the controlled experiment.

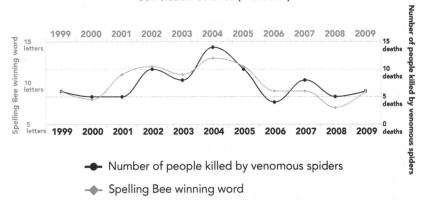

Figure 11.6  Spurious correlation of people killed by venomous spiders and word length in Scripps National Spelling Bee

## SIDEBAR: Refuted Observational Causal Studies

Claiming causality from observational data (uncontrolled) requires multiple assumptions that are impossible to test and are easily violated. While many observational causal studies are later confirmed by randomized controlled experiments (Concato, Shah and Horwitz 2000), others are refuted. Ioannidis (2005) evaluated claims coming from highly cited studies; of six observational causal studies included in his study, five failed to replicate. Stanley Young and Alan Karr (2019) compared published results from medical hypotheses shown to be significant using observational causal studies (i.e., uncontrolled) with randomized clinical trials considered more reliable. Of 52 claims in 12 papers, none replicated in the randomized controlled trials. And in 5 of the 52 cases, the direction was statistically significant in the opposite direction of the observational causal study. Their conclusion: "Any claim coming from an observational study is most likely to be wrong."

One example from the online space is on how to measure the effectiveness of online advertising, in other words, whether online ads led to either increased brand activity or even user engagement. Observational causal studies are often required to measure the effect, since the intervention (the ad) and the effect (user sign-up or engagement) are typically on different sites and therefore different spheres of control. Lewis, Rao and Reiley (2011) compared the effectiveness of online advertising as estimated by observational causal studies relative to the "gold standard" controlled experiments, finding that observational causal studies vastly overestimated the effect. Specifically, they ran three experiments.

First, advertisements (display ads) were shown to users, and the question was: What is the increase (lift) in the number of users who search using keywords related to the brand shown in the ad. Using several observational causal studies of 50 million users, including three regression analyses with Control variables, the estimated lift ranged from 871% to 1198%. This estimated lift is orders of magnitude higher from the lift of 5.4% measured via the controlled experiment. The confound is common cause of users visiting Yahoo! in the first place: Users who actively visit Yahoo! on a given day are much more likely to see the display ad and to perform a Yahoo! search. The ad exposure and the search behavior are highly positively correlated, but the display ads have very little causal impact on the searches.

Next, videos were shown to users, and the question was whether these would lead to increased activity. Users were recruited through Amazon Mechanical Turk, with half exposed to a 30-second video advertisement promoting Yahoo.com services (the Treatment), and half to a political video advertisement (the Control), and the goal was to measure whether there was increased activity on Yahoo! Two analyses were done: an observational causal study of the Treatment group before and after the exposure to the 30-second Yahoo! ads, and an experimental analysis comparing the activity of the two groups after seeing the ad. The observational causal study overstated the effects of the ad by 350%. Here, the common confound is that being active on Amazon Mechanical Turk on a given day increased the chance of participating in the experiment and being active on Yahoo!

Finally, an ad campaign was shown to users on Yahoo! with the goal of measuring whether users who saw the ad were more likely to sign up at the competitor's website on the day they saw the ad. The observational causal study compared users exposed to the ad on the day they saw the ad relative to the week before, while the experiment compared users who did not see the ad but visited Yahoo! on that day to the users who came to Yahoo! on the same day and saw the competitor ad. From the observational causal study, exposed users were more likely to sign up at the competitor's website the day they saw the ad compared to the week before. However, from the experiment, they observed a nearly identical lift. This result is similar to our previous discussion of churn and errors: More active users are simply more likely to do a broad range of activities. Using activity as a factor is typically important.

This is but one story and one comparison. A more recent comparison study also found that observational causal studies were less accurate than online controlled experiments (Gordon et al. 2018). We provide many more stories online at https://bit.ly/experimentGuideRefutedObservationalStudies, showing examples of unidentified common causes, time-sensitive confounds, population differences lack of external validity, and more. Should you need to do an observational causal study, please take care.

# PART IV

## Advanced Topics for Building an Experimentation Platform

Part IV expands on building experiment platforms from Chapter 4, with five short chapters targeted towards engineers and data scientists. Product managers should at least understand the issues discussed here, as they can affect experiment design, as well as the data quality for experiment analysis.

Throughout this book, to make discussions simple, we primarily focus on server-side experimentation. However, there are many thick clients, notably mobile or desktop apps, where we need to run experiments on the client-side. We provide key differences to consider when running *Client-Side Experiments*.

The next two topics are foundational no matter what stage of experimentation maturity you are in.

First, high-quality *Instrumentation* is a pre-requisite for running trustworthy online controlled experiments. Without instrumentation, you cannot get the data or metrics to analyze experiments or even to determine the baseline performance of your system. In this part, we discuss the key points of instrumentation in the context of experimentation.

Next, while we have assumed *user* to be the randomization unit for simplicity throughout this book, there are other choices such as *session* or *page*. *Choosing a Randomization Unit* is typically baked deeply into your system, and it can both impact user experience and the validity of the analysis. We describe various choices you can use and provide guidelines on how to choose among them.

As you scale experimentation, you now need to consider additional areas.

First, ramping up experiments in a principled and controlled manner is crucial for scale. We discuss *Ramping Experiment Exposure: Trading Off Speed, Quality, and Risk*.

Finally, an automated and scalable data analysis pipeline is also critical for scaling experimentation. We provide the common steps needed in *Scaling Experiment Analyses*, including processing, computing and displaying the data.

151

# 12

# Client-Side Experiments

The difference between theory and practice is larger in practice than the difference between theory and practice in theory
– *Jan L.A. van de Snepscheut*

***Why you care:*** *You can run experiments either on a thin client, such as a web browser, or on a thick client, such as a native mobile app or a desktop client app. Changes for a webpage, regardless of whether it is frontend or backend, are fully controlled by the server. This is very different from a thick client. With an explosive growth of mobile usage, the number of experiments running on mobile apps has also grown (Xu and Chen 2016). Understanding the differences between thin and thick clients due to release process, infrastructure, and user behavior is useful to ensure trustworthy experiments.*

For most of this book, we assume thin clients when designing and running experiments to keep the discussions simple. This chapter is devoted to discussing running experiments in thick clients, their differences and implications.

## Differences between Server and Client Side

To simplify the terminology, we will use "client-side experiment" to refer to experiment changes made within a thick client. We will use "server-side experiment" to refer to experiment changes made server side, regardless of whether it impacts a thick or thin client, and regardless of whether it is a UX change or a backend change.

There are two main differences between server and client side that impact online experiments: the release process and the data communication.

153

## Difference #1: Release Process

On an online website, it is common for new feature releases to happen continuously, sometimes multiple times per day. Because changes are controlled by the organization, updating server-side code is relatively easy as part of continuous integration and deployment. When a user visits a site, the server pushes the data (e.g., HTML) to the browser, without interrupting the end-user experience. In a controlled experiment, the variant that the user sees is fully managed by the server and no end user action is required. Whether to show a red or yellow button, whether to show a newly revamped homepage or not—these are all changes that can happen instantaneously after a server-side deployment.

When it comes to client apps, many features can still be affected by services, that is, code on the server side, such as the feed content shown in the Facebook app. Changes affecting them would follow a similar release process as described above for a webpage. In fact, the more we can rely on services, the easier it is to experiment, both with regards to agility and consistency across different clients. For example, many changes on Bing, Google, LinkedIn, and Office are made server side and impact all clients, whether web or thick clients like mobile apps.

However, there is a significant amount of code shipped with the client itself. Any changes to this code must be released differently. For example, in a mobile app, developers do not have full control over the deployment and release cycle. The release process involves three parties: the app owner (e.g., Facebook), the app store (e.g., Google Play or Apple App Store), and the end user.

When the code is ready, the app owner needs to submit a build to the app store for review. Assuming the build passes review (which can take days), releasing it to everyone does not mean that everyone who visits the app will have the new version. Instead, getting the new version is a software upgrade, and users can choose to delay or even ignore the upgrade while continuing to use the old version. Some end users take weeks to adopt. Some enterprise organizations may not want updates and do not allow them for their users.

Some software, such as Exchange, runs in sovereign clouds that are restricted from calling unapproved services. All of these considerations mean that, at any given time, there are multiple versions of the app out there that the app owner has to support. Similar challenges exist for native desktop clients that have their own release mechanisms (e.g., Office, Adobe Acrobat, iTunes), even though there may not be an app store review process involved.

It is worth pointing out that both the Google Play and Apple app stores now support staged rollout (Apple, Inc. 2017, Google Console 2019). They both allow app owners to make the new app available to only a percentage of users and pause if something problematic is discovered. Staged rollouts are essentially randomized experiments, as the eligible users are selected at random. Unfortunately, these rollouts cannot be analyzed as random experiments because the app owners do not know which users are eligible to receive the new app. App owners only know who has "adopted" the new app. We will discuss this more later in this chapter.

App owners may not want to frequently push a new client version. Even though there is no strict limit as how many times they can release a new version, each update costs network bandwidth for users and can potentially be an annoying user experience (depending on update and notification settings). Windows or iOS is a great example of something that cannot update as often because some updates require a reboot.

## Difference #2: Data Communication between Client and Server

Now that the new app is in the hands of users, it has to communicate with the server. The client needs to get the necessary data from the server, and it needs to pass data back to the server on what is happening on the client. While we refer readers to Chapter 13 for client-side instrumentation in general, here we highlight some key factors when it comes to data communication for a native mobile app. While it makes it easier to read this section with mobile in mind, please note that with drastic technology improvement, the divide between mobile and desktop is becoming nominal as a reflection of device capabilities and improvement in network connections.

First, the data connection between the client and server may be limited or delayed:

- **Internet connectivity**. Internet connections may not be reliable or consistent. In some countries, users may be offline for days. Even users who are normally online may not have internet access on a plane or be temporarily in a zone with no available cellular or Wi-Fi networks. As a result, data changes happening server side may not be pushed to these clients. Similarly, data collection on the client may be delayed in transmitting back to the server. These delays vary by country or demographic and must be accounted for in instrumentation and downstream processing.
- **Cellular data bandwidth**. Most users have limited cellular data plans, which raises the question of whether you only upload telemetry when the user is on Wi-Fi or at any point in time. Most apps choose to send telemetry

data over Wi-Fi only, which can delay when that data is received server side. There can also be heterogeneity across countries, as mobile infrastructure in some countries is weaker than others when it comes to bandwidth, cost, and so on.

Not only could the data connection itself be limited, but even if the connection is good, using the network may impact device performance and ultimately user engagement with the app (Dutta and Vadermeer 2018):

- **Battery**. More data communication implies increased battery consumption. For example, the app can wake up more regularly to send more telemetry, but that would impact battery consumption. Moreover, mobile devices in low battery mode have restrictions on what apps are allowed to do (Apple, Inc. 2018).
- **CPU, latency, and performance**. Even though many mobile devices behave like minicomputers nowadays, there are still lower-end mobile devices constrained by CPU power. Frequent data aggregation on the device and sending data back-and-forth with the server can make the app less responsive and hurt the overall performance of the app.
- **Memory and storage**. Caching is one way to reduce data communication but impacts the size of the app, which impacts app performance and increases app uninstallment (Reinhardt 2016). This may be a larger concern for users with lower-end devices with less memory and storage.

Communication bandwidth and device performance are all part of the same device ecosystem, with tradeoffs. For instance, we can get a more consistent internet connection by using more cellular data; we can spend more CPU to compute and aggregate on-device to reduce data sent back to the server; we can wait for Wi-Fi to send tracking data by using more storage on-device. These tradeoffs can impact both visibility into what is happening client side, as well as user engagement and behavior (similar to Chapter 5), making it a fruitful area for experimentation but also an area where care needs to be taken to ensure trustworthy results.

## Implications for Experiments

### Implication #1: Anticipate Changes Early and Parameterize

As client code cannot be shipped to end users easily, controlled experiments on any client-side changes need to be planned. In other words, all experiments, including all variants for each of these experiments, need to be coded and shipped with the current app build. Any new variants, including bug fixes on any existing variant, must wait for the next release. For example, in a typical monthly release, Microsoft Office ships with hundreds of features that rollout in a controlled manner to ensure safe deployment. This has three implications:

1. A new app may be released before certain features are completed, in which case, these features are gated by configuration parameters, called feature flags, that turn the features off by default. Features turned off this way are called dark features. When the feature is finished and ready, sometimes when the server-side service completes, it can be turned on.
2. More features are built so they are configurable from the server side. This allows them to be evaluated in A/B tests, which helps both in measuring performance via controlled experiments, and also provides a safety net. If a feature does not perform well, we can instantly revert by shutting down the feature (the variant in the controlled experiment) without having to go through a lengthy client release cycle. This can prevent end users from being stuck with a faulty app for weeks until the next release.
3. More fine-grained parameterization can be used extensively to add flexibility in creating new variants without needing a client release. This is because even though new code cannot be pushed to the client easily, new configurations can be passed, which effectively creates a new variant if the client understands how to parse the configurations. For instance, we may want to experiment on the number of feed items to fetch from the server at a time. We could put our best guess in the client code and only experiment with what we planned, or we can parameterize the number and have the freedom to experiment post release. Windows 10 parameterized the search box text in the task bar, ran experiments over a year after it shipped, with the winning variant increasing user engagement and Bing revenue by millions of dollars. Another common example is to update machine learning model parameters from the server, so that a model can be tuned over time.

While we believe it is best for the user experience to test new features before launching to all app users, there may be limitations imposed by app stores on which features can be shipped dark. We suggest carefully reading app store policies and appropriately disclosing dark features.

## Implication #2: Expect a Delayed Logging and Effective Starting Time

The limited or delayed data communication between client and server cannot only delay the arrival of data instrumentation, but also the start time of the experiment itself. First, the experiment implementation on the client side needs to be shipped with the new app version. Then, we can activate the experiment for a small percentage of users. However, even then, the experiment is not fully active because:

- User devices may not get the new experiment configuration, either because devices are offline or because they are in limited or low bandwidth situations, where pushing new configurations can lead to increased costs or poor experiences for the user.
- If the new experiment configuration is fetched only when a user opens the app, the new assignment may not take effect until the next session as we do not want to change a user's experience after they have started the current session. For heavy users with multiple sessions a day, this delay is small, but for light users visiting once a week, the experiment may not start until a week later.
- There can be many devices with old versions without the new experiment code, particularly right after the new app release. Based on our experience, the initial adoption phase takes about a week to reach a more stable adoption rate, although this can vary greatly depending on the user population and the type of app.

These delays in experiment start time and instrumentation arriving on the server can impact experiment analysis, especially if the analysis is time sensitive, for example, real-time or near real-time. First, signals at the beginning of the experiment would appear to be weaker (smaller sample size), and also have a strong selection bias towards frequent users and Wi-Fi users who tend to be early adopters. Thus, the duration of an experiment may need to be extended to account for delays. Another important implication is that Treatment and Control variants may have a different effective starting times. Some experiment platforms allow for shared Control variants, in which case the Control variant may be live before the Treatment, and therefore have a different user population due to selection bias. In addition, if the Control runs earlier, the caches are warmed up so responses to service requests are faster, which may introduce additional bias. As a result, the time period to compare the Treatment and Control needs to be carefully chosen.

## Implication #3: Create a Failsafe to Handle Offline or Startup Cases

When users open an app, their device could be offline. For consistency reasons, we should cache experiment assignment in case the next open occurs when the device is offline. In addition, if the server is not responding with the configuration needed to decide on assignment, we should have a default variant for an experiment. Some apps are also distributed as original equipment manufacture (OEM) agreements. In these cases, experiments must be properly set up for a first-run experience. This includes retrieving configurations that would only impact the next startup, and a stable randomization ID before and after users sign up or log in.

## Implication #4: Triggered Analysis May Need Client-Side Experiment Assignment Tracking

You may need to take additional care to enable triggered analysis for client-side experiments. For example, one way to capture triggering information is to send tracking data to the server when an experiment is used. However, to reduce communications from the client to the server, experiment assignment information is usually fetched for all active experiments at once (e.g., at the start of the app), regardless of whether an experiment is triggered or not (see Chapter 20). Relying on the tracking data at fetching time for triggered analysis would lead to over-triggering. One way to address this problem is to send the assignment information when a feature is actually used, thus requiring experiment instrumentation to be sent from the client. Keep in mind that if the volume of these tracking events is high, it could cause latency and performance issues.

## Implication #5: Track Important Guardrails on Device and App Level Health

Device-level performance may impact how the app performs. For instance, the Treatment may be consuming more CPU and draining more battery power. If we only track user engagement data, we may not discover the battery-drain problem. Another example is that the Treatment may send more push notifications to users that then lead to an increased level of notification disablement via device settings. These may not show up as a significant engagement drop during the experiment but have a sizable long-term impact.

It is also important to track the overall health of the app. For example, we should track app size, as a bigger app size is more likely to reduce downloads and cause people to uninstall (Tolomei 2017, Google Developers 2019). Similar behaviors may result due to an app's internet bandwidth consumption, battery usage, or crash rate. For crashes, logging a clean exit allows sending telemetry on a crash on the next app start.

## Implication #6: Monitor Overall App Release through Quasi-experimental Methods

Not all changes on the new app can be put behind an A/B parameter. To truly run a randomized controlled experiment on the new app as a whole, bundle both versions behind the same app and start some users on the new version, while keeping others on the old version. This is not practical or ideal for most apps, as it can double the app size. On the other hand, because not all users adopt the new app version at the same time, there is a period of time where we have both versions of the app serving real users. This effectively offers an A/B comparison if we can correct for the adoption bias. Xu and Chen (2016) share techniques to remove the bias in the mobile adoption setting.

## Implication #7: Watch Out for Multiple Devices/Platforms and Interactions between Them

It is common for a user to access the same site via multiple devices and platforms, for example, desktop, mobile app, and mobile web. This can have two implications.

1. Different IDs may be available on different devices. As a result, the same user may be randomized into different variants on different devices. (Dmitriev et al. 2016).
2. There can be potential interactions between different devices. Many browsers, including Edge, now have a "Continue on desktop" or "Continue on mobile" sync feature to make it easier for users to switch between desktop and mobile. It is also common to shift traffic between the mobile app and mobile web. For example, if a user reads an e-mail from Amazon on their phone and clicks it, the e-mail link can either take them directly to the Amazon app (assuming they have the app installed) or to the mobile website. When analyzing an experiment, it is important to know whether it may cause or suffer from these interactions. If so, we cannot evaluate app performance in isolation, but need to look at user behavior holistically across different platforms. Another thing to watch for is that the user experience on one platform (usually the app) can be better than on another platform. Directing traffic from the app to the web tends to bring down total engagement, which may be a confounding effect not intended by the experiment itself.

# Conclusions

We have devoted this chapter to the differences when experimenting on thin vs. thick clients. While some differences are obvious, many are subtle but critical. We need to put in extra care in order to design and analyze the experiments properly. It is also important to point out that with rapid technological improvement, we expect many of the differences and implications to evolve over time.

# 13

# Instrumentation

Everything that happens happens as it should, and if you observe
carefully, you will find this to be so
– *Marcus Aurelius*

***Why you care:*** *Before you can run any experiments, you must have instru-*
*mentation in place to log what is happening to the users and the system (e.g.,*
*website, application). Moreover, every business should have a baseline under-*
*standing of how the system is performing and how users interact with it, which*
*requires instrumentation. When running experiments, having rich data about*
*what users saw, their interactions (e.g., clicks, hovers, and time-to-click), and*
*system performance (e.g., latencies) is critical.*

A detailed discussion of how to instrument a system is beyond the scope of
this book and highly dependent on system architecture (Wikipedia contributors, List of .NET libraries and frameworks 2019, Wikipedia contributors,
Logging as a Service 2019). This chapter discusses key points of instrumentation in the context of experimentation. Privacy is also a crucial consideration
when it comes to instrumentation, which we discuss in Chapter 9. In the
context of this book, we use the terms "instrument," "track," and "log"
interchangeably.

## Client-Side vs. Server-Side Instrumentation

When implementing instrumentation, understanding what happens client side
vs. server side is important (Edmons et al. 2007, Zhang, Joseph and Rickabaugh 2018). The focus of client-side instrumentation is what the user experiences, including what they see and do, for example:

- **User actions:** What activities does the user do, such as clicks, hovers, scrolls? At what times are these done? What actions are done on the client without a server roundtrip? For example, there could be hovers generating help text or form field errors. Slideshows allow users to click and flip through slides, so capturing the times of those events is important.
- **Performance:** How long does it take the page (webpage or app page) to display or become interactive? In Chapter 5, we discuss the complexities around measuring the time from a search query request to displaying a full page.
- **Errors and crashes:** JavaScript errors are common, and may be browser dependent, and it is critical to track errors and crashes in client software.

System-side instrumentation focuses on what the system does, including:

- **Performance:** How long does it take for the server to generate the response, and which component takes the longest? What is the performance at the 99th percentile?
- **System response rate:** How many requests has the server received from the user? How many pages has the server served? How are retries handled?
- **System information:** How many exceptions or errors does the system throw? What is the cache hit rate?

Client-side instrumentation is useful as it offers a view of what the user sees and does. For example, client-side malware can overwrite what the server sends and this is only discoverable using client-side instrumentation (Kohavi et al. 2014). However, client-side instrumentation has drawbacks in terms of data accuracy and cost to the user. Here are specific concerns for JavaScript-based clients (for mobile-related concerns, see Chapter 12):

1. Client-side instrumentation can utilize significant CPU cycles and network bandwidth and deplete device batteries, impacting the user experience. Large JavaScript snippets will impact load time. This increased latency not only impacts user interaction on that visit, but also how likely those users will return (see Chapter 5).
2. The JavaScript instrumentation can be lossy (Kohavi, Longbotham and Walker 2010): web beacons are often used to track user interactions, such as when users click a link to go to a new site; however, these beacons may be lost when:
   a. A new site loads before the web beacon is successfully sent, meaning that the beacons can be cancelled and lost. The loss rate due to this race condition varies by browser.

b. We force the web beacon to be sent before the new site loads, such as via a synchronous redirect. While the beacon lossiness decreases, latency increases, resulting in a worse user experience and an increased likelihood of the user abandoning the click.

c. You can choose to implement either scenario depending on the application. For example, because ad clicks must be reliably tracked as they relate to payments and compliance requirements, b) is the preferred scenario even though there is added latency.

d. Client clock can be changed, manually or automatically. This means that the actual timing from the client may not be fully synchronized with server time, which must be considered in downstream processing. For example, never subtract client and server times, as they could be significantly off even after adjusting for time zones.

Server-side instrumentation suffers less from these concerns. It offers a less clear view of what the user is actually doing but can provide more granularity of what is happening inside your system and why. For example, you can log the time to generate the HTML for a page; because it is not impacted by the network, the data tend to have lower variance, allowing for more sensitive metrics. In search engine results, there are internal scores indicating why specific search results were returned and their ranking. Instrumenting these scores is useful for debugging and tuning the search algorithm. Another example is logging the actual servers or data center the request is served from, which allows for debugging of bad equipment or finding data centers under stress. It is important to remember that servers also need to be synchronized often. There can be scenarios where the request is served by one server while the beacon is logged by another, creating a mismatch in timestamp.

## Processing Logs from Multiple Sources

It is likely you will have multiple logs from different instrumentation streams (Google 2019), such as:

- Logs from different client types (e.g., browser, mobile)
- Logs from servers
- Per-user state (e.g., opt-ins and opt-outs)

It is important that you ensure that the relevant logs can be easily utilized and combined by downstream processing. First, there must be a way to join logs. The ideal case is to have a common identifier in all logs to serve as a join key.

The join key must indicate which events are for the same user, or randomization unit (see Chapter 14). You may also need a join key for specific events. For instance, there can be a client-side event that indicates a user has seen a particular screen and a corresponding server-side event that explains why the user saw that particular screen and its elements. This join key would let you know that those events were two views of the same event shown to the same user.

Next, have some shared format to make downstream processing easier. This shared format can be common fields (e.g., timestamp, country, language, platform) and customized fields. Common fields are often the basis for segments used for analysis and targeting.

## Culture of Instrumentation

Instrumentation should be treated as critical for the live site. Imagine flying a plane with broken instruments in the panel. It is clearly unsafe, yet teams may claim that there is no user impact to having broken instrumentation. How can they know? Those teams do not have the information to know whether this is a correct assumption because, without proper instrumentation, they are flying blind. Indeed, the most difficult part of instrumentation is getting engineers to instrument in the first place. This difficulty stems from both a time lag (time from when the code is written to when the results are examined), as well as a functional difference (i.e., the engineer creating the feature is often not the one analyzing the logs to see how it performs). Here are a few tips on how to improve this functional dissociation:

- Establish a cultural norm: nothing ships without instrumentation. Include instrumentation as part of the specification. Ensure that broken instrumentation has the same priority as a broken feature. It is too risky to fly a plane if the gas gauge or altimeter is broken, even if it can still fly.
- Invest in testing instrumentation during development. Engineers creating features can add any necessary instrumentation and can see the resulting instrumentation in tests prior to submitting their code (and code reviewers check!).
- Monitor the raw logs for quality. This includes things such as the number of events by key dimensions or invariants that should be true (i.e., timestamps fall within a particular range). Ensure that there are tools to detect outliers on key observations and metrics. When a problem is detected in instrumentation, developers across your organization should fix it right away.

# 14

# Choosing a Randomization Unit

[To generate random digits] a random frequency pulse source, providing on the average about 100,000 pulses per second, was gated about once per second by a constant frequency pulse ... Production from the original machine showed statistically significant biases, and the engineers had to make several modifications and refinements of the circuits before production of apparently satisfactory numbers was achieved. The basic table of a million digits was then produced during May and June of 1947. This table was subjected to fairly exhaustive tests and it was found that it still contained small but statistically significant biases
*A Million Random Digits with 100,000*
*Normal Deviates (RAND 1955)*

**Why you care:** *The choice of randomization unit is critical in experiment design, as it affects both the user experience as well as what metrics can be used in measuring the impact of an experiment. When building an experimentation system, you need to think through what options you want to make available. Understanding the options and the considerations to use when choosing amongst them will lead to improved experiment design and analysis.*

Identifiers are critical as the base randomization unit for experiments. The same identifier can also be used as a join key for the downstream processing of log files (see Chapter 13 and Chapter 16). Note that in this section we are focusing on how to choose which identifier to use, rather than on base criteria for randomization itself, such as ensuring the independence of assignment (i.e., the variant assignment of one identifier should not tell us anything about the variant assignment of another identifier) as well as ensuring the independence of assignment across experiments if an identifier can be assigned to multiple experiments simultaneously (see Chapter 4).

One axis to consider in choosing a randomization unit is granularity. For example, websites have the following natural granularities:

- **Page-level:** Each new web page viewed on a site is considered a unit.
- **Session-level:** This unit is the group of webpages viewed on a single visit. A session, or visit, is typically defined to end after 30 minutes of inactivity.
- **User-level:** All events from a single user is the unit. Note that a user is typically an approximation of a real user, with web cookies or login IDs typically used. Cookies can be erased, or in-private/incognito browser sessions used, leading to overcounting of users. For login IDs, shared accounts can lead to undercounting, whereas multiple accounts (e.g., users may have multiple e-mail accounts) can lead to overcounting.

We'll focus in on the examples on this axis for websites to discuss the main considerations.

For search engines, where there can be multiple pageviews for a single query, a query can be a level of granularity between page and session. We can also consider a combination of user and day to be a unit, where events from the same user on different days are in different units (Hohnhold, O'Brien and Tang 2015).

When trying to decide on the granularity, there are two main questions to consider:

1. How important is the consistency of the user experience?
2. Which metrics matter?

For consistency, the main question is whether the user will notice the changes. As an extreme example, imagine that the experiment is on font color. If we use a fine granularity, such as page-level, then the font color could change with every page. Another example is an experiment that introduces a new feature; the feature may appear and disappear if the randomization is at the page-level or the session-level. These are potentially bad and inconsistent user experiences that can impact key metrics. The more the user will notice the Treatment, the more important it is to use a coarser granularity in randomization to ensure the consistency of the user experience.

Your choice of metrics and your choice of randomization unit also interact. Finer levels of granularity for randomization creates more units, so the variance of the mean of a metric is smaller and the experiment will have more statistical power to detect smaller changes. It is worth noting that randomizing (and analyzing) by pageviews will lead to a tiny underestimation of the variance of the Treatment effect (Deng, Lu and Litz 2017), but that underestimation is very small in practice and is commonly ignored.

While a lower variance in metrics may seem like an advantage for choosing a finer granularity for randomization, there are several considerations to keep in mind:

1. If features act across that level of granularity, you cannot use that level of granularity for randomization. For example, if you have personalization or other inter-page dependences, then randomizing by pageview is no longer valid as what happens on one page affects what a user sees on the subsequent page and the pages are no longer independent. As another specific example, if an experiment is using page-level randomization, and a user's first query is in the Treatment and the feature leads to poor search results, the user may issue a reformulated second query that ends up in the Control.
2. Similarly, if metrics are computed across that level of granularity, then they cannot be used to measure the results. For example, an experiment that uses page-level randomization cannot measure whether the Treatment impacts the total number of user sessions.
3. Exposing users to different variants may violate the stable unit treatment value assumption (SUTVA, see Chapter 3) (Imbens and Rubin 2015), which states that experiment units do not interfere with one another. If users notice the different variants, that knowledge may impact their behavior and interfere (see Chapter 22).

In some enterprise scenarios, such as Office, tenants would like consistent experiences for the enterprise, limiting the ability to randomize by user. In advertising businesses that have auctions where advertisers compete, you could randomize by advertiser or by clusters of advertisers who are often competing in the same auctions. In social networks, you can randomize by clusters of friends to minimize interference (Xu et al. 2015, Ugander et al. 2013, Katzir, Liberty and Somekh 2012, Eckles, Karrer and Ugander 2017), and this generalizes to networks generally if you consider components (Yoon 2018)

## Randomization Unit and Analysis Unit

Generally, we recommend that the randomization unit be the same as (or coarser than) the analysis unit in the metrics you care about.

It is easier to correctly compute the variance of the metrics when the analysis unit is the same as the randomization unit, because the independence assumption between units is reasonable in practice, and Deng et al. (2017) discuss the independent and identical distribution (i.i.d.) assumption with regards to choice of randomization unit in detail. For example, randomizing by page means that clicks on each pageview are independent, so computation for the variance of the mean, click-through rate (clicks/pageviews), is standard. Similarly, if the randomization unit is *user* and the metrics analysis unit is also *user*, such as sessions-per-user, clicks-per-user, and pageviews-per-user, then the analysis is relatively straightforward.

Having the randomization unit be coarser than the analysis unit, such as randomizing by *user* and analyzing the click-through rate (by page), will work, but requires more nuanced analyses methods such as bootstrap or the delta method (Deng et al. 2017, Deng, Knoblich and Lu 2018, Tang et al. 2010, Deng et al. 2011). See Chapter 18 and Chapter 19 for more discussion. In this situation, the experiment results can be skewed by bots that use a single user ID, e.g., a bot that has 10,000 pageviews all done using the same user ID. If this type of scenario is a concern, consider bounding what any individual user can contribute to the finer-grained metric or switching to a user-based metric such as the average click-through rate-per-user, both of which bound the contribution any single user can have on the result.

Conversely, when the metrics are computed at the user-level (e.g., sessions-per-user or revenue-per-user) and the randomization is at a finer granularity (i.e., page-level), the user's experience likely contains a mix of variants. As a result, computing metrics at the user-level is not meaningful; you cannot use user-level metrics to evaluate an experiment when the randomization is by page. If these metrics are part of your OEC, then you cannot use the finer levels of granularity for randomization.

## User-level Randomization

User-level randomization is the most common as it avoids inconsistent experience for the user and allows for long-term measurement such as user retention (Deng et al. 2017). If you are using user-level randomization, you still have several choices to consider:

- A signed-in user ID or login that users can use across devices and platforms. Signed-in IDs are typically stable not just across platforms, but also longitudinally across time.
- A pseudonymous user ID, such as a cookie. On most websites when a user visits, the website writes a cookie containing an identifier (usually mostly random). On mobile devices for native apps, the OS often provides a cookie, such as Apple's idFA or idFV or Android's Advertising ID. These IDs are not persistent across platforms, so the same user visiting through

desktop browser and mobile web would be considered two different IDs. These cookies are controllable by the user through either browser-level controls or device OS-level controls, which means that cookies are typically less persistent longitudinally than a signed-in user ID.

- A device ID is an immutable ID tied to a specific device. Because it is immutable, these IDs are considered identifiable. Device IDs do not have the cross-device or cross-platform consistency that a signed-in identifier has but are typically stable longitudinally.

When debating between these choices, the key aspects to consider are functional and ethical (see Chapter 9).

From a functional perspective, the main difference between these different IDs is their scope. Signed-in user IDs cut across different devices and platforms, so if you need that level of consistency and it is available, a signed-in user ID is really your best choice. If you are testing a process that cuts across the boundary of a user signing in, such as a new user on-boarding process that includes a user signing in for the first time, then using a cookie or device ID is more effective.

The other question about scope is the longitudinal stability of the ID. In some experiments, the goal may be to measure whether there is a long-term effect. Examples may include latency or speed changes (see Chapter 5) or or the users' learned response to ads (Hohnhold et al. 2015). For these cases use a randomization unit with longevity, such as a signed-in user ID, long-lived cookie, or device ID.

One final option that we do not recommend unless it is the only option is IP address. IP-based variant assignment may be the only option for infrastructure changes, such as for comparing latency using one hosting service (or one hosting location) versus another, as this can often only be controlled at the IP level. We do not recommend using IP addresses more generally, however, because they vary in granularity. At one extreme, a user's device IP address may change when a user moves (e.g., a different IP address at home than work), creating inconsistent experiences. At the other extreme, large companies or ISPs have many users sharing a small set of IP addresses representing the firewall. This can lead to low statistical power (i.e., do you have enough IP addresses, especially to handle the wide variance), as well as potential skew and outlier issues from aggregating large numbers of users into a single unit.

Randomization at a sub-user level is useful only if we are not concerned about carryover or leakage from the same user (see Chapter 22), and the success metrics are also at the sub-user level (e.g. clicks-per-page, not clicks-per-user). It is often chosen in favor of increased power that comes from the increase in sample size.

# 15

# Ramping Experiment Exposure: Trading Off Speed, Quality, and Risk

The real measure of success is the number of experiments that can be crowded into 24 hours
– *Thomas A. Edison*

*Why you care: While experimentation is widely adopted to accelerate product innovation, how fast we innovate can be limited by how we experiment. To control the unknown risks associated with new feature launches, we recommend that experiments go through a ramp process, where we gradually increase traffic to new Treatments. If we don't do this in a principled way, this process can introduce inefficiency and risk, decreasing product stability as experimentation scales. Ramping effectively requires balancing three key considerations: speed, quality, and risk.*

## What Is Ramping?

We often talk about running experiments with a given traffic allocation that provides enough statistical power. In practice, it is common that an experiment goes through a *ramping* process to control unknown risks associated with new feature launches (aka. controlled exposure). For example, a new feature may start by exposing the Treatment to only a small percentage of users. If the metrics look reasonable and the system scales well, then we can expose more and more users to the Treatment. We ramp the traffic until the Treatment reaches desired exposure level. One of the most known negative examples is the initial launch of Healthcare.gov. The site collapsed as it was rolled out to 100% users on day one, only to realize that it wasn't ready to handle the load. This could have been mitigated if they had rolled out the site by geographic areas or last names A–Z. Insisting on a ramping process became a key lesson for subsequent launches (Levy 2014).

How do we decide which incremental ramps we need and how long we should stay at each increment? Ramping too slowly wastes time and resources. Ramping too quickly may hurt users and risks making suboptimal decisions. While we can democratize experimentation with a fully self-served platform as described in Chapter 4, we need principles on how to ramp to guide experimenters and ideally, tooling to automate the process and enforce the principles at scale.

We primarily focus on the process of ramping *up*. Ramping *down* is typically used when we have a bad Treatment, in which case we typically shut it down to zero very quickly to limit the user impact. In addition, large enterprises usually control their own client-side updates, so they are effectively excluded from some experiments and ramping exposure.

## SQR Ramping Framework

In the ramp process, how can we iterate fast while controlling risk and improving decision quality? In other words, how do we balance **speed, quality,** and **risk (SQR)**? Consider why we run controlled online experiments:

- **To measure** the impact and Return-On-Investment (ROI) of the Treatment if it launched to 100%.
- **To reduce risk** by minimizing damage and cost to users and business during an experiment (i.e., when there is a negative impact).
- **To learn** about users' reactions, ideally by segments, to identify potential bugs, and to inform future plans. This is either as part of running any standard experiments, or when running experiments designed for learning (see Chapter 5).

If the only reason to run a controlled experiment is to measure, we could run the experiment at the maximum power ramp (MPR)[1], which often means a 50% traffic allocation to the Treatment providing the highest statistical sensitivity, assuming our goal is to ramp that Treatment to 100%. This gives us the fastest and the most precise measurement. However, we may not want to start at MPR – what if something goes wrong? That is why we usually

---

[1] If the experiment has the entire 100% traffic with only one Treatment, the variance in the two-sample t-test is proportional to $1/q(1-q)$, where $q$ is the treatment traffic percentage. The MPR in this case has a 50/50 traffic allocation. If there is only 20% traffic available to experiment between one Treatment and one Control, the MPR has a 10/10 split, and so on. If there are four variants splitting 100% traffic, then each variant should get 25%.

start at a small exposure with the goal to contain the impact and mitigate potential risk.

We may also need intermediate ramp stages between MPR and 100%. For example, for operational reasons we may need to wait at 75% to ensure that the new services or endpoints can scale to the increasing traffic load.

Another common example is to learn. While learning should be part of every ramp, we sometimes conduct a long-term holdout ramp, where a small fraction (e.g., 5–10%) of users do not receive the new Treatment for a period of time (e.g., two months) primarily for learning purposes. The goal is to learn whether the impact measured during MPR is sustainable in the long term. See more discussion in Chapter 23.

## Four Ramp Phases

Figure 15.1 illustrates the principles and techniques for balancing speed, quality, and risk in the four ramp phases. For more discussion, see Xu et al. (2018).

For simplicity, let's assume that our goal is to ramp a single Treatment to 100%, so the MPR has 50% Treatment exposure. Putting all the pieces together, the SQR framework divides the whole ramp process into four phases, each with a primary goal.

The first phase is mainly for risk mitigation, so the SQR framework focuses on trading off speed and risk. The second phase is for precise measurement, so the focus is on trading off speed and quality. The last two phases are optional and address additional operational concerns (third phase) and long-term impact (fourth phase).

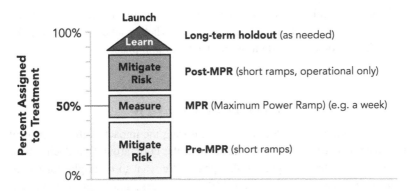

Figure 15.1 Four phases of the ramping process

## Ramp Phase One: Pre-MPR

In this phase, you want to safely determine that the risk is small and ramp quickly to the MPR. You can use these methods:

1. Create "rings" of testing populations and gradually expose the Treatment to successive rings to mitigate risk. The first rings are usually to get qualitative feedbacks, as there simply isn't enough traffic to get a meaningful read on data. The next rings may have quantitative measurement but still be uncontrolled as the statistical power is low. Many bugs can be identified during the early rings. Note that measurements from the early rings can be biased as those users are likely the "insiders." Commonly used rings are:
   a) Whitelisted individuals, such as the team implementing the new feature. You can get verbatim feedback from your team members.
   b) Company employees, as they are typically more forgiving if there are bad bugs.
   c) Beta users or *insiders* who tend to be vocal and loyal, who want to see new features sooner, and who are usually willing to give feedback.
   d) Data centers to isolate interactions that can be challenging to identify, such as memory leaks (death by slow leak) or other inappropriate use of resources (e.g., heavy disk I/O) (see Chapter 22). At Bing, the common ramp-up is single-data center small traffic (e.g., 0.5–2%). When a single data center is ramped up to a decent traffic, then all data centers can ramp up.
2. Automatically dialing up traffic until it reaches the desired allocation. The desired allocation can either be a particular ring or a preset traffic allocation percentage. Even if the desired allocation is only a small percentage (e.g., 5%), taking an extra hour to reach 5% can help limit the impact of bad bugs without adding much delay.
3. Producing real-time or near-real-time measurements on key guardrail metrics. The sooner you can get a read on whether an experiment is risky, the faster you can decide to go to the next ramp phase.

## Ramp Phase Two: MPR

MPR is the ramp phase dedicated to measuring the impact of the experiment. The many discussions we have throughout the book around producing trustworthy results directly apply in this phase. We want to highlight our recommendation to keep experiments at MPR for a week, and longer if novelty or primacy effects are present.

This ramp phase must be long enough to capture time-dependent factors. For example, an experiment that runs for only one day will have results biased towards heavy users. Similarly, users who visit during weekdays tend to be different from users visiting on weekends.

While we usually get smaller variance with a longer experiment, there is a diminishing return as we wait longer. In our experience, the precision gained after a week tends to be small if there are no novelty or primacy trends in the Treatment effect.

## Ramp Phase Three: Post-MPR

By the time an experiment is past the MPR phase, there should be no concerns regarding end-user impact. Optimally, operational concerns should also be resolved in earlier ramps. There are some concerns about increasing traffic load to some engineering infrastructures that may warrant incremental ramps before going to 100%. These ramps should only take a day or less, usually covering peak traffic periods with close monitoring.

## Ramp Phase Four: Long-Term Holdout or Replication

We have seen increasing popularity in long-term *holdouts*, also called *holdbacks*, where certain users do not get exposed to Treatment for a long time. We want to caution not to make a long-term holdout a default step in the ramping process. Besides the cost, it could also be unethical when we know there is a superior experience but deliberately delay the delivery of such experience, especially when customers are paying equally. Decide to do a long-term holdout only if it can be truly useful. Here are three scenarios where we have found a long-term holdout to be useful:

1. When the long-term Treatment effect may be different from the short-term effect (see Chapter 23). This can be because:
   a. The experiment area is known to have a novelty or primacy effect, or
   b. The short-term impact on key metrics is so large that we must ensure that the impact is sustainable for reasons, such as financial forecasting, or
   c. The short-term impact is small-to-none, but teams believe in a delayed effect (e.g., due to adoption or discoverability).
2. When an early indicator metric shows impact, but the true-north metric is a long-term metric, such as a one-month retention.
3. When there is a benefit of variance reduction for holding longer (see Chapter 22).

There is a misconception that holdout should always be conducted with a majority of the traffic in Treatment, such as 90% or 95%. While this may work well in general, for the 1c scenario discussed here where the short-term impact is already too small to be detected at MPR, we should continue the holdout at MPR if possible. The statistical sensitivity gained by running longer is usually not enough to offset the sensitivity loss by going from MPR to 90%.

In addition to holdouts at the experiment level, there are companies that have *uber* holdouts, where some portion of traffic is withheld from any feature launch over a long term (often a quarter) to measure the cumulative impact across experiments. Bing conducts a global holdout to measure the overhead of experimentation platform (Kohavi et al. 2013), where 10% of Bing users are withheld from any experiments. There can also be reverse experiments, where users are put back into Control several weeks (or months) after the Treatment launches to 100% (see Chapter 23).

When experiment results are surprising, a good rule of thumb is to replicate them. Rerun the experiment with a different set of users or with an orthogonal re-randomization. If the results remain the same, you can have a lot more confidence that the results are trustworthy. Replication is a simple yet effective way to eliminate spurious errors. Moreover, when there have been many iterations of an experiment, the results from the final iteration may be biased upwards. A replication run reduces the multiple-testing concern and provides an unbiased estimate. See Chapter 17 see more discussion.

## Post Final Ramp

We have not discussed what happens after an experiment is ramped to 100%. Depending on the implementation details of the experiment (see Chapter 4), there can be different post ramp cleanup needed. If the experiment system uses the architecture that creates a code fork based on variant assignment, one should clean up the dead code path after launch. If the experiment system uses a parameter system, then cleanup would simply mean to use the new parameter value as the default. This process may be overlooked in fast-moving development process, but it is critical for keeping the production system healthy. For example, in the first case, it can be disastrous when a dead code path that is not being maintained for a while is accidentally executed, which could happen when the experiment system has an outage.

# 16

# Scaling Experiment Analyses

If you want to increase your success rate, double your failure rate
– *Thomas J. Watson*

***Why you care:*** *For a company to move to the later phases of experimentation maturity ("Run" or "Fly"), incorporating data analysis pipelines as part of the experimentation platform can ensure that the methodology is solid, consistent, and scientifically founded, and that the implementation is trustworthy. It also helps save teams from needing to do time-consuming ad hoc analysis. If moving in this direction, understanding the common infrastructure steps for data processing, computation, and visualization can be useful.*

## Data Processing

To get the raw instrumented data into a state suitable for computation, we need to *cook* the data. Cooking data typically involves the following steps.

1. **Sort and group the data**. As information about a user request may be logged by multiple systems, including both client- and server-side logs, we start by sorting and joining multiple logs (see Chapter 13). We can sort by both the user ID and timestamp. This allows joining events to create sessions or visits, and to group all activity by a specified time window. You may not need to materialize this join, as a virtual join as a step during processing and computation may suffice. Materialization is useful if the output is used not just for experimentation analysis, but also for debugging, hypothesis generation, and more.
2. **Clean the data**. Having the data sorted and grouped makes it easier to clean the data. We can use heuristics to remove sessions that are unlikely to be

real users (e.g., bots or fraud, see Chapter 3). Some useful heuristics on sessions are whether the sessions have too much or too little activity, too little time between events, too many clicks on a page, users who engage with the site in ways that defy the laws of physics, and so on. We can also fix instrumentation issues, such as duplicate event detection or incorrect timestamp handling. Data cleansing cannot fix missing events, which may be a result of lossiness in the underlying data collection. Click logging, for example, is inherently a tradeoff between fidelity and speed (Kohavi, Longbotham and Walker 2010). Some filtering may unintentionally remove more events from one variant than another, potentially causing a sample ratio mismatch (SRM) (see Chapter 3).

3. **Enrich the data**. Some data can be parsed and enriched to provide useful dimensions or useful measures. For example, we often add browser family and version by parsing a user agent raw string. Day of week may be extracted from dates. Enrichments can happen at a per-event, per-session or per-user levels, such as marking an event as a duplicate or computing event duration, adding the total number of events during the session or the total session duration. Specific to experiments, you may want to annotate whether to include this session in the computation of the experiment results. These annotations are pieces of business logic that are often added during enrichment for performance reasons. Other experimentation specific annotations to consider include experiment transitions information (e.g., starting an experiment, ramping up an experiment, changing the version number) to help determine whether to include this session in the computation of the experiment results. These annotations are pieces of business logic that are often added for performance reasons.

## Data Computation

Given the processed data, you can now compute the segments and metrics, and aggregate the results to get summary statistics for each experiment, including both the estimated Treatment effect itself (e.g., delta of mean or percentiles) and the statistical significance information (p-value, confidence interval, etc.). Additional information, such as which segments are interesting can also occur within the data computation step (Fabijan, Dmitriev and McFarland et al. 2018).

There are many options for how to architect the data computation. We describe two common approaches. Without loss of generality, we assume the experimental unit is user.

1. The first approach is to materialize per-user statistics (i.e., for every user, count the number of pageviews, impressions, and clicks) and join that to a table that maps users to experiments. The advantage of this approach is that you can use the per-user statistics for overall business reporting, not just experiments. To effectively utilize compute resources, you may also consider a flexible way to compute metrics or segments that are only needed for one or a small set of experiments.
2. An alternative architecture is to fully integrate the computation of per-user metrics with the experiment analysis, where per-user metrics are computed along the way as needed without being materialized separately. Typically, in this architecture, there is some way to share the definitions of metrics and segments to ensure consistency among the different pipelines, such as the experiments data computation pipeline and the overall business reporting computation pipeline. This architecture allows more flexibility per-experiment (which may also save machine and storage resources) but requires additional work to ensure consistency across multiple pipelines.

Speed and efficiency increase in importance as experimentation scales across an organization. Bing, LinkedIn, and Google all process terabytes of experiment data daily (Kohavi et al. 2013). As the number of segments and metrics increase, the computation can be quite resource-intensive. Moreover, any delay in experiment scorecard generation can add delay to decision making, which can be costly as experimentation becomes more common and integral to the innovation cycle. In the early days of the experimentation platform, Bing, Google, and LinkedIn generated experiment scorecards daily with a ~24-hour delay (e.g., Monday's data shows up by end-of-day Wednesday). Today, we all have near real-time (NRT) paths. The NRT path has simpler metrics and computations (i.e., sums and counts, no spam filtering, minimal statistical tests) and is used to monitor for egregious problems (such as a misconfigured or buggy experiment), and often operates directly on raw logs without the data processing discussed above (except for some real-time spam processing). The NRT path can then trigger alerts and automatic experiment shut-off. The batch processing pipeline handles intra-day computation and updates to the data processing and computation to ensure that trustworthy experiment results are available in a timely manner.

To ensure speed and efficiency as well as correctness and trustworthiness, we recommend that every experimentation platform:

• Have a way to define common metrics and definitions so that everyone shares a standard vocabulary, everyone builds the same data intuition, and you can discuss the interesting product questions rather than re-litigating definitions and investigating surprising deltas between similar-looking metrics produced by different systems.

- Ensure consistency in the implementation of those definitions, be it a common implementation or some testing or ongoing comparison mechanism.
- Think through change management. As discussed in the experimentation maturity model (see Chapter 4), the metrics, OEC, and segments will all evolve, so specifying and propagating changes is a recurring process. Changing the definition of an existing metric is often more challenging than additions or deletions. For example, do you backfill the data (e.g., do you propagate the changes historically), and if so, for how long?

## Results Summary and Visualization

Ultimately, the goal is to visually summarize and highlight key metrics and segments to guide decision makers. In your summary and visualizations:

- Highlight key tests, such as SRM, to clearly indicate whether the results are trustworthy. For example, Microsoft's experimentation platform (ExP) hides the scorecard if key tests fail.
- Highlight the OEC and critical metrics, but also show the many other metrics, including guardrails, quality, and so on.
- Present metrics as a relative change, with clear indications as to whether the results are statistically significant. Use color-coding and enable filters, so that significant changes are salient.

Segment drill-downs, including automatically highlighting interesting segments, can help ensure that decisions are correct and help determine whether there are ways to improve the product for poorly behaving segments (Wager and Athey 2018, Fabijan, Dmitriev and McFarland et al. 2018). If an experiment has triggering conditions, it is important to include the overall impact in addition to the impact on the triggered population (for more details, see Chapter 20).

Beyond the visualization itself, to truly scale experimentation, scorecard visualizations should be *accessible* to people with various technical backgrounds, from Marketers to Data Scientists and Engineers to Product Managers. This requires ensuring that not just experimenters, but executives and other decision makers see and understand the dashboard. This may also mean hiding some metrics, such as the debugging metrics from the less technical audience, to reduce confusion. Information accessibility helps establish a common language for definitions and a culture of transparency and curiosity, encouraging employees to run experiments and learn about how changes impact the business or how Finance can tie A/B test results to business outlook.

The visualization tool is not just for per-experiment results but is also useful for pivoting to **per-metric results** across experiments. While innovation tends to be decentralized and evaluated through experimentation, the global health of key metrics is usually closely monitored by stakeholders. Stakeholders should have visibility into the top experiments impacting the metrics they care about. If an experiment is hurting their metrics above some threshold, they may want to be involved in making the launch decision. A centralized experimentation platform can unify views of both the experiments and the metrics. Two optional features the platform can provide to cultivate a healthy decision process are:

1. Allow individuals to subscribe to metrics they care about and get an email digest with the top experiments impacting these metrics.
2. If an experiment has a negative impact, the platform can initiate an approval process, where it forces the experiment owner to start a conversation with the metrics owners before the experiment can be ramped up. Not only does this drive transparency regarding experiment launch decisions, it encourages discussion, which increases the overall knowledge of experimentation in the company.

The visualization tools can also be a gateway to accessing **institutional memory** (see Chapter 8).

Finally, as an organization moves into the Run and Fly phases of experimentation maturity, how many metrics your organization uses will continue to grow, even into the thousands, at which point we suggest using these features:

- Categorizing metrics into **different groups**, either by tier or function. For instance, LinkedIn categorizes metrics into three tiers: 1) Companywide 2) Product Specific 3) Feature Specific (Xu et al. 2015). Microsoft groups metrics into 1) Data quality 2) OEC 3) Guardrail 3) Local features/diagnostic (Dmitriev et al. 2017). Google uses categories similar to LinkedIn. The visualization tool provides controls to dig into different groups of metrics.
- **Multiple testing** (Romano et al. 2016) becomes more important as the number of metrics grow, with one common question from experimenters: Why did this metric move significantly when it seems irrelevant? While education helps, one simple yet effective option is using p-value thresholds

smaller than the standard value of 0.05, as it allows experimenters to quickly filter down to the most significant metrics. See Chapter 17 for more discussion on well-studied approaches such as the Benjamini-Hochberg procedure to address multiple testing concerns.

- **Metrics of interest**. When an experimenter goes through the experiment results, they likely already have a set of metrics in mind to review. However, there are always unexpected movements in other metrics that are worth examining. The platform can automatically identify these metrics by combining multiple factors, such as the importance of these metrics for the company, statistical significance, and false positive adjustment.
- **Related metrics.** A metric's movement or lack of movement can often be explained by other related metrics. For example, when click-through rate (CTR) is up, is it because clicks are up or because page views are down? The reason for the movement may lead to different launch decisions. Another example is metrics with high variance such as revenue. Having a more sensitive, lower variance version such as trimmed revenue or other indicators, allows more informed decisions.

# PART V

---

# Advanced Topics for Analyzing Experiments

Part V includes seven advanced analysis topics, targeted primarily at data scientists and those interested in deeper understanding of the design and analysis of controlled experiments.

We begin with *The Statistics behind Online Controlled Experiments,* which outlines the t-test, p-value and confidence-interval calculations, normality assumptions, statistical power, and Type I/II errors. It covers multiple testing and Fisher's method for meta-analysis.

The next chapter is *Variance Estimation and Improved Sensitivity: Pitfalls and Solutions*, where we begin with the standard formula, but then show a very common pitfall that requires the use of the delta method. We then review ways to reduce the variance, which improves the sensitivity of experiments.

*The A/A Test* covers what is perhaps the best way to improve the trustworthiness of the experimentation system and uncover practical problems and bugs in the software or the Statistics used. Many of the pitfalls we discuss were uncovered because of A/A tests.

The chapter on *Triggering Improved Sensitivity* elaborates on a critical concept that organizations need to understand – triggering. Because not every experiment impacts all users, focusing on the impacted population improves sensitivity by reducing the noise of users who could not have been affected. As organizations mature, the use of triggering grows, and with it the tools to help analyze and debug issues.

The next chapter looks at the *Sample Ratio Mismatch (SRM) and Other Trust-Related Guardrail metrics*. SRMs are common in practice and when there is an SRM, the results look extremely positive or extremely negative, but they cannot be trusted. Automatically running this test (and others) is critical for the trustworthiness of the results.

In some practical scenarios, such as multi-sided marketplaces and social networks, the experiment variants may leak information, a topic we deal with in *Leakage and Interference between Variants*.

We conclude this part of the book with an important problem that is still an ongoing research topic: *Measuring Long-Term Treatment Effects*. We present several experimental designs to address the goal.

# 17

# The Statistics behind Online Controlled Experiments

Smoking is one of the leading causes of statistics
– *Fletcher Knebel*

***Why you care***: *Statistics are fundamental to designing and analyzing experiments.*

We introduced several statistical concepts. This chapter goes deeper on the Statistics critical to experimentation, including hypothesis testing and statistical power (Lehmann and Romano 2005, Casella and Berger 2001, Kohavi, Longbotham et al. 2009).

## Two-Sample t-Test

Two-sample t-tests are the most common statistical significance tests for determining whether the difference we see between Treatment and Control is real or just noise (Student 1908; Wasserman 2004). Two-sample t-tests look at the size of the difference between the two means relative to the variance. The significance of the difference is represented by the p-value. The lower the p-value, the stronger the evidence that the Treatment is different from the Control.

To apply the two-sample t-test to a metric of interest $Y$ (e.g., queries-per-user), assume that the observed values of the metric for users in the Treatment and Control are independent realizations of random variables, $Y^t$ and $Y^c$. The Null hypothesis is that $Y^t$ and $Y^c$ have the same mean; the alternative hypothesis is that they do not (see Equation 17.1):

$$H_0 : mean(Y^t) = mean(Y^c)$$

$$H_A : mean(Y^t) \neq mean(Y^c)$$

(17.1)

The two-sample t-test is based on the t-statistic, $T$:

$$T = \frac{\Delta}{\sqrt{var(\Delta)}} \tag{17.2}$$

where, $\Delta = \overline{Y^t} - \overline{Y^c}$ is the difference between the Treatment average and the Control average, an unbiased estimator for the shift of the mean. Because the samples are independent:

$$var(\Delta) = var\left(\overline{Y^t} - \overline{Y^c}\right) = var\left(\overline{Y^t}\right) + var\left(\overline{Y^c}\right) \tag{17.3}$$

The t-statistic $T$ is just a normalized version of $\Delta$.

Intuitively, the larger the $T$, the less likely it is that the means are the same. In other words, you are more likely to reject the Null hypothesis. How do we quantify this?

## p-Value and Confidence Interval

Now that you have the t-statistic $T$, you can compute the p-value, which is the probability that $T$ would be at least this extreme if there really is no difference between Treatment and Control. By convention, any difference with a p-value smaller than 0.05 is considered "statistically significant," though there are ongoing debates calling for lower p-values by default (Benjamin et al. 2017). A p-value less than 0.01 is considered very significant.

Even though p-value is one of the most well-known statistical terms, it is often misinterpreted. One common misinterpretation is that the p-value captures the probability that the Null hypothesis is true given the data observed. This is a reasonable interpretation on the surface as most experimenters would expect to get a probability on whether their Treatment has impact. However, the correct interpretation is almost the opposite, which is the probability of observing the delta, or a more extreme delta, if the Null hypothesis is true. To see how these two interpretations are different yet related, you can break it down using Bayes rule:

$$
\begin{aligned}
P(H_0 \text{ is true } | \Delta \text{ observed}) &= \frac{P(\Delta \text{ observed } | H_0 \text{ is true})P(H_0 \text{ is true})}{P(\Delta \text{ observed})} \\
&= \frac{P(H_0 \text{ is true})}{P(\Delta \text{ observed})} * P(\Delta \text{ observed } | H_0 \text{ is true}) \\
&= \frac{P(H_0 \text{ is true})}{P(\Delta \text{ observed})} * pvalue
\end{aligned}
\tag{17.4}
$$

As indicated in the equation, to know whether the Null hypothesis is true based on data collected (posterior probability), you not only need a p-value but also the likelihood that the Null hypothesis is true.

Another way to examine whether the delta is statistically significant is to check whether the confidence interval overlaps with zero. Some people find confidence intervals a more intuitive way to interpret the noise and uncertainty around the observed delta than the p-value. A 95% confidence interval is the range that covers the true difference 95% of the time and has an equivalence to a p-value of 0.05; the delta is statistically significant at 0.05 significance level if the 95% confidence interval does not contain zero or if the p-value is less than 0.05. In most cases, the confidence interval for the delta centers around the observed delta with an extension of about two standard deviations on each side. This is true for any statistics that (approximately) follow the normal distribution, including the percent delta.

## Normality Assumption

In most cases we compute p-values with the assumption that the t-statistic $T$ follows a normal distribution, and under the Null hypothesis the distribution has a mean 0 and variance 1. The p-value is just the area under the normal curve, as highlighted in Figure 2.1 in Chapter 2. Many people misinterpret the normality assumption to be an assumption on the sample distribution of the metric $Y$, and consider it a poor assumption because almost none of the metrics used in practice follow a normal distribution. However, in most online experiments the sample sizes for both Control and Treatment are at least in the thousands. While the sample distribution of $Y$ does not follow normal distribution, the average $\bar{Y}$ usually does because of the *Central Limit Theorem* (Billingsly 1995). Figure 17.1 illustrates the convergence with samples $Y$ drawn from a beta distribution. As the sample size increases, the distribution of the mean $\bar{Y}$ becomes more normally distributed.

One rule-of-thumb for the minimum number of samples needed for the average $\bar{Y}$ to have normal distribution is $355s^2$ for each variant (Kohavi, Deng et al 2014), where $s$ is the skewness coefficient of the sample distribution of the metric $Y$ defined as in Equation 17.5:

$$s = \frac{E[Y - E(Y)]^3}{[Var(Y)]^{3/2}}. \tag{17.5}$$

Some metrics, especially revenue metrics, tend to have a high skewness coefficient. One effective way to reduce skewness is to transform the metric or

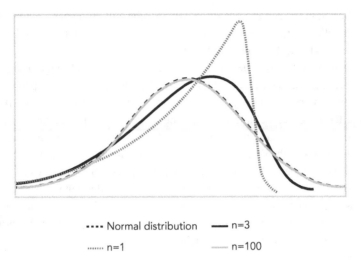

Figure 17.1 Distribution of the mean becomes increasingly normal as the sample size n increases

cap the values. For example, after Bing capped Revenue/User to $10 per user per week, they saw skewness drop from 18 to 5, and the minimum sample needed drop tenfold from 114k to 10k. This rule-of-thumb provides good guidance for when $|s| > 1$ but does not offer a useful lower bound when the distribution is symmetric or has small skewness. On the other hand, it is generally true that fewer samples are needed when skewness is smaller (Tyurin 2009).

For two-sample t-tests, because you are looking at the *difference* of the two variables with similar distributions, the number of samples needed for the normality assumption to be plausible tends to be fewer. This is especially the case if Treatment and Control have equal traffic allocations (Kohavi, Deng et al 2014), as the distribution of the difference is approximately symmetric (it is perfectly symmetric with zero skewness under the Null hypothesis).

If you ever wonder whether your sample size is large enough to assume normality, test it at least once with offline simulation. You can randomly shuffle samples across Treatment and Control to generate the null distribution and compare that distribution with the normal curve using statistical tests such as Kolmogorov–Smirnov and Anderson-Darling (Razali and Wah 2011). As the tail distribution is of interest in hypothesis testing, you can also increase test sensitivity by only focusing on whether the Type I error rate is bounded by the preset threshold, for example, 0.05.

When the normality assumption fails, you can then do a permutation test (Efron and Tibshriani 1994) and see where your observation stands relative to the simulated null distribution. Note that even though a permutation test is very expensive to run at scale, occasions when it is needed are often with small sample sizes, so it works out nicely in practice.

## Type I/II Errors and Power

With any test there are errors. In hypothesis testing, we care about Type I and Type II errors. A Type I error is concluding that there is a significant difference between Treatment and Control when there is no real difference. A Type II error is when we conclude that there is no significant difference when there really is one. You control Type I error rates at 0.05 by concluding statistical significance only if the p-value $< 0.05$. Clearly, there is a tradeoff between these two errors. Using a higher p-value threshold means a higher Type I error rate but a smaller chance of missing a real difference, therefore a lower Type II error rate.

The concept of Type II errors is better known as *power*. Power is the probability of detecting a difference between the variants , that is, rejecting the null, when there really is a difference(see Equation 17.6):

$$\text{Power} = 1 - \text{Type II error} \tag{17.6}$$

Power is typically parameterized by delta, $\delta$, the minimum delta of practical interest. Mathematically, assuming the desired confidence level is 95%, the equation is as in Equation 17.7:

$$\text{Power}_\delta = P(|T| \geq 1.96 \,|\text{true diff is } \delta). \tag{17.7}$$

The industry standard is to achieve at least 80% power in our tests. Therefore, it is common to conduct power analysis before starting the experiment to decide how many samples are needed to achieve sufficient power. Assuming Treatment and Control are of equal size, the total number of samples you need to achieve 80% power can be derived from the power formula above, and is approximately as shown in Equation 17.8 (van Belle 2008):

$$n \approx \frac{16\sigma^2}{\delta^2} \tag{17.8}$$

where, $\sigma^2$ is the sample variance, and $\delta$ is the difference between Treatment and Control. A common question people ask is that how would they know $\delta$ before they run the experiment? It is true that we do not know the true $\delta$ and that is the reason to run the experiment to begin with.

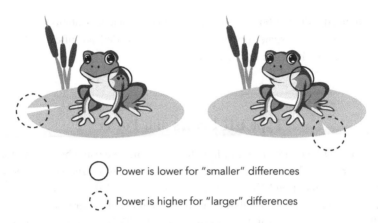

○ Power is lower for "smaller" differences

⟨ ⟩ Power is higher for "larger" differences

Figure 17.2 Analogy of statistical power with the game "Spot the difference."
Power is higher for detecting a larger difference

However, we know the size of $\delta$ that would matter in practice, in other words, that of *practical* significance. For example, you could miss detecting a difference of 0.1% in revenue and that's fine, but a drop of 1% revenue is not fine. In this case, 0.1% is not practically significant while 1% is. To estimate the required minimum sample size, use the smallest $\delta$ that is practically significant (also called the *minimum detectable effect*).

For online experiments, sample size estimation is more complex because online users visit over time, so the duration of the experiment also plays a role in the actual sample size of an experiment. Depending on the randomization unit, the sample variance $\sigma^2$ can also change over time. Another challenge is that with triggered analysis (see Chapter 20), the values $\sigma^2$ and $\delta$ change as the trigger conditions change across experiments. For these reasons, we present a more practical approach in Chapter 15 for deciding traffic allocation and the duration for most online experiments.

We want to highlight a common misinterpretation of the concept of statistical power. Many people consider power an absolute property of a test and forget that it is relative to the size of the effect you want to detect. An experiment that has enough power to detect a 10% difference does not necessarily have enough power to detect a 1% difference. A good analogy is the game "spot the difference." Figure 17.2 demonstrates that relative to difference in the spots (solid circle), it is easier to detect the difference on the lily pads (dashed circle) as it is a larger difference.

As you can tell, power analysis is deeply coupled with Type I and II errors. Gelman and Carlin (2014) argue that for small sample size settings, it is also important to calculate a) the probability of an estimate being in the wrong direction (Type S [sign] error), and b) the factor by which the magnitude of an effect might be overestimated (Type M [magnitude] error or exaggeration ratio).

## Bias

In experiment results, bias arises when the estimate and the true value of the mean are systematically different. It can be caused by a platform bug, a flawed experiment design, or an unrepresentative sample such as company employee or test accounts. We discuss several examples and recommendations for prevention and detection in Chapter 3.

## Multiple Testing

With hundreds of metrics computed for each experiment, we commonly hear from experimenters "Why is this irrelevant metric significant?" Here is a simplified way to look at it. If you compute 100 metrics for your experiment, how many metrics would you see as statistically significant even if your feature does nothing? With the significance level at 5%, the answer is around five (assuming that the metrics are independent). The problem worsens when examining hundreds of experiments and multiple iterations per experiment. When testing multiple things in parallel, the number of false discoveries increases. This is called the "multiple testing" problem.

How can we ensure that Type I and Type II errors are still reasonably controlled under multiple testing? There are many well studied approaches; however, most approaches are either simple but too conservative, or complex and hence less accessible. For example, the popular Bonferroni correction, which uses a consistent but much smaller p-value threshold (0.05 divided by the number of tests), falls into the former category. The Benjamini-Hochberg procedure (Hochberg and Benjamini 1995) uses varying p-value thresholds for different tests and it falls into the latter category.

So, what should you do when a metric is unexpectedly significant? Here's a simple two-step rule-of-thumb:

1. Separate all metrics into three groups:
   - First-order metrics: those you expect to be impacted by the experiment
   - Second-order metrics: those potentially to be impacted (e.g., through cannibalization)

- Third-order metrics: those unlikely to be impacted.
2. Apply tiered significance levels to each group (e.g., 0.05, 0.01 and 0.001 respectively).

These rules-of-thumb are based on an interesting Bayesian interpretation: How much do you believe the Null hypothesis ($H_0$) is true before you even run the experiment? The stronger the belief, the lower the significance level you should use.

## Fisher's Meta-analysis

We discuss how to identify patterns, create and utilize institutional memories based on meta-analysis on historical experiments in Chapter 8. In this section, we are particularly interested in combining results from multiple experiments that test on the *same* hypothesis. For example, it is a common technique to replicate an experiment that had surprising results. Replication is done using either orthogonal randomization or users who were not allocated to the original round of the experiment. These two experiments, the original and the replication, both produce p-values independent of each other. Intuitively, if both p-values are less than 0.05, that's stronger evidence that the Treatment has an impact than if only one p-value is less than 0.05. Fisher formalizes this intuition in his meta-analysis method (Fisher 1925), saying that we can combine p-values from multiple independent statistical tests into one test statistic as shown in Equation 17.9:

$$X_{2k}^2 = -2\sum_{i=1}^{k} ln\,(p_i) \qquad (17.9)$$

where $p_i$ is the p-value for the $i$th hypothesis test. If all $k$ Null hypothesis are true, this test statistic follows a chi-squared distribution with $2k$ degrees of freedom. Brown (1975) extends Fisher's method to cases when the p-values are not independent. There are other p-value combination methods, such as Edgington (1972), Volumne 80 (2) and Mudholkar and George (1979). See Hedges and Olkin (2014) for more discussions.

In general, Fisher's method (or any other meta-analysis technique) is great for increasing power and reducing false-positives. You may have an experiment that is underpowered even after applying all power-increasing techniques, such as maximum power traffic allocation (see Chapter 15) and variance reduction (see Chapter 22). In this case, you can consider two or more (orthogonal) replications of the same experiment (one after another) and achieve higher power by combining the results using Fisher's method.

# 18

# Variance Estimation and Improved Sensitivity: Pitfalls and Solutions

With great power comes small effect size
– *Unknown*

**Why you care:** *What is the point of running an experiment if you cannot analyze it in a trustworthy way? Variance is the core of experiment analysis. Almost all the key statistical concepts we have introduced are related to variance, such as statistical significance, p-value, power, and confidence interval. It is imperative to not only correctly estimate variance, but also to understand how to achieve variance reduction to gain sensitivity of the statistical hypothesis tests.*

This chapter covers variance, which is the most critical element for computing p-values and confidence intervals. We primarily focus on two topics: the common pitfalls (and solutions) in variance estimation and the techniques for reducing variance that result in better sensitivity.

Let's review the standard procedure for computing the variance of an average metric, with $i = 1, \ldots, n$ independent identically distributed (i.i.d.) samples. In most cases, $i$ is a user, but it can also be a session, a page, a user day, and so on:

- Compute the metric (the average): $\bar{Y} = \frac{1}{n} \sum_{i=1}^{n} Y_i$
- Compute the sample variance: $var(Y) = \hat{\sigma}^2 = \frac{1}{n-1} \sum_{i=1}^{n} (Y_i - \bar{Y})^2$
- Compute the variance of the average metric which is the sample variance scaled by a factor of $n$: $var(\bar{Y}) = var\left(\frac{1}{n} \sum_{i=1}^{n} Y_i\right) = \frac{1}{n^2} * n * var(Y) = \frac{\hat{\sigma}^2}{n}$

## Common Pitfalls

If you incorrectly estimate the variance, then the p-value and confidence interval will be incorrect, making your conclusions from the hypothesis test wrong. Overestimated variance leads to false negatives and underestimated variance leads to false positives. Here are a few common pitfalls when it comes to variance estimation.

## Delta vs. Delta %

It is very common to use the relative difference instead of the absolute difference when reporting results from an experiment. It is difficult to know if 0.01 more sessions from an average user are a lot or how it compares with the impact on other metrics. Decision makers usually understand the magnitude of a 1% session increase. The relative difference, called *percent delta* is defined as:

$$\Delta\% = \frac{\Delta}{\overline{Y^c}} \tag{18.1}$$

To properly estimate the confidence interval on $\Delta\%$, we need to estimate its variance. Variance for the delta is the sum of the variances of each component:

$$var(\Delta) = var\left(\overline{Y^t} - \overline{Y^c}\right) = var\left(\overline{Y^t}\right) + var\left(\overline{Y^c}\right) \tag{18.2}$$

To estimate the variance of $\Delta\%$, a common mistake is to divide $var(\Delta)$ by $\overline{Y^c}^2$, that is, $\frac{var(\Delta)}{\overline{Y^c}^2}$. This is incorrect because $\overline{Y^c}$ itself is a random variable. The correct way to estimate the variance is:

$$var(\Delta\%) = var\left(\frac{\overline{Y^t} - \overline{Y^c}}{\overline{Y^c}}\right) = var\left(\frac{\overline{Y^t}}{\overline{Y^c}}\right). \tag{18.3}$$

We will discuss how to estimate the variance of the ratio in the section below.

## Ratio Metrics. When Analysis Unit Is Different from Experiment Unit

Many important metrics come from the ratio of two metrics. For example, click-through rate (CTR) is usually defined as the ratio of total clicks to total pageviews; revenue-per-click is defined as the ratio of total revenue to total clicks. Unlike metrics such as clicks-per-user or revenue-per-user, when you use a ratio of two metrics, the analysis unit is no longer a user, but a pageview or click. When the experiment is randomized by the unit of a user, this can create a challenge for estimating variance.

The variance formula $var(Y) = \hat{\sigma}^2 = \frac{1}{n-1}\sum_{i=1}^{n}(Y_i - \bar{Y})^2$ is so simple and elegant that it's easy to forget a critical assumption behind it: the samples

$(Y_1, \ldots, Y_n)$ need to be i.i.d. (independently identically distributed) or at least uncorrelated. This assumption is satisfied if the analysis unit is the same as the experimental (randomization) unit. It is usually violated otherwise. For user-level metrics, each $Y_i$ represents the measurement for a user. The analysis unit matches the experiment unit and hence the i.i.d. assumption is valid. However, for page-level metrics, each $Y_i$ represents a measurement for a page while the experiment is randomized by user, so $Y_1$, $Y_2$ and $Y_3$ could all be from the same user and are "correlated." Because of such "within user correlation," variance computed using the simple formula would be biased.

To correctly estimate the variance, you can write the ratio metric as the ratio of "average of user level metrics," (see Equation 18.4)

$$M = \frac{\bar{X}}{\bar{Y}}. \tag{18.4}$$

Because $\bar{X}$ and $\bar{Y}$ are jointly bivariate normal in the limit, $M$, as the ratio of the two averages, is also normally distributed. Therefore, by the delta method we can estimate the variance as (Deng et al. 2017) (see Equation 18.5):

$$var(M) = \frac{1}{\bar{Y}^2} var(\bar{X}) + \frac{\bar{X}^2}{\bar{Y}^4} var(\bar{Y}) - 2 \frac{\bar{X}}{\bar{Y}^3} cov(\bar{X}, \bar{Y}). \tag{18.5}$$

In the case of $\Delta\%$, $Y^t$ and $Y^c$ are independent, hence (see Equation 18.6)

$$var(\Delta\%) = \frac{1}{\overline{Y^c}^2} var\left(\overline{Y^t}\right) + \frac{\overline{Y^t}^2}{\overline{Y^c}^4} var\left(\overline{Y^c}\right). \tag{18.6}$$

Note that when the Treatment and Control means differ significantly, this is substantially different from the incorrect estimate of $\frac{var(\Delta)}{\overline{Y^c}^2}$.

Note that there are metrics that cannot be written in the form of the ratio of two user-level metrics, for example, 90th percentile of page load time. For these metrics, we may need to resort to bootstrap method (Efron and Tibshriani 1994) where you simulate randomization by sampling with replacement and estimate the variance from many repeated simulations. Even though bootstrap is computationally expensive, it is a powerful technique, broadly applicable, and a good complement to the delta method.

## Outliers

Outliers come in various forms. The most common are those introduced by bots or spam behaviors clicking or performing many pageviews. Outliers have a big impact on both the mean and variance. In statistical testing, the impact on

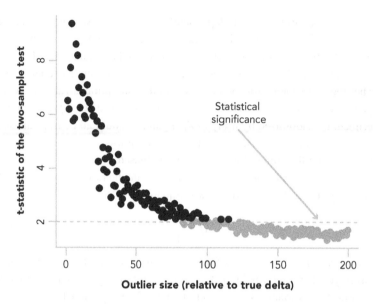

Figure 18.1 In the simulation, as we increase the size of the (single) outlier, the two-sample test goes from being very significant to not significant at all

the variance tends to outweigh the impact on the mean, as we demonstrate using the following simulation.

In the simulation, the Treatment has a positive true delta against Control. We add a single, positive outlier to the Treatment group. The size of the outlier is a multiple of the size of the delta. As we vary the multiplier (the relative size), we notice that while the outlier increases the average of the Treatment, it increases the variance (or the standard deviation) even more. As a result, you can see in Figure 18.1 that the t-statistic decreases as the relative size of the outlier increases and eventually the test is no longer statistically significant.

It is critical to remove outliers when estimating variance. A practical and effective method is to simply cap observations at a reasonable threshold. For example, human users are unlikely to perform a search over 500 times or have over 1,000 pageviews in one day. There are many other outlier removal techniques as well (Hodge and Austin 2004).

## Improving Sensitivity

When running a controlled experiment, we want to detect the Treatment effect when it exists. This detection ability is generally referred to as power or sensitivity. One way to improve sensitivity is reducing variance. Here are some of the many ways to achieve a smaller variance:

- Create an evaluation metric with a smaller variance while capturing similar information. For example, the number of searches has a higher variance than the number of searchers; purchase amount (real valued) has higher variance than purchase (Boolean). Kohavi et al. (2009) gives a concrete example where using conversion rate instead of purchasing spend reduced the sample size needed by a factor of 3.3.
- Transform a metric through capping, binarization, or log transformation. For example, instead of using average streaming hour, Netflix uses binary metrics to indicate whether the user streamed more than x hours in a specified time period (Xie and Aurisset 2016). For heavy long-tailed metrics, consider log transformation, especially if interpretability is not a concern. However, there are some metrics, such as revenue, where a log-transformed version may not be the right goal to optimize for the business.
- Use triggered analysis (see Chapter 20). This is a great way to remove noise introduced by people not affected by the Treatment.
- Use stratification, Control-variates or CUPED (Deng et al. 2013). In strati-fication, you divide the sampling region into strata, sample within each stratum separately, and then combine results from individual strata for the overall estimate, which usually has smaller variance than estimating without stratification. The common strata include platforms (desktop and mobile), browser types (Chrome, Firefox and Edge) and day of week and so on. While stratification is most commonly conducted during the sampling phase (at runtime), it is usually expensive to implement at large scale. Therefore, most applications use post-stratification, which applies stratification retro-spectively during the analysis phase. When the sample size is large, this performs like stratified sampling, though it may not reduce variance as well if the sample size is small and variability among samples is big. Control-variates is based on a similar idea, but it uses covariates as regression variables instead of using them to construct the strata. CUPED is an application of these techniques for online experiments, that emphasizes utilization of pre-experiment data (Soriano 2017, Xie and Aurisset 2016, Jackson 2018, Deb et al. 2018). Xie and Aurisset (2016) compare the performance of stratification, post-stratification, and CUPED on Netflix experiments.
- Randomize at a more granular unit. For example, if you care about the page load time metric, you can substantially increase sample size by randomizing per page. You can also randomize per search query to reduce variance if

you're looking at per query metrics. Note that there are disadvantages with a randomization unit smaller than a user:

- If the experiment is about making a noticeable change to the UI, giving the same user inconsistent UIs makes it a bad user experience.
- It is impossible to measure any user-level impact over time (e.g. user retention).

- Design a paired experiment. If you can show the same user both Treatment and Control in a paired design, you can remove between-user variability and achieve a smaller variance. One popular method for evaluating ranked lists is the interleaving design, where you interleave two ranked lists and present the joint list to user at the same time (Chapelle et al. 2012, Radlinski and Craswell 2013).
- Pool Control groups. If you have several experiments splitting traffic and each has their own Control, consider pooling the separate controls to form a larger, shared Control group. Comparing each Treatment with this shared Control group increases the power for all experiments involved. If you know the sizes of all Treatments you're comparing the Control group with, you can mathematically derive the optimal size for the shared Control. Here are considerations for implementing this in practice:
  - If each experiment has its own trigger condition, it may be hard to instrument them all on the same Control.
  - You may want to compare Treatments against each other directly. How much does statistical power matter in such comparisons relative to testing against the Control?
  - There are benefits of having the same sized Treatment and Control in the comparison, even though the pooled Control is more than likely bigger than the Treatment groups. Balanced variants lead to a faster normality convergence (see Chapter 17) and less potential concern about cache sizes (depending on how you cache implementation).

## Variance of Other Statistics

In most discussions in the book, we assume that the statistic of interest is the mean. What if you're interested in other statistics, such as quantiles? When it comes to time-based metrics, such as page-load-time (PLT), it is common to use quantiles, not the mean, to measure site-speed performance. For instance, the 90th or 95th percentiles usually measure user engagement-related load times, while the 99th percentile is more often server-side latency measurements.

While you can always resort to bootstrap for conducting the statistical test by finding the tail probabilities, it gets expensive computationally as data size grows. On the other hand, if the statistic follows a normal distribution asymptotically, you can estimate variance cheaply. For example, the asymptotic variance for quantile metrics is a function of the density (Lehmann and Romano 2005). By estimating density, you can estimate variance.

There is another layer of complication. Most time-based metrics are at the event/page level, while the experiment is randomized at user level. In this case, apply a combination of density estimation and the delta method (Liu et al. 2018).

# 19

# The A/A Test

If everything seems under control,
you're just not going fast enough
– *Mario Andretti*

If everything is under Control,
then you're running an A/A test
– *Ronny Kohavi*[1]

***Why you care:*** *Running A/A tests is a critical part of establishing trust in an experimentation platform. The idea is so useful because the tests fail many times in practice, which leads to re-evaluating assumptions and identifying bugs.*

The idea of an A/A test is simple: Split the users into two groups as in a regular A/B test but make B identical to A (hence the name A/A test). If the system is operating correctly, then in repeated trials about 5% of the time a given metric should be statistically significant with p-value less than 0.05. When conducting t-tests to compute p-values, the distribution of p-values from repeated trials should be close to a uniform distribution.

## Why A/A Tests?

The theory of controlled experiments is well understood, but practical implementations expose multiple pitfalls. The A/A test (Kohavi, Longbotham et al. 2009), sometimes called a Null test (Peterson 2004), is highly useful for establishing trust in your experimentation platform.

---

[1]  https://twitter.com/ronnyk/status/794357535302029312

A/A tests are the same as A/B tests, but Treatment and Control users receive identical experiences. You can use A/A tests for several purposes, such as to:

- Ensure that Type I errors are controlled (e.g., at 5%) as expected. For example, as will be shown in Example 1 later in this chapter, standard variance calculations may be incorrect for some metrics; or the normality assumption may not hold. A/A tests failing at an unexpected rate will point to issues that must be addressed.
- Assessing metrics' variability. We can examine data from an A/A test to establish how a metric's variance changes over time as more users are admitted into the experiment, and the expected reduction in variance of the mean may not materialize (Kohavi et al. 2012).
- Ensure that no bias exists between Treatment and Control users, especially if reusing populations from prior experiments. A/A tests are very effective at identifying biases, especially those introduced at the platform level. For example, Bing uses continuous A/A testing to identify a carry-over effect (or residual effect), where previous experiments would impact subsequent experiments run on the same users (Kohavi et al. 2012).
- Compare data to the system of record. It is common for the A/A test to be used as the first step before starting to use controlled experiment in an organization. If the data is collected using a separate logging system, a good validation step is to make sure key metrics (e.g., number of users, revenue, click-through rate (CTR)) match the system of record.
- If the system of records shows X users visited the website during the experiment and you ran Control and Treatment at 20% each, do you see around 20% X users in each? Are you leaking users?
- Estimate variances for statistical power calculations. A/A tests provide variances of metrics that can help determine how long to run your A/B tests for a given minimal detectable effect.

We highly recommend running continuous A/A tests in parallel with other experiments to uncover problems, including distribution mismatches and platform anomalies.

The following examples highlight the why and how of running A/A tests.

## Example 1: Analysis Unit Differs from Randomization Unit

As discussed in Chapter 14, randomizing by user and analyzing by pages is something that may be desired. For example, alerting systems typically look at page-load-time (PLT and CTR by aggregating every page in near-real-time. Estimating the Treatment effect by page is therefore often needed.

We now look at CTR and discuss the two common ways to compute it, each with different analysis units. The first is to count the clicks and divide by the number of page views; the second is to average each user's CTR and then average all the CTRs. If randomization is done by user, then the first mechanism uses a different analysis unit than the randomization unit, which violates the independence assumption and makes the variance computation more complex.

We analyze both and compare them in this example.

Here, $n$ is the number of users and $K_i$ the number of pageviews for user $i$. N is the total number of pageviews: $N = \sum_{i=1}^{n} K_i$. $X_{i,j}$ is the number of clicks for user $i$ on their $j$th page.

Now we look at our two reasonable definitions for CTR:

1.  Count all the clicks and divide by the total number of pageviews as shown in Equation 19.1:

$$CTR_1 = \left. \sum_{i=1}^{n} \sum_{j=1}^{K_i} X_{i,j} \middle/ N \right. \tag{19.1}$$

If we have two users, one with no clicks and a single pageview and the other with two clicks, one on each of their two pageviews, then (see Equation 19.2):

$$CTR_1 = \frac{0+2}{1+2} = \frac{2}{3} \tag{19.2}$$

2.  Average each user's CTR and then average all CTRs, essentially getting a double average (see Equation 19.3):

$$CTR_2 = \left. \sum_{i=1}^{n} \frac{\sum_{j=1}^{K_i} X_{i,j}}{K_i} \middle/ n \right. \tag{19.3}$$

To apply the example in definition 1 (see Equation 19.4):

$$CTR_2 = \left. \frac{0}{1} + \frac{2}{2} \middle/ 2 \right. = \frac{1}{2} \tag{19.4}$$

There is no right or wrong in these definitions, both are useful definitions for CTR, but using different user averages yields different results. In practice, it is common to expose both metrics in scorecards, although we generally recommend definition 2 as we find it more robust to outliers, such as bots having many pageviews or clicking often.

It's easy to make mistakes when computing the variance. If the A/B test is randomized by user, then we get this when computing the variance of the first definition (see Equation 19.5):

$$
\text{VAR}(CTR_1) = \left. \sum_{i=1}^{n} \sum_{j=1}^{K_i} \left(X_{ij} - CTR_1\right)^2 \middle/ N^2 \right.
\tag{19.5}
$$

This is incorrect, as it assumes that the $X_{ij}$s are independent (see Chapter 14 and Chapter 18). To compute an unbiased estimate of the variance, use the delta method or bootstrapping (Tang et al. 2010, Deng et al. 2011, Deng, Lu and Litz 2017).

We initially made this observation not because it was an obvious violation of the independence assumption, but because in our A/A tests, $CTR_1$ was statistically significant far more often than the expected 5%.

## Example 2: Optimizely Encouraged Stopping When Results Were Statistically Significant

The book *A/B Testing: The Most Powerful Way to Turn Clicks into Customers* (Siroker and Koomen 2013) suggests an incorrect procedure for ending experiments: "Once the test reaches statistical significance, you'll have your answer," and "When the test has reached a statistically significant conclusion ..." (Kohavi 2014). The statistics commonly used assume that a single test will be made at the end of the experiment and "peeking" violates that assumption, leading to many more false positives than expected using classical hypothesis testing.

Early versions of Optimizely encouraged peeking and thus early stopping, leading to many false successes. When some experimenters started to run A/A tests, they realized this, leading to articles such as "How Optimizely (Almost) Got Me Fired" (Borden 2014). To their credit, Optimizely worked with experts in the field, such as Ramesh Johari, Leo Pekelis, and David Walsh, and updated their evaluations, dubbing it "Optimizely's New Stats Engine" (Pekelis 2015, Pekelis, Walsh and Johari 2015). They address A/A testing in their glossary (Optimizely 2018a).

## Example 3: Browser Redirects

Suppose you are building a new version of your website and would like to run an A/B test of the old versus the new. Users in variant B are redirected to your new website. Spoiler alert: B will lose with high probability. Like many ideas, it is simple and elegant, but flawed.

There are three problems with this approach (Kohavi and Longbotham 2010, section 2):

1. Performance differences. Users who are redirected suffer that extra redirect. This may seem fast in the lab, but users in other regions may see wait times of 1–2 seconds.
2. Bots. Robots handle redirects differently: some may not redirect; some may see this as a new unseen area and crawl deeply, creating a lot of non-human traffic that could impact your key metrics. Normally, it is not critical to remove all small-activity bots, as they are distributed uniformly in all variants, but a new site or updated site is likely to trigger different behavior.
3. Bookmarks and shared links cause contamination. Users that go deep into a website (e.g., to a product detail page) using a bookmark or from a shared link must still be redirected. Those redirects must be symmetric, so you must redirect users in Control to site A.

Our experience is that redirects usually fail A/A tests. Either build things so that there are no redirects (e.g., server-side returns one of two home pages) or execute a redirect for both Control and Treatment (which degrades the Control group).

## Example 4: Unequal Percentages

Uneven splits (e.g., 10%/90%) may suffer from shared resources providing a clear benefit to the larger variant (Kohavi and Longbotham 2010, section 4). Specifically, least recently used (LRU) caches shared between Control and Treatment have more cache entries for the larger variant (note that experiment IDs must always be part of any caching system that could be impacted by the experiment, as the experiments may cache different values for the same hash key). See also Chapter 18.

In some cases, it is easier to run a 10%/10% experiment (not utilizing 80% of the data so useful in theory) to avoid LRU caching issues, but this must be done at runtime; you cannot run 10%/90% and throw away data. Your 50/50% A/A test may pass, but if you run experiments at 90%/10%, run these A/A tests in practice.

Another problem with unequal percentages is that the rate of convergence to a Normal Distribution is different. If you have a highly skewed distribution for a metric, the Central Limit Theorem states that the average will converge to Normal, but when the percentages are unequal, the rate will be different. In an A/B test, it's the delta of the metric for Control and Treatment that matters, and the delta may be more Normal if the two constituents have the same distribution (even if not Normal). See Chapter 17 for details.

## Example 5: Hardware Differences

Facebook had a service running on a fleet of machines. They built a new V2 of the service and wanted to A/B test it. They ran an A/A test between the new and old fleet, and even though they thought the hardware was identical, it failed the A/A test. Small hardware differences can lead to unexpected differences (Bakshy and Frachtenberg 2015).

## How to Run A/A Tests

Always run a series of A/A tests before utilizing an A/B testing system. Ideally, simulate a thousand A/A tests and plot the distribution of p-values. If the distribution is far from uniform, you have a problem. Do not trust your A/B testing system before resolving this issue.

When the metric of interest is continuous and you have a simple Null hypothesis, such as equal means in our A/A test example, then the distribution of p-values under the Null should be uniform (Dickhaus 2014, Blocker et al. 2006).

Figure 19.1 is a real histogram showing far from uniform distribution.

Figure 19.2 shows that after applying the delta method, distribution was much more uniform.

Running a thousand A/A tests may be expensive, but here's a little trick you can use: replay the last week. This of course, assumes that you stored the relevant raw data. This is an example of why we say to store your data for running future tests and applying newly developed metrics. There are limits to this approach, of course: you will not catch performance issues or shared resources such as the LRU cache mentioned above, but it is a highly valuable exercise that leads to identifying many issues.

Because you are not really making a change to your product and the two variants being tested are identical, you can just simulate the A/A test. For each iteration, pick a new randomization hash seed for user assignment and replay

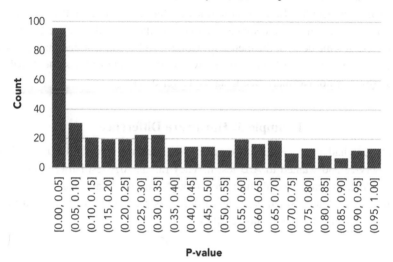

Figure 19.1  Non-uniform p-value distribution from A/A tests for a metric whose variance is not computed correctly because the analysis unit is not equal to the randomization unit

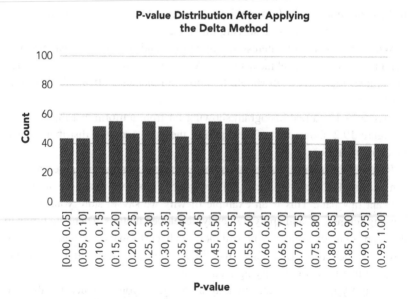

Figure 19.2  Distribution is close to uniform after applying the delta method to compute variance

the last week of data, splitting users into the two groups. Then generate the p-value for each metric of interest (usually tens to hundreds of metrics) and accumulate them into histograms, one for each metric.

Now run a *goodness-of-fit* test, such as Anderson-Darling or Kolmogorov-Smirnoff (Wikipedia contributors, Perverse Incentive 2019, Goodness of fit) to assess whether the distributions are close to uniform.


## When the A/A Test Fails

There are several common p-value scenarios where the test fails the goodness-of-fit for a uniform distribution (Mitchell et al. 2018):

1. The distribution is skewed and clearly not close to uniform. A common problem is a problem with variance estimation of metrics (see Chapter 18). Check for the following:
   a. Is the independence assumption violated (as in the CTR example) because the randomization unit differs from the analysis unit? If so, deploy the delta method or bootstrapping (see Chapter 15).
   b. Does the metric have a highly skewed distribution? Normal approximation may fail for a small number of users. In some cases, the minimum sample size may need to be over 100,000 users (Kohavi et al. 2014). Capped metrics or setting minimum sample sizes may be necessary (see Chapter 17).
2. There is a large mass around p-value of 0.32, indicating a problem with outliers. For example, assume a single very large outlier $o$ in the data.

   When computing the t-statistics (see Equation 19.6):

$$T = \frac{\Delta}{\sqrt{var}}(\Delta) \qquad (19.6)$$

   the outlier will fall into one of the two variants and the delta of the means will be close to $o/n$ (or its negation), as all the other numbers will be swamped by this outlier. The variance of the mean for that variant will also be close to $o^2/n^2$, so the T value will be close to 1 or close to $-1$, which maps to a p-value of about 0.32.

   If you see this, then the reason for the outlier needs to be investigated or the data should be capped. With such large outliers, the t-test will rarely lead to statistically significant results (see Chapter 18).
3. The distribution has a few point masses with large gaps. This happens when the data is single-valued (e.g., 0) with a few rare instances of non-zero

values. The delta of the means can only take a few discrete values in such scenarios, and hence the p-value can only take a few values. Here again, the t-test is not accurate, but this is not as serious as the prior scenario, because if a new Treatment causes the rare event to happen often, the Treatment effect will be large and statistically significant.

Even after an A/A test passes, we recommend regularly running A/A tests concurrently with your A/B tests to identify regressions in the system or a new metric that is failing because its distribution has changed or because outliers started showing up.

# 20

# Triggering for Improved Sensitivity

Be sure you positively identify your target before you pull the trigger
– *Tom Flynn*

***Why you care:*** *Triggering provides experimenters with a way to improve sensitivity (statistical power) by filtering out noise created by users who could not have been impacted by the experiment. As organizational experimentation maturity improves, we see more triggered experiments being run.*

Users are triggered into the analysis of an experiment if there is (potentially) some difference in the system or user behavior between the variant they are in and any other variant (counterfactual). Triggering is a valuable tool for your arsenal, but there are several pitfalls that can lead to incorrect results. It is important that you perform the analysis step, at least for all triggered users. It is easier to identify the triggered population of users if you ensure that triggering events are logged at runtime.

## Examples of Triggering

If you make a change that only impacts some users, the Treatment effect of those who are not impacted is zero. This simple observation of analyzing only users who could have been impacted by your change has profound implications for experiment analysis and can significantly improve sensitivity or statistical power. Let's look at several examples of triggering in increasing complexity.

## Example 1: Intentional Partial Exposure

Suppose you are making a change and running the experiment on a segment of the population: only users from the US. You should only analyze users from the US. Users from other countries were not exposed to the change, so the Treatment effect for them is zero and adding them to the analysis just adds noise and reduces the statistical power. Note that you must include "mixed" users, those from both the United States and other countries, in the analysis if they could have seen the change. Be sure to include all their activities after seeing the change even activities performed outside the United States, because they were exposed and there could be residual effects on the non-US visit.

This observation applies to other partial exposures, such as making a change that only applies to users of the Edge browser, or one that only exposes users whose shipping address is in a given zip code, or making changes to heavy users, users who visited your website at least three times in the last month (note that it's critical that the definition be well-defined based on data prior to the experiment start and not one that could be impacted by the Treatment).

## Example 2: Conditional Exposure

Suppose the change is to users who reach a portion of your website, such as checkout, or users who use a feature, like plotting a graph in Excel, then only analyze those users. In these examples, as soon as the user was exposed to a change, they *triggered* into the experiment because there was some difference. Conditional exposure is a very common triggering scenario; here are some additional examples:

1. A change to checkout: only trigger users who started checkout.
2. A change to collaboration, such as co-editing a document in Microsoft Word or Google Docs: only trigger users participating in collaboration.
3. A change to the unsubscribe screen(s): only trigger users that see these changes.
4. A change to the way the weather answer displays on a search engine results page: only trigger users who issue a query resulting in a weather answer.

## Example 3: Coverage Increase

Suppose that your site is offering free shipping to users with more than $35 in their shopping cart and you are testing a lower threshold of $25. A key observation is that the change only impacts users who at some point started checkout with a shopping cart *between* $25 and $35. Users with shopping carts over $35 and those with shopping carts under $25 have the same behavior in Treatment as Control. Only trigger users who see the free shipping offer when they have $25 to $35 in their shopping cart. For this example, we assume that no "advertisement" of the free shipping promotion is on the site; if at some point free shipping displays for the user and it is different between Control and Treatment, that immediately becomes a trigger point.

Figure 20.1 shows this example as a Venn diagram: Control represents offering some users free shipping and Treatment increases coverage to a broader user population. You don't need to trigger users outside of these groups (as in Example 2), but you also don't need to trigger users meeting the criteria in both Control AND Treatment because the offer is the same.

## Example 4: Coverage Change

Things become a bit more complicated when the coverage isn't increased, but is changed, as shown in the Venn diagram in Figure 20.2. For example, suppose Control offers free shipping to shoppers with at least $35 in their cart

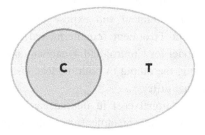

Figure 20.1 Treatment enlarges coverage for a feature. Only users in T\C are triggered. Those in C (and in T) see the same offer, so the Treatment effect is zero

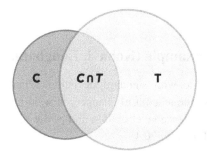

Figure 20.2 Treatment changes the coverage. If users in the intersection see the exact same thing, then only trigger the remaining users

but Treatment offers free shipping to users with at least $25 in their cart except if they returned an item within 60 days before the experiment started.

Both Control and Treatment must evaluate the "other" condition, that is, the counterfactual, and mark users as triggered only if there is a difference between the two variants.

### Example 5: Counterfactual Triggering for Machine Learning Models

Suppose you have a machine learning classifier that classifies users into one of three promotions or a recommender model that recommends related products to the one shown on the page. You trained the new classifier or recommender model, and V2 did well in your offline tests. Now you expose to see if it improves your OEC (see Chapter 7).

The key observation is that if the new model overlaps the old model for most users, as when making the same classifications or recommendations for the same inputs, then the Treatment effect is zero for those users. How would you know? You must generate the counterfactual. The Control would run both the model for Control and Treatment and expose users to the Control while logging the Control and Treatment (counterfactual) output; the Treatment would run both the model for Control and Treatment and expose users to the Treatment while logging the output of both models. Users are triggered if the actual and counterfactual differ.

Note that the computational cost in this scenario rises (e.g., the model inference cost doubles with one Treatment) as both machine learning models must be executed. Latency could also be impacted if the two models are not run concurrently and the controlled experiment cannot expose differences in the model's execution (e.g., if one is faster or takes less memory) as both executed.

### A Numerical Example (Kohavi, Longbotham et al. 2009)

Given an OEC metric with standard deviation $\sigma$ and a desired level of sensitivity, $\Delta$, that is, the amount of change you want to detect, the minimum sample size for a confidence level of 95% and power of 80% (van Belle 2008, 31) is as shown in Equation 20.1:

$$n = \frac{16\,\sigma^2}{\Delta^2}$$

(20.1)

Let's take an e-commerce site with 5% of users who visit during the experiment period ending up making a purchase. The conversion event is a Bernoulli trial with $p = 0.05$. The standard deviation, $\sigma$, of a Bernoulli is $\sqrt{p(1 - p)}$ and thus $\sigma^2 = 0.05(1 - 0.05) = 0.0475$. According to the above formula, you need at least $16 * 0.0475/(0.05 \cdot 0.05)^2 = 121{,}600$ users.

If you made a change to the checkout process, as in Example 2, only analyze triggered users who started the checkout process. Assume that 10% of users initiate checkout, so that given the 5% purchase rate, half of them complete checkout, or $p = 0.5$. The variance $\sigma^2 = 0.5(1 - 0.5) = 0.25$. You therefore need at least $16 * 0.25/(0.5 \cdot 0.05)^2 = 6{,}400$ users to go through checkout. Because 90% of users do not initiate checkout, the number of users in the experiment should be at least 64,000, almost half, thus the experiment could have the same power in about half the time (because there are repeat users, reaching half the users typically takes less than half the time).

## Optimal and Conservative Triggering

When comparing two variants, the optimal trigger condition is to trigger into the analysis only users for which there was some difference between the two variants compared, such as between the variant the user was in and the counterfactual for the other variant.

If there are multiple Treatments, ideally information representing all variants is logged, the actual plus all counterfactuals. This then allows for optimal triggering of users who were impacted. However, multiple Treatments can present significant cost as multiple models must be executed to generate the counterfactuals.

In practice, it is sometimes easier to do a non-optimal but conservative triggering, such as including more users than is optimal. This does not invalidate the analysis, but rather loses statistical power. If the conservative trigger does not identify many more users than the ideal trigger, the simplicity tradeoff may be worthwhile. Here are some examples:

1. Multiple Treatments. Any difference between the variants triggers the user into the analysis. Instead of logging the output of each variant, just log a Boolean to indicate that they differed. It is possible that the behavior for Control and Treatment1 was identical for some users but differed for Treatment2. So, when comparing just Control and Treatment1, include users with a known zero Treatment effect.
2. Post-hoc analysis. Suppose the experiment was run and there was something wrong with counterfactual logging, perhaps the recommendation

model used during checkout did not properly log counterfactuals. You can use a trigger condition such as "user-initiated checkout." While it identifies more users than those for which the recommendation model at checkout differed, it may still remove the 90% of users who never initiated checkout, thus had zero Treatment effect.

## Overall Treatment Effect

When computing the Treatment effect on the triggered population, you must dilute the effect to the overall user base, sometimes called diluted impact or side-wide impact (Xu et al. 2015). If you improved the revenue by 3% for 10% of users, did you improve your overall revenue by 10%*3% = 0.3%? NO! (common pitfall). The overall impact could be anywhere from 0% to 3%!

### Example 1

If the change was made to the checkout process, the triggered users were those who initiated checkout. If the only way to generate revenue is to initiate checkout, then you improved both triggered and overall revenue by 3% and there is no need to dilute that percentage.

### Example 2

If the change was made to very low spenders who spend 10% of the average user, then you improved revenue by 3% for 10% of users who spend 10%, so you improved revenue by 3% of 10% of 10% = 0.03%, a negligible improvement.

- Let $\omega$ denote the overall user universe and let $\theta$ denote the triggered population.
- Let $C$ and $T$ denote Control and Treatment, respectively.

For a given metric $M$, we have

- $M_{\omega C}$ is the metric value for the untriggered Control.
- $M_{\omega T}$ is the metric value for the untriggered Treatment.
- $M_{\theta C}$ is the metric value for the triggered Control.
- $M_{\theta T}$ is the metric value for the triggered Treatment.

Let N denote the number of users and define $\Delta_\theta = M_{\theta T} - M_{\theta C}$, that is, the absolute effect on the triggered population.

Define $\delta_\theta = \Delta_\theta / M_{\theta C}$, that is, the relative effect on the triggered population. The triggering rate, $\tau$, is the percent of users that were triggered, is $N_{\theta C}/N_{\omega C}$.

The Treatment can be used instead of Control or can be combined as shown in Equation 20.2:

$$(N_{\theta C} + N_{\theta T})/(N_{\omega C} + N_{\omega T}). \tag{20.2}$$

Here are two ways to think of the diluted percent impact:

1. What is the absolute Treatment effect divided by the total (see Equation 20.3):

$$\frac{\Delta_\theta * N_{\theta C}}{M_{\omega C} * N_{\omega C}} \tag{20.3}$$

2. What is the "ratio of the Treatment effect relative to the untriggered metric" times the triggering rate (see Equation 20.4):

$$\frac{\Delta_\theta}{M_{\omega C}} * \tau \tag{20.4}$$

Because $\tau$ is $N_{\theta C}/N_{\omega C}$, we can see that this is equivalent to the prior equation.

What is a common pitfall with diluting by the trigger rate directly? The computation is essentially as shown in Equation 20.5:

$$\frac{\Delta_\theta}{M_{\theta C}} * \tau \tag{20.5}$$

The computation holds when the triggered population is a random sample, but if the triggered population is skewed, as is often the case, then this computation is inaccurate by a factor $M_{\omega C}/M_{\theta C}$.

To dilute ratio metrics, more refined formulas need to be used (Deng and Hu 2015). Note that ratio metrics can cause Simpson's paradox (see Chapter 3), where the ratio in the triggered population improves, but the diluted global impact regresses.

## Trustworthy Triggering

There are two checks you should do to ensure a trustworthy use of triggering. We have found these to be highly valuable and they regularly point to issues.

1. Sample Ratio Mismatch (SRM; see Chapter 3).

If the overall experiment has no SRM, but the triggered analysis shows an SRM, then there is some bias being introduced. Usually, the counterfactual triggering is not done properly.

2. Complement analysis. Generate a scorecard for *never* triggered users, and you should get an A/A scorecard (see Chapter 19). If more than the expected metrics are statistically significant, then there is a good chance your trigger condition is incorrect; you influenced users not included in the trigger condition.

## Common Pitfalls

Triggering is a powerful concept, but there are several pitfalls to be aware of.

### Pitfall 1: Experimenting on Tiny Segments That Are Hard to Generalize

If you are trying to improve a metric for the overall population, then it is the diluted value of your experiment that matters. Even if you improve a metric by a massive 5%, if the triggered population is 0.1% of the overall users, then your diluted value will have $\tau = 0.001$ when you compute the diluted value based on Equation 20.6:

$$\frac{\Delta_\theta}{M_{\omega C}} * \tau \tag{20.6}$$

In computer architecture, Amdahl's law is often mentioned as a reason to avoid focusing on speeding up parts of the system that are a small portion of the overall execution time.

There is one important exception to this rule, which is generalizations of a small idea. For example, in Aug 2008, MSN UK ran an experiment whereby the link to Hotmail opened in a new tab (or new window for older browsers), which increased MSN users' engagement, as measured by clicks/user on the homepage, by 8.9% for the triggered users who clicked the Hotmail link (Gupta et al. 2019). This was a massive improvement, but a relatively small segment. However, over several years a series of experiments were run to generalize this idea, which at the time was very controversial. By 2011, MSN US ran a very large experiment, with over 12 million users, which opened the search results in a new tab/window and engagement as measured by clicks-per-user increased by a whopping 5%. This was one of the best features that MSN ever implemented in terms of increasing user engagement (Kohavi et al. 2014, Kohavi and Thomke 2017).

### Pitfall 2: A Triggered User Is Not Properly Triggered for the Remaining Experiment Duration

As soon as a user triggers, the analysis must include them going forward. The Treatment might impact their future behavior because of some difference in the experience. Analyses of triggered users by day or session are susceptible to impact from prior experience. For example, assume that the Treatment provides such a terrible experience that users significantly reduce visits. If you analyze users by day or by session, you will underestimate the Treatment effect. If visits-per-user has not significantly changed statistically, you can get statistical power by looking at triggered visits.

### Pitfall 3: Performance Impact of Counterfactual Logging

To log the counterfactual, both Control and Treatment will execute each other's code (e.g., model). If the model for one variant is significantly slower than the other, this will not be visible in the controlled experiment. These two things can help:

1. Awareness of this issue. The code can log the timing for each model so that they can be directly compared.
2. Run an A/A'/B experiment, where A is the original system (Control), A' is the original system with counterfactual logging, and B is the new Treatment with counterfactual logging. If A and A' are significantly different, you can raise an alert that counterfactual logging is making an impact.

It is worth noting that counterfactual logging makes it very hard to use shared controls (see Chapter 12 and Chapter 18), as those shared controls are typically running without code changes. In some cases, triggering conditions can be determined through other means, although this can result in suboptimal triggering or erroneous conditions.

## Open Questions

The following are issues that we face where we have no clear answer. Awareness is important, even when we have pros and cons and not the "answer."

## Question 1: Triggering Unit

When a user is triggered, you could take only the logged activities after the triggering point. Clearly the data prior to the triggering point was not impacted by the Treatment. We have done this, but those triggered sessions are now partial, and their metrics are abnormal (e.g., the metric clicks prior to checkout are zero). Is it better to take the whole session? The whole day? Perhaps all user activities from the start of the experiment?

Computationally, it is easier to take the user, including data from the beginning of the experiment, if they trigger at any point; however, this causes a small loss of statistical power.

## Question 2: Plotting Metrics over Time

Plotting a metric over time with increasing numbers of users usually leads to false trends (Kohavi et al. 2012, Chen, Liu and Xu 2019). It's best to look at graphs over time where each day shows the user who visited that day. When users are triggered, we have the same problem: 100% of users on the first day were triggered, but a smaller portion of users on day 2 were triggered, as some triggered on day 1 but just visited on day 2. False trends start to appear, usually as a decreasing Treatment effect over time. Perhaps it's better to plot each day with the users who visited that day and triggered on that day. The key issue is that the overall Treatment effect must include *all* days, so the single-day and overall (or cross-day) numbers do not match.

# 21

# Sample Ratio Mismatch and Other Trust-Related Guardrail Metrics

The major difference between a thing that might go wrong and a thing that cannot possibly go wrong is that when a thing that cannot possibly go wrong goes wrong it usually turns out to be impossible to get at or repair
– *Douglas Adams*

***Why you care:*** *Guardrail metrics are critical metrics designed to alert experimenters about violated assumptions. There are two types of guardrail metrics: organizational and trust-related. Chapter 7 discusses organizational guardrails that are used to protect the business, and this chapter describes the Sample Ratio Mismatch (SRM) in detail, which is a trust-related guardrail. The SRM guardrail should be included for every experiment, as it is used to ensure the internal validity and trustworthiness of the experiment results. A few other trust-related guardrail metrics are also described here.*

As the Douglas Adams quotation shows, many people assume that the experiment will execute according to the design. When that assumption fails, and it fails more often than people expect, the analysis is usually heavily biased, and some conclusions are invalid. Multiple companies have reported seeing SRMs and have highlighted the value of this test as a guardrail (Kohavi and Longbotham 2017, Zhao et al. 2016, Chen, Liu and Xu 2019, Fabijan et al. 2019).

## Sample Ratio Mismatch

The Sample Ratio Mismatch (SRM) metric looks at the ratio of users (or other units, see Chapter 14) between two variants, usually a Treatment and the Control. If the experiment design calls for exposing a certain ratio of users (say 1:1) to the two variants, then the results should closely match the design. Unlike metrics that could be impacted by the Treatment, the decision to expose a user to a variant must be independent of the Treatment, so the ratio of the users in the variants should match the experimental design. For example, if you flip a fair coin 10 times and turn up 4 heads and 6 tails, a ratio of 0.67, it's no surprise. However, the Law of Large Numbers implies that, with high probability, the ratio should get closer to one as your sample size grows.

When the p-value for the Sample Ratio metric is low, that is, the probability of observing such a ratio or more extreme conditioned on the design ratio, there is a sample ratio mismatch (SRM), and all other metrics are probably invalid. You can use a standard t-test or chi-squared test to compute the p-value. An example Excel spreadsheet is available at http://bit.ly/srmCheck.

## Scenario 1

In this experiment, Control and Treatment are each assigned 50% of users. You expect to see an approximately equal number of users in each, but your results are:

- Control: 821,588 users
- Treatment: 815,482 users

The ratio between the two is 0.993 whereas, per design, the ratio should be 1.0.

The p-value of the above .993 Sample Ratio is 1.8E-6, so the probability of seeing this ratio or more extreme, in a design with an equal number of users in Control and Treatment, is 1.8E-6, or less than 1 in 500,000!

You just observed an extremely unlikely event. It is therefore more likely that there is a bug in the implementation of the experiment, and you should not trust any of the other metrics.

## Scenario 2

This experiment also runs with Control and Treatment each assigned 50% of users and the ratio ends up at 0.994. You compute the p-value, and it's 2E-5, which is still very unlikely. It's a small percentage, so how far off can the metrics be? Do you really have to throw away the results?

Figure 21.1 shows an actual scorecard from Bing.

The middle column shows Treatment, Control, Delta, Delta %, P-Value, and P-Move (a Bayesian probability not germane for this example). The values for Treatment and Control are hidden to avoid disclosing confidential data, but they are not germane for our example. You can see that all five success metrics

| | Treatment | Control | Delta | Delta % | P-Value | P-Move | Treatment | Control | Delta | Delta % | P-Value | P-Move |
|---|---|---|---|---|---|---|---|---|---|---|---|---|
| **▾ Metadata** | | | | | | | | | | | | |
| ScorecardId | 96699772 | | | | | | 96762547 | | | | | |
| Sample Ratio [by user] | 0.9938 = 959,716 (T) / 965,679 (C) | | | | | P=2e-5 | 0.9993 = 924,240 (T) / 924,842 (C) | | | | | P=0.6580 |
| Sample Ratio [by page] | 0.9914 = 6,906,537 (T) / 6,966,740 (C) | | | | | | 0.9955 = 6,652,169 (T) / 6,682,151 (C) | | | | | |
| Trigger Rate [by user] | | | | | | | 0.9604 = 1,849,082 (T+C) / 1,925,395 (T+C) | | | | | |
| Trigger Rate [by page] | | | | | | | 0.9612 = 13,334,320 (T+C) / 13,873,277 (T+C) | | | | | |
| **▾ Main Metrics** | | | | | | | | | | | | |
| **▾ Success Metrics** | | | | | | | | | | | | |
| Sessions/UU | | | | +0.54% | 0.0094 | 12.8% | | | | +0.19% | 0.3754 | 0.2% |
| | | | | +0.20% | 7e-11 | >99.5% | | | | +0.04% | 0.1671 | 10.1% |
| | | | | +0.49% | 2e-10 | >99.5% | | | | +0.13% | 0.0727 | 24.6% |
| | | | | -0.46% | 4e-5 | 99.5% | | | | -0.12% | 0.2877 | 7.4% |
| | | | | +0.24% | 0.0001 | 99.0% | | | | +0.03% | 0.8275 | 0.7% |

Figure 21.1 Scorecard from Bing. The left column shows the meta-data, or metric names. The center column shows the statistics for each metric for the overall experiment. The right column shows the statistics for each metric for a segment of the population

improved, starting with Sessions/UU (UU = Unique User), and that the p-values are small (below 0.05 for all) to extremely small (below 0.0001 for the bottom four metrics).

The right column represents slightly over 96% of users; the excluded users were those that used an old version of the Chrome browser, which was the cause of the SRM. Also, a bot was not properly classified due to some changes in the Treatment, causing an SRM. Without the segment, the remaining 96% of users are properly balanced, and the metrics show no statistically significant movement in the five success metrics.

## SRM Causes

There are many examples of SRMs causing incorrect results that have been documented (Zhao et al. 2016, Chen et al. 2019, Fabijan et al. 2019), and at Microsoft about 6% of experiments exhibited an SRM.

Here are some causes of SRMs:

- Buggy randomization of users. While simple Bernoulli randomization of users based on the percentages that get assigned to Control and Treatment is easy to imagine, things get more complex in practice because of ramp-up procedures discussed in Chapter 15 (e.g., starting an experiment at 1%, and ramping up to 50%), exclusions (users in experiment X should not be in experiment Y), and attempts to balance covariates by looking at historical data (see hash seed in Chapter 19).

  In one real example, the experiment Treatment was exposed to the Microsoft Office organization within Microsoft at 100%, and then an experiment was started exposing external users equally at 10%/10%. The relatively small set of additional Office users in Treatment was enough to skew the results and make the Treatment look artificially good (as these are heavy users). The SRM provided a useful guardrail for trustworthiness of the result; when these internal-to-Microsoft users were removed, the strong Treatment effect disappeared.

- Data pipeline issues, such as the bot filtering mentioned in Scenario 2 above.
- Residual effects. Experiments are sometimes restarted after fixing a bug. When the experiment is visible to users, there is a desire not to re-randomize the users, so the analysis start date is set to the point after introducing the bug fix. If the bug was serious enough for users to abandon, then there will be an SRM (Kohavi et al. 2012).
- Bad trigger condition. The trigger condition should include any user that *could* have been impacted. A common example is a redirect: website A redirects a percentage of users to website A', their new website being built and tested. Because the redirect generates some loss, there will be typically be an SRM if only users that make it to website A'; are assumed to be in the Treatment. See Chapter 20.
- Triggering based on attributes impacted by the experiment. For example, suppose you are running a campaign on dormant users based on a *dormant* attribute stored in the user profile database. If the Treatment is effective enough to make some dormant users more active, then identifying users based on this attribute at the end of the experiment will give an SRM: The users that were dormant early and are now active will be excluded by the trigger condition. The analysis should be triggered to the state of the *dormant* attribute before the experiment started (or before each user was assigned). Trigger conditions based on machine learning algorithms are especially suspect because models may be updated while the experiment is running and impacted by Treatment effect.

## Debugging SRMs

As noted above, when the p-value for the Sample Ratio guardrail metric is low, you should reject the hypothesis that the design is properly implemented and assume there is a bug someplace in the system. Don't even look at any other metrics, except to help debug what went wrong. Debugging an SRM is hard, and internal tools are usually built to help debug SRMs, such as by implementing some of the suggestions below.

Here are common directions to investigate that we have found to be useful:

- Validate that there is no difference upstream of the randomization point or trigger point. For example, if you are analyzing users starting at the check-out point because you changed a checkout feature, make sure that there is no difference between the variants upstream of that point. If you're evaluating 50% off vs. two-for-one at the checkout point, you cannot mention any of these options on the homepage; if you do, you must analyze users starting from the homepage.

  The Bing Image team runs experiments on users searching using Bing Image. They found that sometimes the experiment impacts the regular Bing web search results by serving image search results inline, often causing SRMs.

- Validate that variant assignment is correct. Are users properly randomized at the top of the data pipeline? While most variant-assignment systems start with simple randomization schemes based on hashing the user ID, assignment gets complicated over time supporting concurrent experiments and isolation groups, where different experiments are guaranteed to not be exposed to the same users (Kohavi et al. 2013).

  For example, suppose one experiment changes the font color from black to dark blue and a concurrent experiment starts that changes the background color, but that experiment filters to users who have their font set to black. Due to the way the code is run, the second experiment "steals" users from the first, but only from the font-set-to-black variant. Of course, this causes an SRM.

- Follow the stages of the data processing pipeline to see whether any cause an SRM. For example, a very common source of SRMs is bot filtering. Heuristics are typically used to remove bots, as they increase noise and make analysis less sensitive. At Bing over 50% of traffic in the United States is filtered out as bots, and 90% of traffic in China and Russia is bot generated! In one extreme case at MSN, the Treatment was so good at increasing usage, that the best users passed one heuristic threshold and were classified as bots — a bug. Except for triggering the SRM, the result appeared that the Treatment was significantly worse because the best users were excluded (Kohavi 2016).

- Exclude the initial period. Is it possible that both variants did not start together? In some systems, a Control is shared across multiple experiments. Starting the Treatment later can cause multiple problems even if the analysis period starts after the Treatment started. For example, caches take time to prime, apps take time to push, phones may be offline causing delays.

- Look at the Sample Ratio for segments.
  - Look at each day separately; was there an event on some day that was anomalous? For example, did someone ramp the experiment percentages for Treatment on some day? Or did another experiment start and "steal" traffic?
  - Is there a browser segment that stands out, as in Scenario 2 above?
  - Do new users and returning users show different ratios?
- Look at the intersection with other experiments. Treatment and Control should have similar percentages of variants from other experiments.

In some cases, if the SRM is understood, it is possible to fix the cause (e.g., bots) during the analysis phase. However, in other cases the removal of traffic (e.g., removal of browser due to a bug for that browser) implies that some segments have not been properly exposed to the Treatment, and it is better to rerun the experiment.

## Other Trust-Related Guardrail Metrics

There are other metrics besides the SRM to indicate that something is wrong (Dmitriev et al. 2017). Sometimes these follow deep investigations and relate to software bugs, as the following examples show.

- Telemetry fidelity. Click tracking is typically done using web beacons, which is known to be lossy, that is, less than 100% of clicks are properly recorded (Kohavi, Messner et al. 2010). If the Treatment impacts the loss rate, the results may appear better or worse than the actual user experience. Having a metric to assess the loss, such as through internal referrers to the website or through clicks that use dual logging (sometimes used in ad clicks, which require high fidelity), fidelity issues may be uncovered.
- Cache hit rates. As noted in Chapter 3, shared resources can violate SUTVA (Kohavi and Longbotham 2010). Having metrics for shared resources, such as cache hit rates, may help identify unexpected factors that impact the trustworthiness of the experiment.
- Cookie write rate – the rate that the variant writes permanent (non-session) cookies. This phenomenon, dubbed *cookie clobbering* (Dmitriev et al. 2016), can cause severe distortion to other metrics due to browser bugs. One experiment at Bing wrote a cookie that was not used anywhere and set it to a random number with every search response page. The results showed massive user degradations in all key metrics, including sessions-per-user, queries-per-user, and revenue-per-user.

- Quick queries are two or more search queries that arrive from the same user to a search engine within one second of each other. Google and Bing have both observed this phenomenon, but to date have been unable to explain their cause. What we know is that some Treatments increase or decrease the proportion of quick queries and those results are deemed untrustworthy.

# 22

# Leakage and Interference between Variants

It doesn't matter how beautiful your theory is, it doesn't matter how smart you are. If it doesn't agree with experiment, it's wrong
– *Richard Feynman*

***Why you care***: *In most experiment analyses, we assume that the behavior of each unit in the experiment is unaffected by variant assignment to other units. This is a plausible assumption in most practical applications. However, there are also many cases where this assumption fails.*

In most of the discussions in the book, we assume the Rubin causal model (Imbens and Rubin 2015), a standard framework for analyzing controlled experiments. In this chapter, we discuss these assumptions, scenarios where they fail, and approaches to address them.

A key assumption made in the Rubin causal model is the Stable Unit Treatment Value Assumption (SUTVA), which states that the behavior of each unit in the experiment is unaffected by variant assignment to other units (Rubin 1990, Cox 1958, Imbens and Rubin 2015) as shown in Equation 22.1:

$$Y_i(z) = Y_i(z_i) \qquad (22.1)$$

with variant assignment vector $z = (z_1, z_2, \ldots, z_n)$ for all $n$ units.

This is a plausible assumption in most practical applications. For example, a user who likes the new checkout flow described in Chapter 2 is more likely to purchase, and that behavior is independent of others who are using the same eCommerce site. However, if the SUTVA assumption does not hold (see examples later in this chapter), the analysis results in potentially incorrect conclusions. We define *interference* as a violation of SUTVA, sometimes called *spillover* or *leakage* between the variants.

There are two ways interference may arise: through *direct* or *indirect* connections. As an example, two units can be directly connected if they are friends on a social network or if they visited the same physical space at the same time. Indirect connections are connections that exist because of certain latent variables or shared resources, such as units in Treatment and Control that share the same ad campaign budget. These two categories are similar in that in both cases there is a medium that connects the Treatment and Control groups and allows them to interact. The medium can either be a materialized friendship connection on a social network or a shared advertising budget that clicks from both Treatment and Control users are billed against. It is important to understand the mechanism through which interference can manifest, as the best solution to address them can differ.

To make the problems more concrete, here are examples with more detailed discussions.

## Examples

### Direct Connections

Two units can be directly connected if they are friends on a social network or if they visited the same physical space at the same time. Two units that are directly connected can be separated into Treatment and Control groups and hence cause interference between variants.

**Facebook/LinkedIn**. In social networks, such as Facebook or LinkedIn, user behavior is likely impacted by that of their social neighborhood (Eckles, Karrer and Ugander 2017, Gui et al. 2015). Users find a new social-engagement feature more valuable as more of their neighbors use it and are thus more likely to use it themselves. For example, from the user perspective:

- I am more likely to use video chat on Facebook if my friends use it.
- I am more likely to message my friends on LinkedIn if they message me.
- I am more likely to post on LinkedIn if friends in my network post on it.

In an A/B experiment, this implies that if the Treatment has a significant impact on a user, the effect could spill over to their social circles, regardless whether the neighbors are in Treatment or Control. For example, a better recommendation algorithm in Treatment for the "People You May Know" algorithm on LinkedIn encourages users to send more connect invitations. However, users who receive these invitations may be in the Control variant and when they visit LinkedIn to accept the invitation, they may discover more people to connect with. If the primary metric of interest is the total number of invitations sent, both Treatment and Control invitations are likely to increase,

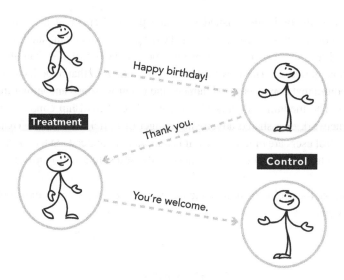

Figure 22.1 As users in Treatment send more messages to their network, users in Control will also send more messages as they reply to those messages.

so the delta is biased downwards and does not fully capture the benefit of the new algorithm. Similarly, if the Treatment encourages users to send more messages, the Control group will also see an increase in messages sent as users reply. See Figure 22.1.

**Skype calls**. As a communication tool, every call on Skype involves at least two parties. Clearly, if a user decides to call a friend on Skype, the friend ends up using Skype more, at least to answer this call. It is likely that the friend will also use Skype to call their friends. In an A/B setting, assume that Skype improved call quality for Treatment, increasing calls made from the Treatment group. Those calls can go to users who are in Treatment or Control. The result is that users in Control also increase using Skype for calls, so the delta between Treatment and Control is underestimated.

## Indirect Connections

Two units can have an indirect connection because of certain latent variables or shared resources. Like direct connections, these indirect connections can also cause interference and biased estimates of Treatment effect.

- **Airbnb** If the AirBnB marketplace site of homes for rent improved conversion flow for Treatment users, resulting in more booking, it would naturally lead to less inventory for Control users. This means that revenue generated from the Control group is less than what it would have been if there were no Treatment group. Comparing Treatment and Control leads to an over-estimation of the Treatment effect (Holtz 2018).

- **Uber/Lyft**. Imagine that Uber wants to test a different "surge price" algorithm that is so awesome that riders in Treatment are more likely to opt-in for a ride. Now there are fewer drivers available on the road, the price for the Control group goes up leading to fewer riders. As a result, the delta comparing the Treatment and Control groups is overestimated (Chamandy 2016).

- **eBay.** Assume that the Treatment for buyers encourages up bidding, like a rebate or promotion. Because the Treatment and Control users are competing for the same items, the higher bid price from Treatment certainly makes Control users less likely to win the auction. If the metric of interest is the total number of transactions, the delta between Treatment and Control is overestimated (Blake and Coey 2014, Kohavi, Longbotham et al. 2009).

- **Ad Campaigns**. Consider an experiment that shows users different rankings for the same ads. If the Treatment encourages more clicks on the ads, it uses up campaign budget faster. Because the budget on a given campaign is shared between Treatment and Control groups, the Control group ends up with a smaller budget. As a result, the delta between Treatment and Control is overestimated. Also, because of the budget constraints, experiments impacting ad revenue tend to yield a different result at the beginning of the month (or quarter) than the end of the month (or quarter) (Blake and Coey 2014, Kohavi, Longbotham et al. 2009).

- **Relevance Model Training**. Relevance models usually rely heavily on user engagement data to learn what is relevant and what is not. Just to explain the concept, imagine a search engine that uses a simple click-based relevance model for ranking. In this case, if more users click target.com when searching for "shoes," the search engine would learn and rank target.com higher for the keyword "shoes." This learning process is *model training*, and it happens continuously as fresh data flows in. Consider a Treatment relevance model that can better predict what users like to click. If we use data collected from all users to train both Treatment and Control models, the longer the experiment runs, the more the "good" clicks from Treatment benefit Control.

- **CPU**. When a user performs an action on a website, such as adding an item to the shopping cart or clicking a search result, it usually results in a request to the website server. Simplified, the request is processed by the server machines and information returned to the user. In an A/B setting, requests from both Treatment and Control are usually processed by the same machines. We have experienced examples where a bug in Treatment unexpectedly held up CPUs and memory on the machines, and as a result, requests from both Treatment and Control took longer to process. This negative Treatment effect on latency is underestimated if we do the usual Treatment and Control comparison.

- **Sub-user experiment unit**. As we discussed in Chapter 14, even though *user* is a more commonly used experiment unit, there are cases where an experiment randomizes on different units, such as a page visit, or session. Experiment units smaller than a user, such as a pageview, can cause potential leakage among units from the same user if there is a strong learning effect from the Treatment. In this case, "user" is the latent connection. As an example, assume we have a Treatment that dramatically improves latency and we randomize on a pageview, so the same user experiences pageviews in both Treatment and Control. Faster page-load-times usually lead to more clicks and more revenue (see Chapter 5); however, because the user experiences a mixed experience, their behavior on the fast pages may be influenced by that of the slow pages, and vice versa. Again, the Treatment effect is underestimated.

## Some Practical Solutions

While the interference in these examples may be caused by different reasons, they can all lead to biased results. In an ad campaign, for example, you might see a positive delta on revenue during the experiment, but when the Treatment launches to all users, the impact could be neutral because of budget constraints. When we run an experiment, we want to estimate the delta between two parallel universes: the universe where every unit is in Treatment, and the universe where every unit is in Control. Leakage between the Treatment and Control units biases the estimate. How can we prevent or correct for it?

There are a few categories of practical approaches to address interference in controlled experiments. Gupta et al. (2019) also have good discussions around some of these methods.

### Rule-of-Thumb: Ecosystem Value of an Action

Not all user actions spill over from Treatment to Control. You can identify actions that can potentially spill over, and only have concern about interference if these actions are materially impacted in an experiment. This usually means not only the first-order action, but also the potential responses to actions. For example, consider the following metrics for an experiment on a social network:

- Total number of messages sent, and messages responded to
- Total number of posts created, and total number of likes/comments they received
- Total number of likes and comments, and total number of creators receiving these likes and comments.

These metrics can indicate the downstream impact. Measuring responses gives an estimate of the depth and breadth of the potential ecosystem impact from first-order actions (Barrilleaux and Wang 2018). An experiment with positive impact on the first-order action and no impact on downstream metrics is not likely to have a measurable spillover effect.

Once you identify metrics indicative of a downstream impact, you can establish *general* guidance for how each action translates to values or engagement for the whole ecosystem. For example, how much does a message from user A translate to visit sessions from both A and their neighbors? One approach for establishing this rule-of-thumb is using historical experiments shown to have downstream impact and extrapolating this impact to the downstream impact of actions X/Y/Z using the Instrumental Variable approach (Tutterow and Saint-Jacques 2019).

This rule-of-thumb approach is relatively easy to implement, because it takes a one-time effort to establish the ecosystem value and you then apply it on any Bernoulli randomized experiment. It is more sensitive than other approaches because it relies on Bernoulli randomization to measure significant impact on downstream metrics. The approach does have limitations, however. By nature, rule-of-thumb is only an approximation and may not work for all scenarios. For example, additional messages resulting from a certain Treatment may have an ecosystem impact larger than average.

## Isolation

Interference happens through a medium connecting the Treatment and Control groups. You can remove potential interference by identifying the medium and isolating each variant. The rule-of-thumb approach uses the Bernoulli randomization design to allow you to estimate the ecosystem impact during analysis. To create isolation, you must consider other experimental designs to ensure that your Treatment and Control units are well separated. Here are a few practical isolation approaches.

- **Splitting shared resources.** If a shared resource is causing interference, splitting it between Treatment and Control is the obvious first choice. For example, you can split the ad budget according to variant allocation and only allow 20% budget to be consumed by a variant allocated 20% of traffic. Similarly, in a relevance algorithm training case, you can split the training data according to the variants they are collected from.

  There are two things to watch out for when applying this approach:
  1. Can your interfering resources be split exactly according to the traffic allocation for your variants? While this is easily achieved for budget or training data, it often isn't possible. For example, with shared machines there is heterogeneity among individual machines and simply serving Treatment and Control traffic different machines introduces too much other confounding factors difficult to correct for.
  2. Does your traffic allocation (the resource split size) introduce bias? For training data, model performance increases as it gets more training data. If the Treatment model only gets 5% data to train on and the Control model gets 95% data, this introduces bias against the Control model. This is one of the reasons we recommend a 50/50 split for traffic allocations.

- **Geo-based randomization**. There are many examples where interference happens when two units are geographically close, for example, two hotels competing for the same tourists or two taxis competing for the same riders. It's reasonable to assume that units (hotels, taxis, riders, etc.) from different regions are isolated from each other. This lets you randomize at the region level to isolate the interference between Treatment and Control (Vaver and Koehler 2011, 2012). One caveat: randomizing at the geo level limits the sample size by the number of available geo locations. This leads to a bigger variance and less power for A/B tests. See Chapter 18 for discussions on reducing variance and achieving better power.

- **Time-based randomization**. You can create isolation using time. At any time $t$, you could flip a coin and decide whether to give all users Treatment or all users Control (Bojinov and Shephard 2017, Hohnhold, O'Brien and Tang 2015). Of course, for this to work, the interference that can be caused by the same user over time is not a concern (see the sub-user experiment unit discussion above). The time unit can be short (seconds) or long (weeks), depending on what is practical and how many sample points you need. For example, if "day" is your unit, you can only collect seven sample points in a week, which is probably not fast enough. One thing to keep in mind is that there is usually strong temporal variation, like the day-of-week or hour-of-day effects. This usually helps reduce variance by utilizing this information in paired t-tests or covariate adjustments. See Chapter 18 for more details. A similar technique called interrupted time series (ITS) is discussed in Chapter 11.

- **Network-cluster randomization**. Similar to geo-based randomization, on social networks, we construct "clusters" of nodes that are close to each other based on their likelihood to interfere. We use each cluster as "mega" units and randomize them independently into Treatment or Control groups (Gui et al. 2015, Backstrom and Kleinberg 2011, Cox 1958, Katzir, Liberty and Somekh 2012).

  There are two limitations to this approach:
  1. It is rare to have perfect isolation in practice. With most social networks, the connection graphs are usually too dense to be cut into perfectly isolated clusters. For example, when attempting to create 10,000 isolated and balanced clusters from the entire LinkedIn graph, there were still more than 80% of the connections between clusters (Saint-Jacques et al. 2018).
  2. Like other mega-unit randomization approaches, the effective sample size (number of clusters) is usually small, which leads to a variance-bias tradeoff when we built the clusters. The larger number of clusters leads to a smaller variance, but also gave us a larger bias with less isolation.

- **Network ego-centric randomization**. In the network-cluster randomization approach, clusters are constructed by minimizing the edge cut between the clusters and each cluster does not employ a specific structure. During experiment assignment, every node in the cluster is also treated the same. Ego-centric randomization addresses similar interference problems on social networks but has fewer limitations. It achieves better isolation and smaller variance by creating clusters each comprised of an "ego" (a focal individual) and its "alters" (the individuals it is immediately connected to). This allows you to decide variant assignment for egos and alters separately. For example, give all alters Treatment and only half of your egos Treatment. By comparing the egos in Treatment to the egos in Control, you can measure first-order impact and downstream impact. You can find a good discussion of this in Saint-Jacques et. al. (2018b).

Whenever applicable, always combine isolation methods to get a larger sample size. For example, while applying network-cluster randomization, you can expand the sample size by leveraging time $t$ as a sampling dimension. If most of interference has a short time span and the Treatment effect itself is transactional, you can use a coin flip each day to determine variant assignment for each cluster. Sometimes, you can create a better isolation by predicting where interference could happen. For example, a user does not message every neighbor in their social network. Knowing that the connection network itself is usually too dense to create isolated clusters, identifying a subgraph where messages are likely to be exchanged can create better clusters.

## Edge-Level Analysis

Some leakage happens in a clearly defined interaction between two users. These interactions (edges) are easy to identify. You can use Bernoulli randomization on users and then label the edges based on the experiment assignment of the users (nodes) as one of these four types: Treatment-to-Treatment, Treatment-to-Control, Control-to-Control, and Control-to-Treatment. Contrasting interactions (e.g., messages, likes) that happen on different edges, allows you to understand important network effects. For example, use the contrast between the Treatment-to-Treatment and Control-to-Control edges to estimate unbiased delta, or identify whether units in Treatment prefer to message other Treatment units over Control units (Treatment affinity), and whether new actions created by Treatment get a higher response rate. You can read up on edge-level analysis in Saint-Jacques et. al. (2018b).

## Detecting and Monitoring Interference

Understanding the mechanism of the interference is the key to identifying a good solution. But while getting a precise measurement may not be practical for every experiment, it is important to have a strong monitoring and alert system for detecting interference. For example, if all ad revenue during the experiment comes from budget-constrained vs. budget-non-constrained advertisers, the experiment result could not generalize after launch. Ramp phases can also detect really bad interference (e.g., a Treatment consumes all CPU), such as first ramping to employees or a small datacenter. See Chapter 15 for details.

# 23

# Measuring Long-Term Treatment Effects

We tend to overestimate the effect of a technology in the short run and underestimate the effect in the long run
– *Roy Amara*

***Why you care****: Sometimes the effect that you care to measure can take months or even years to accumulate – a long-term effect. In an online world where products and services are developed quickly and iteratively in an agile fashion, trying to measure a long-term effect is challenging. While an active area of research, understanding the key challenges and current methodology is useful if you are tackling a problem of this nature.*

## What Are Long-Term Effects?

In most scenarios discussed in this book, we recommend running experiments for one to two weeks. The Treatment effect measured in this short timeframe is called the *short-term* effect. For most experiments, understanding this short-term effect is all we need, as it is stable and generalizes to the *long-term* Treatment effect, which is usually what we care about. However, there are scenarios where the long-term effect is different from the short-term effect. For example, raising prices is likely to increase short-term revenue but reduce long-term revenue as users abandon the product or service. Showing poor search results on a search engine will cause users to search again (Kohavi et al. 2012); the query share increases in the short-term but decreases in the long-term as users switch to a better search engine. Similarly, showing more ads – including more low-quality ads – can increase ad clicks and revenue in the short-term but decreases revenue via decreased ad clicks, and even searches, in the long-term (Hohnhold, O'Brien and Tang 2015, Dmitriev, Frasca, et al. 2016).

The long-term effect is defined as the asymptotic effect of a Treatment, which, in theory, can be years out. Practically, it is common to consider long-term to be 3+ months, or based on the number of exposures (e.g., the Treatment effect for users exposed to the new feature at least 10 times).

We explicitly exclude from discussion changes that have a short life span. For example, you may run an experiment on news headlines picked by editors that have a life span of only a few hours. However, the question of whether headlines should be "catchy" or "funny" is a good long-term hypothesis, as an initial increase in short-term engagement may also be associated with long-term increased abandonment. Except when you are specifically running experiments on such short life-span changes, when testing a new Treatment, you would really like to know how it would perform in the long term.

In this chapter, we cover the reasons that long-term effects can be different from short-term effects and discuss measurement methods. We only focus on scenarios where short-term and long-term Treatment effects differ. We are not considering other important differences between short-term and long-term, such as sample size difference, which may cause the *estimated* Treatment effects and variance to differ.

One key challenge in determining the OEC (see Chapter 7) is that it must be measurable in the short term but believed to causally impact long-term objectives. Measuring long-term effects discussed in this chapter can provide insights to improve and devise short-term metrics that impact the long-term goals.

## Reasons the Treatment Effect May Differ between Short-Term and Long-Term

There are several reasons why short-term and long-term Treatment effects may differ. We have discussed some in the context of trustworthiness in Chapter 3.

- **User-learned effects**. As users learn and adapt to a change, their behavior changes. For example, product crashes are a terrible user experience that may not turn users away with the first occurrence. However, if crashes are frequent, users learn and may decide to leave the product. Users may adjust the rate they click on ads if they realize the ads' quality is poor. The behavior change may also be due to discoverability, maybe a new feature that may take time for users to notice, but once they discover its usefulness, they engage heavily. Users may also need time to adapt to a new feature because they are primed in the old feature, or they explore a new change more when it is first introduced (see Chapter 3). In such cases, a long-term effect may differ from a short-term effect because users eventually reach an equilibrium point (Huang, Reiley and Raibov 2018, Hohnhold, O'Brien and Tang 2015, Chen, Liu and Xu 2019, Kohavi, Longbotham et al. 2009).

- **Network effects**. When users see friends using the Live Video feature on a communication app such as Facebook Messenger, WhatsApp, or Skype, it is more likely that they will use it too. User behavior tends to be influenced by people in their network though it may take a while for a feature to reach its full effect as it propagates through their network (see Chapter 22, which discusses interference in marketplaces with limited or shared resources, focusing on biased estimation in the *short-term* due to leakage between variants). The limited resources introduce additional challenges as we measure long-term impact. For example, in two-sided marketplaces, such as Airbnb, eBay, and Uber, a new feature can be very effective at driving demand for an item, such as a house to rent, computer keyboard, or ride, but the supply may take longer to catch up. As a result, the impact on revenue may take longer to realize as supply is unavailable. Similar examples exist for other areas, such as hiring marketplaces (job seekers and jobs), ad marketplaces (advertisers and publishers), recommendation systems for content (news feeds), or connections (LinkedIn's People You May Know). Because there are a limited number of people one person knows ("supply"), a new algorithm may perform better at the beginning but may reach a lower equilibrium long term because of supply constraints (an analogous effect can be seen in recommendation algorithms more generally, where a new algorithm may perform better initially due to diversity, or simply showing new recommendations).

- **Delayed experience and measurement.** There can be a time gap before a user experiences the entirety of the Treatment effect. For example, for companies like Airbnb and Booking.com, there can be months between a user's online experience and when the user physically arrives at the destination. The metrics that matter, such as user retention, can be affected by the user's delayed offline experience. Another example is annual contracts: Users who sign up have a decision point when the year ends and their cumulative experience over that year determines whether they renew.

- **Ecosystem change.** Many things in your ecosystem change over time and can impact how users react to the Treatment, including:
  - **Launching other new features**. For example, if more teams embed the Live Video feature in their product, Live Video becomes more valuable.
  - **Seasonality**. For example, experiments on gift cards that perform well during the Christmas season may not have the same performance during the non-holiday season due to users having different purchasing intent.

- ◦ **Competitive landscape**. For example, if your competition launches the same feature, the value of the feature may decline.
- ◦ **Government policies**. For example, the European Union General Data Protection Regulation (GDPR) changes how users control their online data, and hence what data you can use for online ad targeting (European Commission 2016, Basin, Debois and Hildebrandt 2018, Google, Helping advertisers comply with the GDPR 2019).
- ◦ **Concept drift**. The performance of machine learning models trained on data that is not refreshed may degrade over time as distributions change.
- ◦ **Software rot**. After features ship, unless they are maintained, they tend to degrade with respect to the environment around them. This can be caused, for example, by system assumptions made by code that becomes invalid over time.

## Why Measure Long-Term Effects?

While the long-term effect can certainly differ from short-term effect for various reasons, not all such differences are worth measuring. What you want to achieve with the long-term effect plays a critical role in determining what you should measure and how you should measure it. We summarize the top reasons.

- • **Attribution**. Companies with strong data-driven culture use experiment results to track team goals and performance, potentially incorporating experiment gains into long-term financial forecasting. In these scenarios, proper measurement and attribution of the long-term impact of an experiment is needed. What would the world look like in the long term with vs. without introducing the new feature now? This type of attribution is challenging because we need to consider both endogenous reasons such as user-learned effects, and exogenous reasons such as competitive landscape changes. In practice, because future product changes are usually built on top of past launches, it may be hard to attribute such compounding impacts.
- • **Institutional learning**. What is the difference between short term and long term? If the difference is sizable, what is causing it? If there is a strong novelty effect, this may indicate a suboptimal user experience. For example, if it takes a user too long to discover a new feature they like, you may expedite uptake by using in-product education. On the other hand, if many users are attracted to the new feature but only try it once, it may indicate low quality or click-bait. Learning about the difference can offer insights into an improved subsequent iteration.

- **Generalization**. In many cases, we measure the long-term effect on some experiments so we can extrapolate to other experiments. How much long-term impact does a similar change have? Can we derive a general principle for certain product areas (e.g., search ads in Hohnhold et. al. (2015)? Can we create a short-term metric that is predictive of long term (see the last section of this chapter)? If we can generalize or predict the long-term effect, we can take that generalization into account in the decision-making process. For this purpose, you may want to isolate the long-term impact from exogenous factors, especially big shocks that are unlikely to repeat over time.

## Long-Running Experiments

The simplest and most popular approach for measuring long-term effects is to keep an experiment running for a long time. You can measure the Treatment effect at the beginning of the experiment (in the first week) and at the end of the experiment (in the last week). Note that this analysis approach differs from a typical experiment analysis that would measure the average effect over the entire Treatment period. The first percent-delta measurement $p\varDelta_1$ is considered the short-term effect and the last measurement $p\varDelta_T$ is the long-term effect as shown in Figure 23.1.

While this is a viable solution, there are several challenges and limitations in this type of long-term experiment design. We focus on a few that are relevant

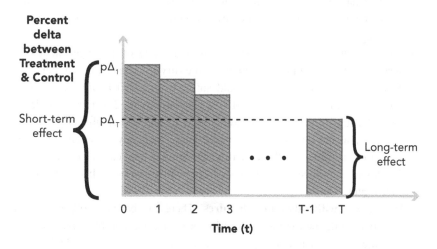

Figure 23.1 Measuring long-term effect based on a long-running experiment

to measuring long-term effects, organized around the purpose of attribution and institutional learning.

- **For attribution**: The measurement from the last week of the long-running experiment ($p\Delta_T$) may not represent the true long-term Treatment effect for the following reasons:
  - Treatment effect dilution.
  - The user may use multiple devices or entry points (e.g., web and app), while the experiment is only capturing a subset. The longer the experiment runs, the more likely a user will have used multiple devices during the experiment period. For users who visit during the last week, only a fraction of their experience during the entire time period $T$ is actually in Treatment. Therefore, if users are learning, what is measured in $p\Delta_T$ is not the long-term impact of what users learned after being exposed to Treatment for time $T$, but a diluted version. Note that this dilution may not matter for all features, but rather the subset where the dosage matters.
  - If you randomize the experiment units based on cookies, cookies can churn due to user behavior or get clobbered due to browser issues (Dmitriev et al. 2016). A user who was in Treatment could get randomized into Control with a new cookie. As in the two previous bullet points, the longer the experiment runs, the more likely that a user will have experienced both Treatment and Control.
  - If network effects are present, unless you have perfect isolation between the variants, the Treatment effect can "leak" from Treatment to Control (see Chapter 22). The longer the experiment runs, it is likely that the effect will cascade more broadly through the network, creating larger leakage.
- **Survivorship bias.** Not all users at the beginning of the experiment will survive to the end of the experiment. If the survival rate is different between Treatment and Control, $p\Delta_T$ would suffer from *survivorship bias*, which should also trigger an SRM alert (see Chapters 3 and 21). For example, if those Treatment users who dislike the new feature end up abandoning over time, $p\Delta_T$ would only capture a biased view of those who remain (and the new users admitted to the experiment). Similar bias can also exist if the Treatment introduces a bug or side-effect that causes a different cookie churn rate.
- **Interaction with other new features**. There can be many other features launched while the long-term experiment is running, and they may interact with the specific feature being tested. These new features can erode the wins of the experiment over time. For example, a first experiment that sends push

notifications to users can be hugely effective at driving sessions, but as other teams start sending notifications, the effect of the first notification diminishes.

- **For measuring a time-extrapolated effect**: Without further study – including more experiments – we need to be cautious to not interpret the difference between $p\Delta_0$ and $p\Delta_T$ as a meaningful difference caused by the Treatment itself. Besides the attribution challenges discussed above that complicate the interpretation of $p\Delta_T$ itself, the difference may be purely due to exogenous factors, such as seasonality. In general, if the underlying population or external environment has changed between the two time periods, we can no longer directly compare short-term and long-term experiment results.

Of course, challenges around attribution and measuring time-extrapolated effects also make it hard to generalize the results from specific long-running experiments to more extensible principles and techniques. There are also challenges around how to know that the long-term result is stabilized and when to stop the experiment. The next section explores experiment design and analysis methodologies that partially address these challenges.

## Alternative Methods for Long-Running Experiments

Different methods have been proposed to improve measurements from long-running experiments (Hohnhold, O'Brien and Tang 2015, Dmitriev, Frasca, et al. 2016). Each method discussed in this section offers some improvements, but none fully address the limitations under all scenarios. We highly recommend that you always evaluate whether these limitations apply, and if so, how much they impact your results or your interpretation of the results.

### Method #1: Cohort Analysis

You can construct a stable cohort of users before starting the experiment and only analyze the short-term and long-term effects on this cohort of users. One method is to select the cohort based on a stable ID, for example, logged-in user IDs. This method can be effective at addressing dilution and survivorship bias, especially if the cohort can be tracked and measured in a stable way. There are two important considerations to keep in mind:

- You need to evaluate how stable the cohort is, as it is crucial for the effectiveness of the method. For example, if the ID is based on cookies and when cookie churn rate is high, this method does not work well for correcting bias (Dmitriev et al. 2016).

- If the cohort is not representative of the overall population, there may be external validity concerns because the analysis results may not be generalizable to the full population. For example, analyzing logged-in users only may introduce bias because they differ from non-logged-in users. You can use additional methods to improve the generalizability, such as a weighting adjustment based on stratification (Park, Gelman and Bafumi 2004, Gelman 1997, Lax and Phillips 2009). In this approach, you first stratify users into subgroups (e.g., based on pre-experiment high/medium/low engagement levels), and then compute a weighted average of the Treatment effects from each subgroup, with the weights reflecting the population distribution. This approach has similar limitations as observational studies discussed extensively in Chapter 11.

## Method #2: Post-Period Analysis

In this method, you turn off the experiment after it has been running for a while (time $T$) and then measure the difference between the users in Treatment and those in Control during time $T$ and $T+1$, as shown in Figure 23.2. In the event where you cannot ramp down the new Treatment due to user experience concerns, you can still apply this method by "ramping up" the Treatment for all users. A key aspect of this method is that during the measurement period, users in the Treatment and Control groups are both exposed to the exact same

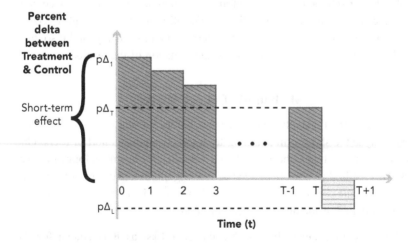

Figure 23.2 Measuring long-term effect based on post-period A/A measurement

features. The difference between the groups, however, is that in the first case, the Treatment group was exposed to a set of features that the Control group was not exposed to, or in the second "ramping up" case, the Treatment group was exposed to the features for a longer time than the Control group.

Hohnhold et al. (2015) calls the effect measured during the post-period the *learning effect*. To properly interpret it, you need to understand the specific change tested in the experiment. There are two types of learned effect:

1. **User-learned effect**. Users have learned and adapted to the change over time. Hohnhold et al. (2015) studies the impact of increasing ad-load on users' ad clicking behavior. In their case study, user learning is considered the key reason behind the post-period effect.
2. **System-learned effect**. The system may have "remembered" information from the Treatment period. For example, the Treatment may encourage more users to update their profile and this updated information stays in the system even after the experiment ends. Or, if more Treatment users are annoyed by emails and opt out during the experiment, they will not receive emails during the post-period. Another common example is personalization through machine learning models, such as models that show more ads to users who click more on ads. After a Treatment that causes users to click more on ads, the system that uses a sufficiently long time period for personalization may learn about the user and thus show them more ads even after they are back to experiencing the Control Treatment.

Given enough experiments, the method can estimate a learned effect based on the system parameters and subsequently extrapolate from new short-term experiments to estimate the anticipated long-term effect (Gupta et al. 2019). This extrapolation is reasonable when the system-learned effects are zero, that is, in the A/A post-period, both Treatment and Control users are exposed to the exact same set of features. Examples of where this system-learned effect is non-zero might include permanent user state changes, such as more time-persistent personalization, opt-outs, unsubscribes, hitting impression limits, and so on.

That said, this approach is effective at isolating impact from exogenous factors that change over time and from potential interactions with other newly launched features. Because the learned effect is measured separately, it offers more insights on why the effects are different short term vs. long term. This method suffers from potential dilution and survivorship bias (Dmitriev et al. 2016). However, because the learned effect is measured separately in the post-period, you could attempt to apply an adjustment to the learned effect to account for dilution or by combining with the cohort analysis method discussed earlier.

## Method #3: Time-Staggered Treatments

The methods discussed so far simply require experimenters to wait "enough" time before taking the long-term measurement. But how long is "long enough?" A poor man's approach is to observe the Treatment effect trend line and decide that enough time has passed when the curve stabilizes. This does not work well in practice because Treatment effect is rarely stable over time. With big events or even day-of-week effect, the volatility over time tends to overwhelm the long-term trend.

To determine the measurement time, you can have two versions of the same Treatment running with staggered start times. One version ($T_0$) starts at time $t=0$, while the other ($T_1$) starts at time $t=1$. At any given time, $t>1$, you can measure the difference between the two versions of Treatment. Note that at time $t$, $T_0$ and $T_1$ are effectively an A/A test with the only difference being the duration their users are exposed to Treatment. We can conduct a two-sample t-test to check whether the difference between $T_1(t)$ and $T_0(t)$ is statistically significant, and conclude that the two Treatments have converged if the difference is small, as shown in Figure 23.3. Note that it is important to determine the practically significant delta and ensure that the comparison has enough statistical power to detect it. At this point, we can apply the post-period

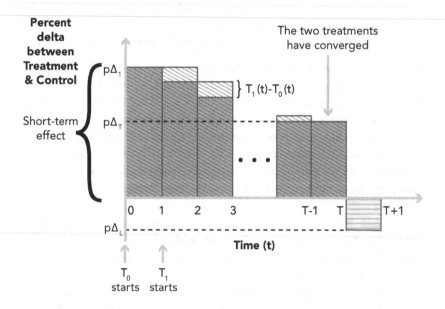

Figure 23.3 Measuring long-term effect after we observe the two time-staggered Treatments have converged

method after time $t$ to measure the long-term effect (Gupta, Kohavi et al. 2019). While testing the difference between the two Treatments, it may be more important to control for a lower type II error rate than the typical 20%, even at the cost of increasing the Type I error rate to be higher than 5%.

This method assumes that the difference between the two Treatments grows smaller over time. In other words, $T_1(t) - T_0(t)$ is a decreasing function of $t$. While this is a plausible assumption, in practice, you also need to ensure that there is enough time gap between the two staggered Treatments. If the learned effect takes some time to manifest, and the two Treatments start right after one another, there may not be enough time for the two Treatments to have a difference at the start of $T_1$.

## Method #4: Holdback and Reverse Experiment

Long-term experiments may not be feasible if there is time pressure to launch a Treatment to all users. Control groups can be expensive: they have an opportunity cost as they don't receive the Treatment (Varian 2007). An alternative is to conduct a *holdback*: keeping 10% of users in Control for several weeks (or months) after launching the Treatment to 90% users (Xu, Duan and Huang 2018). Holdback experiments are a typical type of long-running experiment. Because they have a small Control variant, they tend to have less power than may be optimal. It is important to make sure that the reduced sensitivity does not impact what you want to learn from the holdout. See more discussion in Chapter 15.

There is an alternative version called *reverse* experiments. In a reverse experiment, we ramp 10% of users back into the Control several weeks (or months) after launching the Treatment to 100% of users. The benefit of this approach is that everyone has received the Treatment for a while. If the Treatment introduces a new feature where network effect plays a role in user adoption, or if supply is constrained in the marketplace, the reverse experiment allows the network or the marketplace time to reach the new equilibrium. The disadvantage is that if the Treatment may introduce a visible change, ramping the users back into the Control may confuse them.

# References

Abadi, Martin, Andy Chu, Ian Goodfellow, H. Brendan Mironov, Ilya Mcmahan, Kunal Talwar, and Li Zhang. 2016. "Deep Learning with Differential Privacy." *Proceedings of the 2016 ACM SIGSAC Conference on Computer and Communications Security.*

Abrahamse, Peter. 2016. "How 8 Different A/B Testing Tools Affect Site Speed." *CXL: All Things Data-Driven Marketing.* May 16. https://conversionxl.com/blog/testing-tools-site-speed/.

ACM. 2018. *ACM Code of Ethics and Professional Conduct.* June 22. www.acm.org/code-of-ethics.

Alvarez, Cindy. 2017. *Lean Customer Development: Building Products Your Customers Will Buy.* O'Reilly.

Angrist, Joshua D., and Jörn-Steffen Pischke. 2014. *Mastering 'Metrics: The Path from Cause to Effect.* Princeton University Press.

Angrist, Joshua D., and Jörn-Steffen Pischke. 2009. *Mostly Harmless Econometrics: An Empiricist's Companion.* Princeton University Press.

Apple, Inc. 2017. "Phased Release for Automatic Updates Now Available." June 5. https://developer.apple.com/app-store-connect/whats-new/?id=31070842.

Apple, Inc. 2018. "Use Low Power Mode to Save Battery Life on Your iPhone." *Apple.* September 25. https://support.apple.com/en-us/HT205234.

Athey, Susan, and Guido Imbens. 2016. "Recursive Partitioning for Heterogeneous Causal Effects." *PNAS: Proceedings of the National Academy of Sciences.* 7353–7360. doi: https://doi.org/10.1073/pnas.1510489113.

Azevedo, Eduardo M., Alex Deng, Jose Montiel Olea, Justin M. Rao, and E. Glen Weyl. 2019. "A/B Testing with Fat Tails." February 26. Available at SSRN: https://ssrn.com/abstract=3171224 or http://dx.doi.org/10.2139/ssrn.3171224.

Backstrom, Lars, and Jon Kleinberg. 2011. "Network Bucket Testing." *WWW '11 Proceedings of the 20th International Conference on World Wide Web.* Hyderabad, India: ACM. 615–624.

Bailar, John C. 1983. "Introduction." In *Clinical Trials: Issues and Approaches*, by Stuart Shapiro and Thomas Louis. Marcel Dekker.

Bakshy, Eytan, Max Balandat, and Kostya Kashin. 2019. "Open-sourcing Ax and BoTorch: New AI tools for adaptive experimentation." Facebook Artificial Intelligence. May 1. https://ai.facebook.com/blog/open-sourcing-ax-and-botorch-new-ai-tools-for-adaptive-experimentation/.

Bakshy, Eytan, and Eitan Frachtenberg. 2015. "Design and Analysis of Benchmarking Experiments for Distributed Internet Services." *WWW '15: Proceedings of the 24th International Conference on World Wide Web*. Florence, Italy: ACM. 108–118. doi: https://doi.org/10.1145/2736277.2741082.

Bakshy, Eytan, Dean Eckles, and Michael Bernstein. 2014. "Designing and Deploying Online Field Experiments." *International World Wide Web Conference (WWW 2014)*. https://facebook.com//download/255785951270811/planout.pdf.

Barajas, Joel, Ram Akella, Marius Hotan, and Aaron Flores. 2016. "Experimental Designs and Estimation for Online Display Advertising Attribution in Marketplaces." *Marketing Science: the Marketing Journal of the Institute for Operations Research and the Management Sciences* 35: 465–483.

Barrilleaux, Bonnie, and Dylan Wang. 2018. "Spreading the Love in the LinkedIn Feed with Creator-Side Optimization." *LinkedIn Engineering*. October 16. https://engineering.linkedin.com/blog/2018/10/linkedin-feed-with-creator-side-optimization.

Basin, David, Soren Debois, and Thomas Hildebrandt. 2018. "On Purpose and by Necessity: Compliance under the GDPR." *Financial Cryptography and Data Security 2018*. IFCA. Preproceedings 21.

Benbunan-Fich, Raquel. 2017. "The Ethics of Online Research with Unsuspecting Users: From A/B Testing to C/D Experimentation." *Research Ethics* 13 (3–4): 200–218. doi: https://doi.org/10.1177/1747016116680664.

Benjamin, Daniel J., James O. Berger, Magnus Johannesson, Brian A. Nosek, E.-J. Wagenmakers, Richard Berk, Kenneth A. Bollen, et al. 2017. "Redefine Statistical Significance." *Nature Human Behaviour* 2 (1): 6–10. https://www.nature.com/articles/s41562-017-0189-z.

Beshears, John, James J. Choi, David Laibson, Brigitte C. Madrian, and Katherine L. Milkman. 2011. *The Effect of Providing Peer Information on Retirement Savings Decisions*. NBER Working Paper Series, National Bureau of Economic Research. www.nber.org/papers/w17345.

Billingsly, Patrick. 1995. *Probability and Measure*. Wiley.

Blake, Thomas, and Dominic Coey. 2014. "Why Marketplace Experimentation is Harder Than it Seems: The Role of Test-Control Interference." *EC '14 Proceedings of the Fifteenth ACM Conference on Economics and Computation*. Palo Alto, CA: ACM. 567–582.

Blank, Steven Gary. 2005. *The Four Steps to the Epiphany: Successful Strategies for Products that Win*. Cafepress.com.

Blocker, Craig, John Conway, Luc Demortier, Joel Heinrich, Tom Junk, Louis Lyons, and Giovanni Punzi. 2006. "Simple Facts about P-Values." *The Rockefeller University*. January 5. http://physics.rockefeller.edu/luc/technical_reports/cdf8023_facts_about_p_values.pdf.

Bodlewski, Mike. 2017. "When Slower UX is Better UX." *Web Designer Depot*. Sep 25. https://www.webdesignerdepot.com/2017/09/when-slower-ux-is-better-ux/.

Bojinov, Iavor, and Neil Shephard. 2017. "Time Series Experiments and Causal Estimands: Exact Randomization Tests and Trading." *arXiv of Cornell University*. July 18. arXiv:1706.07840.

Borden, Peter. 2014. "How Optimizely (Almost) Got Me Fired." *The SumAll Blog: Where E-commerce and Social Media Meet*. June 18. https://blog.sumall.com/journal/optimizely-got-me-fired.html.

Bowman, Douglas. 2009. "Goodbye, Google." *stopdesign.* March 20. https://stop
design.com/archive/2009/03/20/goodbye-google.html.

Box, George E.P., J. Stuart Hunter, and William G. Hunter. 2005. *Statistics for Experimenters: Design, Innovation, and Discovery.* 2nd edition. John Wiley & Sons, Inc.

Brooks Bell. 2015. "Click Summit 2015 Keynote Presentation." *Brooks Bell.*
www.brooksbell.com/wp-content/uploads/2015/05/BrooksBell_ClickSummit15_
Keynote1.pdf.

Brown, Morton B. 1975. "A Method for Combining Non-Independent, One-Sided
Tests of Signficance." *Biometrics* 31 (4) 987–992. www.jstor.org/stable/2529826.

Brutlag, Jake, Zoe Abrams, and Pat Meenan. 2011. "Above the Fold Time: Measuring
Web Page Performance Visually." *Velocity: Web Performance and Operations
Conference.*

Buhrmester, Michael, Tracy Kwang, and Samuel Gosling. 2011. "Amazon's Mechanical Turk: A New Source of Inexpensive, Yet High-Quality Data?" *Perspectives
on Psychological Science,* Feb 3.

Campbell, Donald T. 1979. "Assessing the Impact of Planned Social Change." *Evaluation and Program Planning* 2: 67–90. https://doi.org/10.1016/0149-7189(79)
90048-X.

Campbell's law. 2018. *Wikipedia.* https://en.wikipedia.org/wiki/Campbell%27s_law.

Card, David, and Alan B Krueger. 1994. "Minimum Wages and Employment: A Case
Study of the Fast-Food Industry in New Jersey and Pennsylvania." *The American
Economic Review* 84 (4): 772–793. https://www.jstor.org/stable/2118030.

Casella, George, and Roger L. Berger. 2001. *Statistical Inference.* 2nd edition. Cengage
Learning.

CDC. 2015. *The Tuskegee Timeline.* December. https://www.cdc.gov/tuskegee/
timeline.htm.

Chamandy, Nicholas. 2016. "Experimentation in a Ridesharing Marketplace." *Lyft
Engineering.* September 2. https://eng.lyft.com/experimentation-in-a-risharing-mar
ketplace-b39db027a66e.

Chan, David, Rong Ge, Ori Gershony, Tim Hesterberg, and Diane Lambert. 2010.
"Evaluating Online Ad Campaigns in a Pipeline: Causal Models at Scale." *Proceedings of ACM SIGKDD.*

Chapelle, Olivier, Thorsten Joachims, Filip Radlinski, and Yisong Yue. 2012. "Large-
Scale Validation and Analysis of Interleaved Search Evaluation." *ACM Transactions on Information Systems,* February.

Chaplin, Charlie. 1964. *My Autobiography.* Simon Schuster.

Charles, Reichardt S., and Mark M. Melvin. 2004. "Quasi Experimentation." In *Handbook of Practical Program Evaluation,* by Joseph S. Wholey, Harry P. Hatry and
Kathryn E. Newcomer. Jossey-Bass.

Chatham, Bob, Bruce D. Temkin, and Michelle Amato. 2004. *A Primer on A/B Testing.*
Forrester Research.

Chen, Nanyu, Min Liu, and Ya Xu. 2019. "How A/B Tests Could Go Wrong:
Automatic Diagnosis of Invalid Online Experiments." *WSDM '19 Proceedings
of the Twelfth ACM International Conference on Web Search and Data Mining.*
Melbourne, VIC, Australia: ACM. 501–509. https://dl.acm.org/citation.cfm?id=
3291000.

Chrystal, K. Alec, and Paul D. Mizen. 2001. *Goodhart's Law: Its Origins, Meaning and Implications for Monetary Policy.* Prepared for the Festschrift in honor of Charles Goodhart held on 15–16 November 2001 at the Bank of England. http://cyberlibris.typepad.com/blog/files/Goodharts_Law.pdf.

Coey, Dominic, and Tom Cunningham. 2019. "Improving Treatment Effect Estimators Through Experiment Splitting." *WWW '19: The Web Conference.* San Francisco, CA, USA: ACM. 285–295. doi:https://dl.acm.org/citation.cfm?doid= 3308558.3313452.

Collis, David. 2016. "Lean Strategy." *Harvard Business Review* 62–68. https://hbr.org/2016/03/lean-strategy.

Concato, John, Nirav Shah, and Ralph I Horwitz. 2000. "Randomized, Controlled Trials, Observational Studies, and the Hierarchy of Research Designs." *The New England Journal of Medicine* 342 (25): 1887–1892. doi:https://www.nejm.org/doi/10.1056/NEJM200006223422507.

Cox, David Roxbee. 1958. *Planning of Experiments.* New York: John Wiley.

Croll, Alistair, and Benjamin Yoskovitz. 2013. *Lean Analytics: Use Data to Build a Better Startup Faster.* O'Reilly Media.

Crook, Thomas, Brian Frasca, Ron Kohavi, and Roger Longbotham. 2009. "Seven Pitfalls to Avoid when Running Controlled Experiments on the Web." *KDD '09: Proceedings of the 15th ACM SIGKDD international conference on Knowledge discovery and data mining,* 1105–1114.

Cross, Robert G., and Ashutosh Dixit. 2005. "Customer-centric Pricing: The Surprising Secret for Profitability." *Business Horizons,* 488.

Deb, Anirban, Suman Bhattacharya, Jeremey Gu, Tianxia Zhuo, Eva Feng, and Mandie Liu. 2018. "Under the Hood of Uber's Experimentation Platform." *Uber Engineering.* August 28. https://eng.uber.com/xp.

Deng, Alex. 2015. "Objective Bayesian Two Sample Hypothesis Testing for Online Controlled Experiments." Florence, IT: ACM. 923–928.

Deng, Alex, and Victor Hu. 2015. "Diluted Treatment Effect Estimation for Trigger Analysis in Online Controlled Experiments." *WSDM '15: Proceedings of the Eighth ACM International Conference on Web Search and Data Mining.* Shanghai, China: ACM. 349–358. doi:https://doi.org/10.1145/2684822.2685307.

Deng, Alex, Jiannan Lu, and Shouyuan Chen. 2016. "Continuous Monitoring of A/B Tests without Pain: Optional Stopping in Bayesian Testing." *2016 IEEE International Conference on Data Science and Advanced Analytics (DSAA).* Montreal, QC, Canada: IEEE. doi:https://doi.org/10.1109/DSAA.2016.33.

Deng, Alex, Ulf Knoblich, and Jiannan Lu. 2018. "Applying the Delta Method in Metric Analytics: A Practical Guide with Novel Ideas." *24th ACM SIGKDD Conference on Knowledge Discovery and Data Mining.*

Deng, Alex, Jiannan Lu, and Jonathan Litz. 2017. "Trustworthy Analysis of Online A/B Tests: Pitfalls, Challenges and Solutions." *WSDM: The Tenth International Conference on Web Search and Data Mining.* Cambridge, UK.

Deng, Alex, Ya Xu, Ron Kohavi, and Toby Walker. 2013. "Improving the Sensitivity of Online Controlled Experiments by Utilizing Pre-Experiment Data." *WSDM 2013: Sixth ACM International Conference on Web Search and Data Mining.*

Deng, Shaojie, Roger Longbotham, Toby Walker, and Ya Xu. 2011. "Choice of Randomization Unit in Online Controlled Experiments." *Joint Statistical Meetings Proceedings*. 4866–4877.

Denrell, Jerker. 2005. "Selection Bias and the Perils of Benchmarking." *(Harvard Business Review)* 83 (4): 114–119.

Dickhaus, Thorsten. 2014. *Simultaneous Statistical Inference: With Applications in the Life Sciences*. Springer. https://www.springer.com/cda/content/document/cda_downloaddocument/9783642451812-c2.pdf.

Dickson, Paul. 1999. *The Official Rules and Explanations: The Original Guide to Surviving the Electronic Age With Wit, Wisdom, and Laughter*. Federal Street Pr.

Djulbegovic, Benjamin, and Iztok Hozo. 2002. "At What Degree of Belief in a Research Hypothesis Is a Trial in Humans Justified?" *Journal of Evaluation in Clinical Practice*, June 13.

Dmitriev, Pavel, and Xian Wu. 2016. "Measuring Metrics." *CIKM: Conference on Information and Knowledge Management*. Indianapolis, In. http://bit.ly/measuringMetrics.

Dmitriev, Pavel, Somit Gupta, Dong Woo Kim, and Garnet Vaz. 2017. "A Dirty Dozen: Twelve Common Metric Interpretation Pitfalls in Online Controlled Experiments." *Proceedings of the 23rd ACM SIGKDD International Conference on Knowledge Discovery and Data Mining (KDD 2017)*. Halifax, NS, Canada: ACM. 1427–1436. http://doi.acm.org/10.1145/3097983.3098024.

Dmitriev, Pavel, Brian Frasca, Somit Gupta, Ron Kohavi, and Garnet Vaz. 2016. "Pitfalls of Long-Term Online Controlled Experiments." *2016 IEEE International Conference on Big Data (Big Data)*. Washington DC. 1367–1376. http://bit.ly/expLongTerm.

Doerr, John. 2018. *Measure What Matters: How Google, Bono, and the Gates Foundation Rock the World with OKRs*. Portfolio.

Doll, Richard. 1998. "Controlled Trials: the 1948 Watershed." *BMJ*. doi:https://doi.org/10.1136/bmj.317.7167.1217.

Dutta, Kaushik, and Debra Vadermeer. 2018. "Caching to Reduce Mobile App Energy Consumption." *ACM Transactions on the Web (TWEB)*, February 12(1): Article No. 5.

Dwork, Cynthia, and Aaron Roth. 2014. "The Algorithmic Foundations of Differential Privacy." *Foundations and Trends in Computer Science* 211–407.

Eckles, Dean, Brian Karrer, and Johan Ugander. 2017. "Design and Analysis of Experiments in Networks: Reducing Bias from Interference." *Journal of Causal Inference* 5(1). www.deaneckles.com/misc/Eckles_Karrer_Ugander_Reducing_Bias_from_Interference.pdf.

Edgington, Eugene S. 1972, "An Additive Method for Combining Probablilty Values from Independent Experiments." *The Journal of Psychology* 80 (2): 351–363.

Edmonds, Andy, Ryan W. White, Dan Morris, and Steven M. Drucker. 2007. "Instrumenting the Dynamic Web." *Journal of Web Engineering*. (3): 244–260. www.microsoft.com/en-us/research/wp-content/uploads/2016/02/edmondsjwe2007.pdf.

Efron, Bradley, and Robert J. Tibshriani. 1994. *An Introduction to the Bootstrap*. Chapman & Hall/CRC.

EGAP. 2018. "10 Things to Know About Heterogeneous Treatment Effects." *EGAP: Evidence in Government and Politics.* egap.org/methods-guides/10-things-hetero geneous-treatment-effects.

Ehrenberg, A.S.C. 1975. "The Teaching of Statistics: Corrections and Comments." *Journal of the Royal Statistical Society. Series A* 138 (4): 543–545. https://www .jstor.org/stable/2345216.

Eisenberg, Bryan 2005. "How to Improve A/B Testing." *ClickZ Network.* April 29. www.clickz.com/clickz/column/1717234/how-improve-a-b-testing.

Eisenberg, Bryan. 2004. *A/B Testing for the Mathematically Disinclined.* May 7. http:// www.clickz.com/showPage.html?page=3349901.

Eisenberg, Bryan, and John Quarto-vonTivadar. 2008. *Always Be Testing: The Complete Guide to Google Website Optimizer.* Sybex.

eMarketer. 2016. "Microsoft Ad Revenues Continue to Rebound." April 20. https:// www.emarketer.com/Article/Microsoft-Ad-Revenues-Continue-Rebound/1013854.

European Commission. 2018. https://ec.europa.eu/commission/priorities/justice-and-fundamental-rights/data-protection/2018-reform-eu-data-protection-rules_en.

European Commission. 2016. EU GDPR.ORG. https://eugdpr.org/.

Fabijan, Aleksander, Pavel Dmitriev, Helena Holmstrom Olsson, and Jan Bosch. 2018. "Online Controlled Experimentation at Scale: An Empirical Survey on the Current State of A/B Testing." *Euromicro Conference on Software Engineering and Advanced Applications (SEAA).* Prague, Czechia. doi:10.1109/SEAA.2018.00021.

Fabijan, Aleksander, Pavel Dmitriev, Helena Holmstrom Olsson, and Jan Bosch. 2017. "The Evolution of Continuous Experimentation in Software Product Development: from Data to a Data-Driven Organization at Scale." *ICSE '17 Proceedings of the 39th International Conference on Software Engineering.* Buenos Aires, Argentina: IEEE Press. 770–780. doi:https://doi.org/10.1109/ ICSE.2017.76.

Fabijan, Aleksander, Jayant Gupchup, Somit Gupta, Jeff Omhover, Wen Qin, Lukas Vermeer, and Pavel Dmitriev. 2019. "Diagnosing Sample Ratio Mismatch in Online Controlled Experiments: A Taxonomy and Rules of Thumb for Practitioners." *KDD '19: The 25th SIGKDD International Conference on Knowledge Discovery and Data Mining.* Anchorage, Alaska, USA: ACM.

Fabijan, Aleksander, Pavel Dmitriev, Colin McFarland, Lukas Vermeer, Helena Holmström Olsson, and Jan Bosch. 2018. "Experimentation Growth: Evolving Trustworthy A/B Testing Capabilities in Online Software Companies." *Journal of Software: Evolution and Process* 30 (12:e2113). doi:https://doi.org/10.1002/ smr.2113.

FAT/ML. 2019. *Fairness, Accountability, and Transparency in Machine Learning.* http://www.fatml.org/.

Fisher, Ronald Aylmer. 1925. *Statistical Methods for Research Workers.* Oliver and Boyd. http://psychclassics.yorku.ca/Fisher/Methods/.

Forte, Michael. 2019. "Misadventures in experiments for growth." The Unofficial Google Data Science Blog. April 16. www.unofficialgoogledatascience.com/ 2019/04/misadventures-in-experiments-for-growth.html.

Freedman, Benjamin. 1987. "Equipoise and the Ethics of Clinical Research." *The New England Journal of Medicine* 317 (3): 141–145. doi:https://www.nejm.org/doi/ full/10.1056/NEJM198707163170304.

Gelman, Andrew, and John Carlin. 2014. "Beyond Power Calculations: Assessing Type S (Sign) and Type M (Magnitude) Errors." *Perspectives on Psychological Science* 9 (6): 641–651. doi:10.1177/1745691614551642.

Gelman, Andrew, and Thomas C. Little. 1997. "Poststratification into Many Categories Using Hierarchical Logistic Regression." *Survey Methdology* 23 (2): 127–135. www150.statcan.gc.ca/n1/en/pub/12-001-x/1997002/article/3616-eng.pdf.

Georgiev, Georgi Zdravkov. 2019. Statistical Methods in Online A/B Testing: Statistics for Data-Driven Business Decisions and Risk Management in e-Commerce. Independently published. www.abtestingstats.com

Georgiev, Georgi Zdravkov. 2018. "Analysis of 115 A/B Tests: Average Lift is 4%, Most Lack Statistical Power." *Analytics Toolkit.* June 26. http://blog.analytics-toolkit.com/2018/analysis-of-115-a-b-tests-average-lift-statistical-power/.

Gerber, Alan S., and Donald P. Green. 2012. *Field Experiments: Design, Analysis, and Interpretation.* W. W. Norton & Company. https://www.amazon.com/Field-Experiments-Design-Analysis-Interpretation/dp/0393979954.

Goldratt, Eliyahu M. 1990. *The Haystack Syndrome.* North River Press.

Goldstein, Noah J., Steve J. Martin, and Robert B. Cialdini. 2008. *Yes!: 50 Scientifically Proven Ways to Be Persuasive.* Free Press.

Goodhart, Charles A. E. 1975. *Problems of Monetary Management: The UK Experience.* Vol. 1, in *Papers in Monetary Economics*, by Reserve Bank of Australia.

Goodhart's law. 2018. *Wikipedia.* https://en.wikipedia.org/wiki/Goodhart%27s_law.

Goodman, Steven. 2008. "A Dirty Dozen: Twelve P-Value Misconceptions." Seminars in Hematology. doi:https://doi.org/10.1053/j.seminhematol.2008.04.003.

Google. 2019. *Processing Logs at Scale Using Cloud Dataflow.* March 19. https://cloud.google.com/solutions/processing-logs-at-scale-using-dataflow.

Google. 2018. *Google Surveys.* https://marketingplatform.google.com/about/surveys/.

Google. 2011. "Ads Quality Improvements Rolling Out Globally." *Google Inside AdWords.* October 3. https://adwords.googleblog.com/2011/10/ads-quality-improvements-rolling-out.html.

Google Console. 2019. "Release App Updates with Staged Rollouts." *Google Console Help.* https://support.google.com/googleplay/android-developer/answer/6346149?hl=en.

Google Developers. 2019. *Reduce Your App Size.* https://developer.andriod.com/topic/performance/reduce-apk-size.

Google, Helping Advertisers Comply with the GDPR. 2019. *Google Ads Help.* https://support.google.com/google-ads/answer/9028179?hl=en.

Google Website Optimizer. 2008. http://services.google.com/websiteoptimizer.

Gordon, Brett R., Florian Zettelmeyer, Neha Bhargava, and Dan Chapsky. 2018. "A Comparison of Approaches to Advertising Measurement: Evidence from Big Field Experiments at Facebook (forthcoming at Marketing Science)." https://papers.ssrn.com/sol3/papers.cfm?abstract_id=3033144.

Goward, Chris. 2015. "Delivering Profitable 'A-ha!' Moments Everyday." *Conversion Hotel.* Texel, The Netherlands. www.slideshare.net/webanalisten/chris-goward-strategy-conversion-hotel-2015.

Goward, Chris. 2012. *You Should Test That: Conversion Optimization for More Leads, Sales and Profit or The Art and Science of Optimized Marketing.* Sybex.

Greenhalgh, Trisha. 2014. *How to Read a Paper: The Basics of Evidence-Based Medicine*. BMJ Books. https://www.amazon.com/gp/product/B00IPG7GLC.

Greenhalgh, Trisha. 1997. "How to Read a Paper : Getting Your Bearings (deciding what the paper is about)." *BMJ* 315 (7102): 243–246. doi:10.1136/bmj.315.7102.243.

Greenland, Sander, Stephen J. Senn, Kenneth J. Rothman, John B. Carlin, Charles Poole, Steven N. Goodman, and Douglas G. Altman. 2016. "Statistical Tests, P Values, Confidence Intervals, and Power: a Guide to Misinterpretations." *European Journal of Epidemiology* 31 (4): 337–350. https://dx.doi.org/10.1007%2Fs10654-016-0149-3.

Grimes, Carrie, Diane Tang, and Daniel M. Russell. 2007. "Query Logs Alone are not Enough." *International Conference of the World Wide Web*, May.

Grove, Andrew S. 1995. *High Output Management*. 2nd edition. Vintage.

Groves, Robert M., Floyd J. Fowler Jr, Mick P. Couper, James M. Lepkowski, Singer Eleanor, and Roger Tourangeau. 2009. *Survey Methodology, 2nd edition.* Wiley.

Gui, Han, Ya Xu, Anmol Bhasin, and Jiawei Han. 2015. "Network A/B Testing From Sampling to Estimation." *WWW '15 Proceedings of the 24th International Conference on World Wide Web*. Florence, IT: ACM. 399–409.

Gupta, Somit, Lucy Ulanova, Sumit Bhardwaj, Pavel Dmitriev, Paul Raff, and Aleksander Fabijan. 2018. "The Anatomy of a Large-Scale Online Experimentation Platform." *IEEE International Conference on Software Architecture*.

Gupta, Somit, Ronny Kohavi, Diane Tang, Ya Xu, and etal. 2019. "Top Challenges from the first Practical Online Controlled Experiments Summit." Edited by Xin Luna Dong, Ankur Teredesai and Reza Zafarani. *SIGKDD Explorations* (ACM) 21 (1). https://bit.ly/OCESummit1.

Guyatt, Gordon H., David L. Sackett, John C. Sinclair, Robert Hayward, Deborah J. Cook, and Richard J. Cook. 1995. "Users' Guides to the Medical Literature: IX. A method for Grading Health Care Recommendations." *Journal of the American Medical Association (JAMA)* 274 (22): 1800–1804. doi:https://doi.org/10.1001%2Fjama.1995.03530220066035.

Harden, K. Paige, Jane Mendle, Jennifer E. Hill, Eric Turkheimer, and Robert E. Emery. 2008. "Rethinking Timing of First Sex and Delinquency." *Journal of Youth and Adolescence* 37 (4): 373–385. doi:https://doi.org/10.1007/s10964-007-9228-9.

Harford, Tim. 2014. *The Undercover Economist Strikes Back: How to Run – or Ruin – an Economy*. Riverhead Books.

Hauser, John R., and Gerry Katz. 1998. "Metrics: You Are What You Measure!" *European Management Journal* 16 (5): 516–528. http://www.mit.edu/~hauser/Papers/metrics%20you%20are%20what%20you%20measure.pdf.

Health and Human Services. 2018a. *Guidance Regarding Methods for De-identification of Protected Health Information in Accordance with the Health Insurance Portability and Accountability Act (HIPAA) Privacy Rule*. https://www.hhs.gov/hipaa/for-professionals/privacy/special-topics/de-identification/index.html.

Health and Human Services. 2018b. *Health Information Privacy*. https://www.hhs.gov/hipaa/index.html.

Health and Human Services. 2018c. *Summary of the HIPAA Privacy Rule*. https://www.hhs.gov/hipaa/for-professionals/privacy/laws-regulations/index.html.

Hedges, Larry, and Ingram Olkin. 2014. *Statistical Methods for Meta-Analysis*. Academic Press.

Hemkens, Lars, Despina Contopoulos-Ioannidis, and John Ioannidis. 2016. "Routinely Collected Data and Comparative Effectiveness Evidence: Promises and Limitations." *CMAJ*, May 17.

HIPAA Journal. 2018. *What is Considered Protected Health Information Under HIPAA*. April 2. https://www.hipaajournal.com/what-is-considered-protected-health-information-under-hipaa/.

Hochberg, Yosef, and Yoav Benjamini. 1995. "Controlling the False Discovery Rate: a Practical and Powerful Approach to Multiple Testing Series B." *Journal of the Royal Statistical Society* 57 (1): 289–300.

Hodge, Victoria, and Jim Austin. 2004. "A Survey of Outlier Detection Methodologies." *Journal of Artificial Intelligence Review*. 85–126.

Hohnhold, Henning, Deirdre O'Brien, and Diane Tang. 2015. "Focus on the Long-Term: It's better for Users and Business." *Proceedings 21st Conference on Knowledge Discovery and Data Mining (KDD 2015)*. Sydney, Australia: ACM. http://dl.acm.org/citation.cfm?doid=2783258.2788583.

Holson, Laura M. 2009. "Putting a Bolder Face on Google." *NY Times*. February 28. https://www.nytimes.com/2009/03/01/business/01marissa.html.

Holtz, David Michael. 2018. "Limiting Bias from Test-Control Interference In Online Marketplace Experiments." *DSpace@MIT*. http://hdl.handle.net/1721.1/117999.

Hoover, Kevin D. 2008. "Phillips Curve." In R. David Henderson, *Concise Encyclopedia of Economics*. http://www.econlib.org/library/Enc/PhillipsCurve.html.

Huang, Jason, David Reiley, and Nickolai M. Raibov. 2018. "David Reiley, Jr." *Measuring Consumer Sensitivity to Audio Advertising: A Field Experiment on Pandora Internet Radio*. April 21. http://davidreiley.com/papers/PandoraListenerDemandCurve.pdf.

Huang, Jeff, Ryen W. White, and Susan Dumais. 2012. "No Clicks, No Problem: Using Cursor Movements to Understand and Improve Search." *Proceedings of SIGCHI*.

Huang, Yanping, Jane You, Iris Wang, Feng Cao, and Ian Gao. 2015. *Data Science Interviews Exposed*. CreateSpace.

Hubbard, Douglas W. 2014. *How to Measure Anything: Finding the Value of Intangibles in Business*. 3rd edition. Wiley.

Huffman, Scott. 2008. *Search Evaluation at Google*. September 15. https://googleblog.blogspot.com/2008/09/search-evaluation-at-google.html.

Imbens, Guido W., and Donald B. Rubin. 2015. *Causal Inference for Statistics, Social, and Biomedical Sciences: An Introduction*. Cambridge University Press.

Ioannidis, John P. 2005. "Contradicted and Initially Stronger Effects in Highly Cited Clinical Research." *(The Journal of the American Medical Association)* 294 (2).

Jackson, Simon. 2018. "How Booking.com increases the power of online experiments with CUPED." *Booking.ai*. January 22. https://booking.ai/how-booking-com-increases-the-power-of-online-experiments-with-cuped-995d186fff1d.

Joachims, Thorsten, Laura Granka, Bing Pan, Helene Hembrooke, and Geri Gay. 2005. "Accurately Interpreting Clickthrough Data as Implicit Feedback." *SIGIR*, August.

Johari, Ramesh, Leonid Pekelis, Pete Koomen, and David Walsh. 2017. "Peeking at A/B Tests." *KDD '17: Proceedings of the 23rd ACM SIGKDD International Conference on Knowledge Discovery and Data Mining*. Halifax, NS, Canada: ACM. 1517–1525. doi:https://doi.org/10.1145/3097983.3097992.

Kaplan, Robert S., and David P. Norton. 1996. *The Balanced Scorecard: Translating Strategy into Action*. Harvard Business School Press.

Katzir, Liran, Edo Liberty, and Oren Somekh. 2012. "Framework and Algorithms for Network Bucket Testing." *Proceedings of the 21st International Conference on World Wide Web* 1029–1036.

Kaushik, Avinash. 2006. "Experimentation and Testing: A Primer." *Occam's Razor*. May 22. www.kaushik.net/avinash/2006/05/experimentation-and-testing-a-primer.html.

Keppel, Geoffrey, William H. Saufley, and Howard Tokunaga. 1992. *Introduction to Design and Analysis*. 2nd edition. W.H. Freeman and Company.

Kesar, Alhan. 2018. *11 Ways to Stop FOOC'ing up your A/B tests*. August 9. www.widerfunnel.com/stop-fooc-ab-tests/.

King, Gary, and Richard Nielsen. 2018. *Why Propensity Scores Should Not Be Used for Matching*. Working paper. https://gking.harvard.edu/publications/why-propensity-scores-should-not-be-used-formatching.

King, Rochelle, Elizabeth F. Churchill, and Caitlin Tan. 2017. *Designing with Data: Improving the User Experience with A/B Testing*. O'Reilly Media.

Kingston, Robert. 2015. *Does Optimizely Slow Down a Site's Performance*. January 18. https://www.quora.com/Does-Optimizely-slow-down-a-sites-performance/answer/Robert-Kingston.

Knapp, Michael S., Juli A. Swinnerton, Michael A. Copland, and Jack Monpas-Huber. 2006. *Data-Informed Leadership in Education*. Center for the Study of Teaching and Policy, University of Washington, Seattle, WA: Wallace Foundation. https://www.wallacefoundation.org/knowledge-center/Documents/1-Data-Informed-Leadership.pdf.

Kohavi, Ron. 2019. "HiPPO FAQ." *ExP Experimentation Platform*. http://bitly.com/HIPPOExplained.

Kohavi, Ron. 2016. "Pitfalls in Online Controlled Experiments." *CODE '16: Conference on Digital Experimentation*. MIT. https://bit.ly/Code2016Kohavi.

Kohavi, Ron. 2014. "Customer Review of A/B Testing: The Most Powerful Way to Turn Clicks Into Customers." *Amazon.com*. May 27. www.amazon.com/gp/customer-reviews/R44BH2HO30T18.

Kohavi, Ron. 2010. "Online Controlled Experiments: Listening to the Customers, not to the HiPPO." *Keynote at EC10: the 11th ACM Conference on Electronic Commerce*. www.exp-platform.com/Documents/2010-06%20EC10.pptx.

Kohavi, Ron. 2003. *Real-world Insights from Mining Retail E-Commerce Data*. Stanford, CA, May 22. http://ai.stanford.edu/~ronnyk/realInsights.ppt.

Kohavi, Ron, and Roger Longbotham. 2017. "Online Controlled Experiments and A/B Tests." In *Encyclopedia of Machine Learning and Data Mining*, by Claude Sammut and Geoffrey I Webb. Springer. www.springer.com/us/book/9781489976857.

Kohavi, Ron, and Roger Longbotham. 2010. "Unexpected Results in Online Controlled Experiments." *SIGKDD Explorations*, December. http://bit.ly/expUnexpected.

Kohavi, Ron and Parekh, Rajesh. 2003. "Ten Supplementary Analyses to Improve E-commerce Web Sites." *WebKDD*. http://ai.stanford.edu/~ronnyk/supplementaryAnalyses.pdf.

Kohavi, Ron, and Stefan Thomke. 2017. "The Surprising Power of Online Experiments." *Harvard Business Review* (September–October): 74–92. http://exp-platform.com/hbr-the-surprising-power-of-online-experiments/.

Kohavi, Ron, Thomas Crook, and Roger Longbotham. 2009. "Online Experimentation at Microsoft." *Third Workshop on Data Mining Case Studies and Practice Prize.* http://bit.ly/expMicrosoft.

Kohavi, Ron, Roger Longbotham, and Toby Walker. 2010. "Online Experiments: Practical Lessons." *IEEE Computer,* September: 82–85. http://bit.ly/expPracticalLessons.

Kohavi, Ron, Diane Tang, and Ya Xu. 2019. "History of Controlled Experiments." *Practical Guide to Trustworthy Online Controlled Experiments.* https://bit.ly/experimentGuideHistory.

Kohavi, Ron, Alex Deng, Roger Longbotham, and Ya Xu. 2014. "Seven Rules of Thumb for Web Site." *Proceedings of the 20th ACM SIGKDD International Conference on Knowledge Discovery and Data Mining (KDD '14).* http://bit.ly/expRulesOfThumb.

Kohavi, Ron, Roger Longbotham, Dan Sommerfield, and Randal M. Henne. 2009. "Controlled Experiments on the Web: Survey and Practical Guide." *Data Mining and Knowledge Discovery* 18: 140–181. http://bit.ly/expSurvey.

Kohavi, Ron, Alex Deng, Brian Frasca, Roger Longbotham, Toby Walker, and Ya Xu. 2012. "Trustworthy Online Controlled Experiments: Five Puzzling Outcomes Explained." *Proceedings of the 18th Conference on Knowledge Discovery and Data Mining.* http://bit.ly/expPuzzling.

Kohavi, Ron, Alex Deng, Brian Frasca, Toby Walker, Ya Xu, and Nils Pohlmann. 2013. "Online Controlled Experiments at Large Scale." *KDD 2013: Proceedings of the 19th ACM SIGKDD International Conference on Knowledge Discovery and Data Mining.*

Kohavi, Ron, David Messner, Seth Eliot, Juan Lavista Ferres, Randy Henne, Vignesh Kannappan, and Justin Wang. 2010. "Tracking Users' Clicks and Submits: Trade-offs between User Experience and Data Loss." *Experimentation Platform.* September 28. www.exp-platform.com/Documents/TrackingUserClicksSubmits.pdf

Kramer, Adam, Jamie Guillory, and Jeffrey Hancock. 2014. "Experimental evidence of massive-scale emotional contagion through social networks." *PNAS,* June 17.

Kuhn, Thomas. 1996. *The Structure of Scientific Revolutions.* 3rd edition. University of Chicago Press.

Laja, Peep. 2019. "How to Avoid a Website Redesign FAIL." *CXL.* March 8. https://conversionxl.com/show/avoid-redesign-fail/.

Lax, Jeffrey R., and Justin H. Phillips. 2009. "How Should We Estimate Public Opinion in The States?" *American Journal of Political Science* 53 (1): 107–121. www.columbia.edu/~jhp2121/publications/HowShouldWeEstimateOpinion.pdf.

Lee, Jess. 2013. *Fake Door.* April 10. www.jessyoko.com/blog/2013/04/10/fake-doors/.

Lee, Minyong R, and Milan Shen. 2018. "Winner's Curse: Bias Estimation for Total Effects of Features in Online Controlled Experiments." *KDD 2018: The 24th ACM Conference on Knowledge Discovery and Data Mining.* London: ACM.

Lehmann, Erich, L., and Joseph P. Romano. 2005. *Testing Statistical Hypothesis.* Springer.

Levy, Steven. 2014. "Why The New Obamacare Website is Going to Work This Time." www.wired.com/2014/06/healthcare-gov-revamp/.

Lewis, Randall A, Justin M Rao, and David Reiley. 2011. "Here, There, and Everywhere: Correlated Online Behaviors Can Lead to Overestimates of the Effects of Advertising." Proceedings of the 20th ACM International World Wide Web Conference (WWW). 157–166. https://ssrn.com/abstract=2080235.

Li, Lihong, Wei Chu, John Langford, and Robert E. Schapire. 2010. "A Contextual-Bandit Approach to Personalized News Article Recommendation." *WWW 2010: Proceedings of the 19th International Conference on World Wide Web*. Raleigh, North Carolina. https://arxiv.org/pdf/1003.0146.pdf.

Linden, Greg. 2006. *Early Amazon: Shopping Cart Recommendations.* April 25. http://glinden.blogspot.com/2006/04/early-amazon-shopping-cart.html.

Linden, Greg. 2006. "Make Data Useful." *December.* http://sites.google.com/site/glinden/Home/StanfordDataMining.2006-11-28.ppt.

Linden, Greg. 2006. "Marissa Mayer at Web 2.0 ." *Geeking with Greg* . November 9. http://glinden.blogspot.com/2006/11/marissa-mayer-at-web-20.html.

Linowski, Jakub. 2018a. *Good UI: Learn from What We Try and Test.* https://goodui .org/.

Linowski, Jakub. 2018b. *No Coupon.* https://goodui.org/patterns/1/.

Liu, Min, Xiaohui Sun, Maneesh Varshney, and Ya Xu. 2018. "Large-Scale Online Experimentation with Quantile Metrics." *Joint Statistical Meeting, Statistical Consulting Section.* Alexandria, VA: American Statistical Association. 2849–2860.

Loukides, Michael, Hilary Mason, and D.J. Patil. 2018. *Ethics and Data Science.* O'Reilly Media.

Lu, Luo, and Chuang Liu. 2014. "Separation Strategies for Three Pitfalls in A/B Testing." *KDD User Engagement Optimization Workshop.* New York. www.ueo-workshop.com/wp-content/uploads/2014/04/Separation-strategies-for-three-pitfalls-in-AB-testing_withacknowledgments.pdf.

Lucas critique. 2018. *Wikipedia.* https://en.wikipedia.org/wiki/Lucas_critique.

Lucas, Robert E. 1976. *Econometric Policy Evaluation: A Critique.* Vol. 1. In *The Phillips Curve and Labor Markets*, by K. Brunner and A. Meltzer, 19–46. Carnegie-Rochester Conference on Public Policy.

Malinas, Gary, and John Bigelow. 2004. "Simpson's Paradox." *Stanford Encyclopedia of Philosophy.* February 2. http://plato.stanford.edu/entries/paradox-simpson/.

Manzi, Jim. 2012. *Uncontrolled: The Surprising Payoff of Trial-and-Error for Business, Politics, and Society.* Basic Books.

Marks, Harry M. 1997. *The Progress of Experiment: Science and Therapeutic Reform in the United States, 1900–1990.* Cambridge University Press.

Marsden, Peter V., and James D. Wright. 2010. *Handbook of Survey Research*, 2nd Edition. Emerald Publishing Group Limited.

Marsh, Catherine, and Jane Elliott. 2009. *Exploring Data: An Introduction to Data Analysis for Social Scientists.* 2nd edition. Polity.

Martin, Robert C. 2008. *Clean Code: A Handbook of Agile Software Craftsmanship.* Prentice Hall.

Mason, Robert L., Richard F. Gunst, and James L. Hess. 1989. *Statistical Design and Analysis of Experiments With Applications to Engineering and Science.* John Wiley & Sons.

McChesney, Chris, Sean Covey, and Jim Huling. 2012. *The 4 Disciplines of Execution: Achieving Your Wildly Important Goals.* Free Press.

McClure, Dave. 2007. *Startup Metrics for Pirates: AARRR!!!* August 8. www.slide share.net/dmc500hats/startup-metrics-for-pirates-long-version.

McClure, Dave. 2007. *Startup Metrics for Pirates: AARRR!!!* August 8. www.slide share.net/dmc500hats/startup-metrics-for-pirates-long-version.

McCrary, Justin. 2008. "Manipulation of the Running Variable in the Regression Discontinuity Design: A Density Test." *Journal of Econometrics* (142): 698–714.

McCullagh, Declan. 2006. *AOL's Disturbing Glimpse into Users' Lives.* August 9. www.cnet.com/news/aols-disturbing-glimpse-into-users-lives/.

McFarland, Colin. 2012. *Experiment!: Website Conversion Rate Optimization with A/B and Multivariate Testing.* New Riders.

McGue, Matt. 2014. *Introduction to Human Behavioral Genetics, Unit 2: Twins: A Natural Experiment .* Coursera. https://www.coursera.org/learn/behavioralge netics/lecture/u8Zgt/2a-twins-a-natural-experiment.

McKinley, Dan. 2013. *Testing to Cull the Living Flower.* January. http://mcfunley.com/ testing-to-cull-the-living-flower.

McKinley, Dan. 2012. *Design for Continuous Experimentation: Talk and Slides.* December 22. http://mcfunley.com/design-for-continuous-experimentation.

Mechanical Turk. 2019. *Amazon Mechanical Turk.* http://www.mturk.com.

Meenan, Patrick. 2012. "Speed Index." *WebPagetest.* April. https://sites.google.com/a/ webpagetest.org/docs/using-webpagetest/metrics/speed-index.

Meenan, Patrick, Chao (Ray) Feng, and Mike Petrovich. 2013. "Going Beyond Onload – How Fast Does It Feel?" *Velocity: Web Performance and Operations* conference, October 14–16. http://velocityconf.com/velocityny2013/public/sched ule/detail/31344.

Meyer, Michelle N. 2018. "Ethical Considerations When Companies Study – and Fail to Study – Their Customers." In *The Cambridge Handbook of Consumer Privacy,* by Evan Selinger, Jules Polonetsky and Omer Tene. Cambridge University Press.

Meyer, Michelle N. 2015. "Two Cheers for Corporate Experimentation: The A/B Illusion and the Virtues of Data-Driven Innovation." *13 Colo. Tech. L.J. 273.* https://ssrn.com/abstract=2605132.

Meyer, Michelle N. 2012. *Regulating the Production of Knowledge: Research Risk– Benefit Analysis and the Heterogeneity Problem.* 65 *Administrative Law Review* 237; Harvard Public Law Working Paper. doi:http://dx.doi.org/10.2139/ ssrn.2138624.

Meyer, Michelle N., Patrick R. Heck, Geoffrey S. Holtzman, Stephen M. Anderson, William Cai, Duncan J. Watts, and Christopher F. Chabris. 2019. "Objecting to Experiments that Compare Two Unobjectionable Policies or Treatments." *PNAS: Proceedings of the National Academy of Sciences* (National Academy of Sciences). doi:https://doi.org/10.1073/pnas.1820701116.

Milgram, Stanley. 2009. *Obedience to Authority: An Experimental View.* Harper Perennial Modern Thought.

Mitchell, Carl, Jonathan Litz, Garnet Vaz, and Andy Drake. 2018. "Metrics Health Detection and AA Simulator." *Microsoft ExP (internal).* August 13. https://aka .ms/exp/wiki/AASimulator.

Moran, Mike. 2008. *Multivariate Testing in Action: Quicken Loan's Regis Hadiaris on multivariate testing.* December. www.biznology.com/2008/12/multivariate_testing_in_action/.

Moran, Mike. 2007. *Do It Wrong Quickly: How the Web Changes the Old Marketing Rules* . IBM Press.

Mosavat, Fareed. 2019. *Twitter.* Jan 29. https://twitter.com/far33d/status/1090400421842018304.

Mosteller, Frederick, John P. Gilbert, and Bucknam McPeek. 1983. "Controversies in Design and Analysis of Clinical Trials." In *Clinical Trials*, by Stanley H. Shapiro and Thomas A. Louis. New York, NY: Marcel Dekker, Inc.

MR Web. 2014. "Obituary: Audience Measurement Veteran Tony Twyman." *Daily Research News Online.* November 12. www.mrweb.com/drno/news20011.htm.

Mudholkar, Govind S., and E. Olusegun George. 1979. "The Logit Method for Combining Probablilities." Edited by J. Rustagi. Symposium on Optimizing Methods in Statistics." Academic Press. 345–366. https://apps.dtic.mil/dtic/tr/fulltext/u2/a049993.pdf.

Mueller, Hendrik, and Aaron Sedley. 2014. "HaTS: Large-Scale In-Product Measurement of User Attitudes & Experiences with Happiness Tracking Surveys." *OZCHI*, December.

Neumann, Chris. 2017. *Does Optimizely Slow Down a Site's Performance?* October 18. https://www.quora.com/Does-Optimizely-slow-down-a-sites-performance.

Newcomer, Kathryn E., Harry P. Hatry, and Joseph S. Wholey. 2015. *Handbook of Practical Program Evaluation (Essential Tests for Nonprofit and Publish Leadership and Management).* Wiley.

Neyman, J. 1923. "On the Application of Probability Theory of Agricultural Experiments." *Statistical Science* 465–472.

NSF. 2018. *Frequently Asked Questions and Vignettes: Interpreting the Common Rule for the Protection of Human Subjects for Behavioral and Social Science Research.* www.nsf.gov/bfa/dias/policy/hsfaqs.jsp.

Office for Human Research Protections. 1991. *Federal Policy for the Protection of Human Subjects ('Common Rule').* www.hhs.gov/ohrp/regulations-and-policy/regulations/common-rule/index.html.

Optimizely. 2018. "A/A Testing." *Optimizely.* www.optimizely.com/optimization-glossary/aa-testing/.

Optimizely. 2018. "Implement the One-Line Snippet for Optimizely X." *Optimizely.* February 28. https://help.optimizely.com/Set_Up_Optimizely/Implement_the_one-line_snippet_for_Optimizely_X.

Optimizely. 2018. *Optimizely Maturity Model.* www.optimizely.com/maturity-model/.

Orlin, Ben. 2016. *Why Not to Trust Statistics.* July 13. https://mathwithbaddrawings.com/2016/07/13/why-not-to-trust-statistics/.

Owen, Art, and Hal Varian. 2018. *Optimizing the Tie-Breaker Regression Discontinuity Design.* August. http://statweb.stanford.edu/~owen/reports/tiebreaker.pdf.

Owen, Art, and Hal Varian. 2009. *Oxford Centre for Evidence-based Medicine – Levels of Evidence.* March. www.cebm.net/oxford-centre-evidence-based-medicine-levels-evidence-march-2009/.

Park, David K., Andrew Gelman, and Joseph Bafumi. 2004. "Bayesian Multilevel Estimation with Poststratification: State-Level Estimates from National Polls." *Political Analysis* 375–385.

Parmenter, David. 2015. *Key Performance Indicators: Developing, Implementing, and Using Winning KPIs*. 3rd edition. John Wiley & Sons, Inc.

Pearl, Judea. 2009. *Causality: Models, Reasoning and Inference*. 2nd edition. Cambridge University Press.

Pekelis, Leonid. 2015. "Statistics for the Internet Age: The Story behind Optimizely's New Stats Engine." *Optimizely*. January 20. https://blog.optimizely.com/2015/01/20/statistics-for-the-internet-age-the-story-behind-optimizelys-new-stats-engine/.

Pekelis, Leonid, David Walsh, and Ramesh Johari. 2015. "The New Stats Engine." *Optimizely*. www.optimizely.com/resources/stats-engine-whitepaper/.

Pekelis, Leonid, David Walsh, and Ramesh Johari. 2005. *Web Site Measurement Hacks*. O'Reilly Media.

Peterson, Eric T. 2005. *Web Site Measurement Hacks*. O'Reilly Media.

Peterson, Eric T. 2004. *Web Analytics Demystified: A Marketer's Guide to Understanding How Your Web Site Affects Your Business*. Celilo Group Media and CafePress.

Pfeffer, Jeffrey, and Robert I Sutton. 1999. *The Knowing-Doing Gap: How Smart Companies Turn Knowledge into Action*. Harvard Business Review Press.

Phillips, A. W. 1958. "The Relation between Unemployment and the Rate of Change of Money Wage Rates in the United Kingdom, 1861–1957." *Economica, New Series* 25 (100): 283–299. www.jstor.org/stable/2550759.

Porter, Michael E. 1998. *Competitive Strategy: Techniques for Analyzing Industries and Competitors*. Free Press.

Porter, Michael E. 1996. "What is Strategy." *Harvard Business Review* 61–78.

Quarto-vonTivadar, John. 2006. "AB Testing: Too Little, Too Soon." *Future Now*. www.futurenowinc.com/abtesting.pdf.

Radlinski, Filip, and Nick Craswell. 2013. "Optimized Interleaving For Online Retrieval Evaluation." *International Conference on Web Search and Data Mining*. Rome, IT: ASM. 245–254.

Rae, Barclay. 2014. "Watermelon SLAs – Making Sense of Green and Red Alerts." *Computer Weekly*. September. https://www.computerweekly.com/opinion/Watermelon-SLAs-making-sense-of-green-and-red-alerts.

RAND. 1955. *A Million Random Digits with 100,000 Normal Deviates*. Glencoe, Ill: Free Press. www.rand.org/pubs/monograph_reports/MR1418.html.

Rawat, Girish. 2018. "Why Most Redesigns fail." *freeCodeCamp*. December 4. https://medium.freecodecamp.org/why-most-redesigns-fail-6ecaaf1b584e.

Razali, Nornadiah Mohd, and Yap Bee Wah. 2011. "Power comparisons of Shapiro-Wilk, Kolmogorov-Smirnov, Lillefors and Anderson-Darling tests." *Journal of Statistical Modeling and Analytics, January* 1: 21–33.

Reinhardt, Peter. 2016. *Effect of Mobile App Size on Downloads*. October 5. https://segment.com/blog/mobile-app-size-effect-on-downloads/.

Resnick, David. 2015. *What is Ethics in Research & Why is it Important?* December 1. www.niehs.nih.gov/research/resources/bioethics/whatis/index.cfm.

Ries, Eric. 2011. *The Lean Startup: How Today's Entrepreneurs Use Continuous Innovation to Create Radically Successful Businesses*. Crown Business.

Rodden, Kerry, Hilary Hutchinson, and Xin Fu. 2010. "Measuring the User Experience on a Large Scale: User-Centered Metrics for Web Applications." *Proceedings of CHI*, April. https://ai.google/research/pubs/pub36299

Romano, Joseph, Azeem M. Shaikh, and Michael Wolf. 2016. "Multiple Testing." In *The New Palgrave Dictionary of Economics*. Palgram Macmillan.

Rosenbaum, Paul R, and Donald B Rubin. 1983. "The Central Role of the Propensity Score in Observational Studies for Causal Effects." *Biometrika* 70 (1): 41–55. doi:http://dx.doi.org/10.1093/biomet/70.1.41.

Rossi, Peter H., Mark W. Lipsey, and Howard E. Freeman. 2004. *Evaluation: A Systematic Approach*. 7th edition. Sage Publications, Inc.

Roy, Ranjit K. 2001. *Design of Experiments using the Taguchi Approach : 16 Steps to Product and Process Improvement*. John Wiley & Sons, Inc.

Rubin, Donald B. 1990. "Formal Mode of Statistical Inference for Causal Effects." *Journal of Statistical Planning and Inference* 25, (3) 279–292.

Rubin, Donald 1974. "Estimating Causal Effects of Treatment in Randomized and Nonrandomized Studies." *Journal of Educational Psychology* 66 (5): 688–701.

Rubin, Kenneth S. 2012. *Essential Scrum: A Practical Guide to the Most Popular Agile Process*. Addison-Wesley Professional.

Russell, Daniel M., and Carrie Grimes. 2007. "Assigned Tasks Are Not the Same as Self-Chosen Web Searches." HICSS'07: 40th Annual Hawaii International Conference on System Sciences, January. https://doi.org/10.1109/HICSS.2007.91.

Saint-Jacques, Guillaume B., Sinan Aral, Edoardo Airoldi, Erik Brynjolfsson, and Ya Xu. 2018. "The Strength of Weak Ties: Causal Evidence using People-You-May-Know Randomizations." 141–152.

Saint-Jacques, Guillaume, Maneesh: Simpson, Jeremy Varshney, and Ya Xu. 2018. "Using Ego-Clusters to Measure Network Effects at LinkedIn." *Workshop on Information Systems and Exonomics*. San Francisco, CA.

Samarati, Pierangela, and Latanya Sweeney. 1998. "Protecting Privacy When Disclosing Information: k-anonymity and its Enforcement through Generalization and Suppression." *Proceedings of the IEEE Symposium on Research in Security and Privacy*.

Schrage, Michael. 2014. *The Innovator's Hypothesis: How Cheap Experiments Are Worth More than Good Ideas*. MIT Press.

Schrijvers, Ard. 2017. "Mobile Website Too Slow? Your Personalization Tools May Be to Blame." *Bloomreach*. February 2. www.bloomreach.com/en/blog/2017/01/server-side-personalization-for-fast-mobile-pagespeed.html.

Schurman, Eric, and Jake Brutlag. 2009. "Performance Related Changes and their User Impact." Velocity 09: Velocity Web Performance and Operations Conference. www.youtube.com/watch?v=bQSE51-gr2s and www.slideshare.net/dyninc/the-user-and-business-impact-of-server-delays-additional-bytes-and-http-chunking-in-web-search-presentation.

Scott, Steven L. 2010. "A modern Bayesian look at the multi-armed bandit." *Applied Stochastic Models in Business and Industry* 26 (6): 639–658. doi:https://doi.org/10.1002/asmb.874.

Segall, Ken. 2012. *Insanely Simple: The Obsession That Drives Apple's Success*. Portfolio Hardcover.

Senn, Stephen. 2012. "Seven myths of randomisation in clinical trials." *Statistics in Medicine.* doi:10.1002/sim.5713.

Shadish, William R., Thomas D. Cook, and Donald T. Campbell. 2001. *Experimental and Quasi-Experimental Designs for Generalized Causal Inference.* 2nd edition. Cengage Learning.

Simpson, Edward H. 1951. "The Interpretation of Interaction in Contingency Tables." *Journal of the Royal Statistical Society, Ser. B*, 238–241.

Sinofsky, Steven, and Marco Iansiti. 2009. *One Strategy: Organization, Planning, and Decision Making.* Wiley.

Siroker, Dan, and Pete Koomen. 2013. *A/B Testing: The Most Powerful Way to Turn Clicks Into Customers.* Wiley.

Soriano, Jacopo. 2017. "Percent Change Estimation in Large Scale Online Experiments." *arXiv.org.* November 3. https://arciv.org/pdf/1711.00562.pdf.

Souders, Steve. 2013. "Moving Beyond window.onload()." *High Performance Web Sites Blog.* May 13. www.stevesouders.com/blog/2013/05/13/moving-beyond-window-onload/.

Souders, Steve. 2009. *Even Faster Web Sites: Performance Best Practices for Web Developers.* O'Reilly Media.

Souders, Steve. 2007. *High Performance Web Sites: Essential Knowledge for Front-End Engineers.* O'Reilly Media.

Spitzer, Dean R. 2007. *Transforming Performance Measurement: Rethinking the Way We Measure and Drive Organizational Success.* AMACOM.

Stephens-Davidowitz, Seth, Hal Varian, and Michael D. Smith. 2017. "Super Returns to Super Bowl Ads?" *Quantitative Marketing and Economics*, March 1: 1–28.

Sterne, Jim. 2002. *Web Metrics: Proven Methods for Measuring Web Site Success.* John Wiley & Sons, Inc.

Strathern, Marilyn. 1997. "'Improving ratings': Audit in the British University System." *European Review* 5 (3): 305–321. doi:10.1002/(SICI)1234-981X (199707)5:33.0.CO;2-4.

Student. 1908. "The Probable Error of a Mean." *Biometrika* 6 (1): 1–25. https://www.jstor.org/stable/2331554.

Sullivan, Nicole. 2008. "Design Fast Websites." *Slideshare.* October 14. www.slideshare.net/stubbornella/designing-fast-websites-presentation.

Tang, Diane, Ashish Agarwal, Deirdre O'Brien, and Mike Meyer. 2010. "Overlapping Experiment Infrastructure: More, Better, Faster Experimentation." *Proceedings 16th Conference on Knowledge Discovery and Data Mining.*

The Guardian. 2014. *OKCupid: We Experiment on Users. Everyone does.* July 29. www.theguardian.com/technology/2014/jul/29/okcupid-experiment-human-beings-dating.

The National Commission for the Protection of Human Subjects of Biomedical and Behavioral Research. 1979. *The Belmont Report.* April 18. www.hhs.gov/ohrp/regulations-and-policy/belmont-report/index.html.

Thistlewaite, Donald L., and Donald T. Campbell. 1960. "Regression-Discontinuity Analysis: An Alternative to the Ex-Post Facto Experiment." *Journal of Educational Psychology* 51 (6): 309–317. doi:https://doi.org/10.1037%2Fh0044319.

Thomke, Stefan H. 2003. "Experimentation Matters: Unlocking the Potential of New Technologies for Innovation."

Tiffany, Kaitlyn. 2017. "This Instagram Story Ad with a Fake Hair in It is Sort of Disturbing." *The Verge*. December 11. www.theverge.com/tldr/2017/12/11/16763664/sneaker-ad-instagram-stories-swipe-up-trick.

Tolomei, Sam. 2017. *Shrinking APKs, growing installs*. November 20. https://medium.com/googleplaydev/shrinking-apks-growing-installs-5d3fcba23ce2.

Tutterow, Craig, and Guillaume Saint-Jacques. 2019. *Estimating Network Effects Using Naturally Occurring Peer Notification Queue Counterfactuals*. February 19. https://arxiv.org/abs/1902.07133.

Tyler, Mary E., and Jerri Ledford. 2006. *Google Analytics*. Wiley Publishing, Inc.

Tyurin, I.S. 2009. "On the Accuracy of the Gaussian Approximation." *Doklady Mathematics* 429 (3): 312–316.

Ugander, Johan, Brian Karrer, Lars Backstrom, and Jon Kleinberg. 2013. "Graph Cluster Randomization: Network Exposure to Multiple Universes." *Proceedings of the 19th ACM SIGKDD International Conference on Knowledge Discovery and Data Mining* 329–337.

van Belle, Gerald. 2008. *Statistical Rules of Thumb*. 2nd edition. Wiley-Interscience.

Vann, Michael G. 2003. "Of Rats, Rice, and Race: The Great Hanoi Rat Massacre, an Episode in French Colonial History." *French Colonial History* 4: 191–203. https://muse.jhu.edu/article/42110.

Varian, Hal. 2016. "Causal inference in economics and marketing." *Proceedings of the National Academy of Sciences of the United States of America* 7310–7315.

Varian, Hal R. 2007. "Kaizen, That Continuous Improvement Strategy, Finds Its Ideal Environment." *The New York Times*. February 8. www.nytimes.com/2007/02/08/business/08scene.html.

Vaver, Jon, and Jim Koehler. 2012. *Periodic Measuement of Advertising Effectiveness Using Multiple-Test Period Geo Experiments*. Google Inc.

Vaver, Jon, and Jim Koehler. 2011. *Measuring Ad Effectiveness Using Geo Experiments*. Google, Inc.

Vickers, Andrew J. 2009. *What Is a p-value Anyway? 34 Stories to Help You Actually Understand Statistics*. Pearson. www.amazon.com/p-value-Stories-Actually-Understand-Statistics/dp/0321629302.

Vigen, Tyler. 2018. *Spurious Correlations*. http://tylervigen.com/spurious-correlations.

Wager, Stefan, and Susan Athey. 2018. "Estimation and Inference of Heterogeneous Treatment Effects using Random Forests." *Journal of the American Statistical Association* 13 (523): 1228–1242. doi:https://doi.org/10.1080/01621459.2017.1319839.

Wagner, Jeremy. 2019. "Why Performance Matters." *Web Fundamentals. May.* https://developers.google.com/web/fundamentals/performance/why-performance-matters/#performance_is_about_improving_conversions.

Wasserman, Larry. 2004. *All of Statistics: A Concise Course in Statistical Inference*. Springer.

Weiss, Carol H. 1997. *Evaluation: Methods for Studying Programs and Policies*. 2nd edition. Prentice Hall.

Wider Funnel. 2018. "The State of Experimentation Maturity 2018." *Wider Funnel*. www.widerfunnel.com/wp-content/uploads/2018/04/State-of-Experimentation-2018-Original-Research-Report.pdf.

Wikipedia contributors, Above the Fold. 2014. *Wikipedia, The Free Encyclopedia*. Jan. http://en.wikipedia.org/wiki/Above_the_fold.

Wikipedia contributors, Cobra Effect. 2019. *Wikipedia, The Free Encyclopedia*. https://en.wikipedia.org/wiki/Cobra_effect.

Wikipedia contributors, Data Dredging. 2019. *Data dredging*. https://en.wikipedia.org/wiki/Data_dredging.

Wikipedia contributors, Eastern Air Lines Flight 401. 2019. *Wikipedia, The Free Encyclopedia*. https://en.wikipedia.org/wiki/Eastern_Air_Lines_Flight_401.

Wikipedia contributors, List of .NET libraries and frameworks. 2019. https://en.wikipedia.org/wiki/List_of_.NET_libraries_and_frameworks#Logging_Frameworks.

Wikipedia contributors, Logging as a Service. 2019. *Logging as a Service*. https://en.wikipedia.org/wiki/Logging_as_a_service.

Wikipedia contributors, Multiple Comparisons Problem. 2019. *Wikipedia, The Free Encyclopedia*. https://en.wikipedia.org/wiki/Multiple_comparisons_problem.

Wikipedia contributors, Perverse Incentive. 2019. https://en.wikipedia.org/wiki/Perverse_incentive.

Wikipedia contributors, Privacy by Design. 2019. *Wikipedia, The Free Encyclopedia*. https://en.wikipedia.org/wiki/Privacy_by_design.

Wikipedia contributors, Semmelweis Reflex. 2019. *Wikipedia, The Free Encyclopedia*. https://en.wikipedia.org/wiki/Semmelweis_reflex.

Wikipedia contributors, Simpson's Paradox. 2019. *Wikipedia, The Free Encyclopedia*. Accessed February 28, 2008. http://en.wikipedia.org/wiki/Simpson%27s_paradox.

Wolf, Talia. 2018. "Why Most Redesigns Fail (and How to Make Sure Yours Doesn't)." *GetUplift*. https://getuplift.co/why-most-redesigns-fail.

Xia, Tong, Sumit Bhardwaj, Pavel Dmitriev, and Aleksander Fabijan. 2019. "Safe Velocity: A Practical Guide to Software Deployment at Scale using Controlled Rollout." *ICSE: 41st ACM/IEEE International Conference on Software Engineering*. Montreal, Canada. www.researchgate.net/publication/333614382_Safe_Vel ocity_A_Practical_Guide_to_Software_Deployment_at_Scale_using_Controlled_ Rollout.

Xie, Huizhi, and Juliette Aurisset. 2016. "Improving the Sensitivity of Online Controlled Experiments: Case Studies at Netflix." *KDD '16: Proceedings of the 22nd ACM SIGKDD International Conference on Knowledge Discovery and Data Mining*. New York, NY: ACM. 645–654. http://doi.acm.org/10.1145/2939672.2939733.

Xu, Ya, and Nanyu Chen. 2016. "Evaluating Mobile Apps with A/B and Quasi A/B Tests." *KDD '16: Proceedings of the 22nd ACM SIGKDD International Conference on Knowledge Discovery and Data Mining*. San Francisco, California, USA: ACM. 313–322. http://doi.acm.org/10.1145/2939672.2939703.

Xu, Ya, Weitao Duan, and Shaochen Huang. 2018. "SQR: Balancing Speed, Quality and Risk in Online Experiments." *24th ACM SIGKDD Conference on Knowledge Discovery and Data Mining*. London: Association for Computing Machinery. 895–904.

Xu, Ya, Nanyu Chen, Adrian Fernandez, Omar Sinno, and Anmol Bhasin. 2015. "From Infrastructure to Culture: A/B Testing Challenges in Large Scale Social Networks." *KDD '15: Proceedings of the 21th ACM SIGKDD International*

*Conference on Knowledge Discovery and Data Mining.* Sydney, NSW, Australia: ACM. 2227–2236. http://doi.acm.org/10.1145/2783258.2788602.

Yoon, Sangho. 2018. *Designing A/B Tests in a Collaboration Network.* www .unofficialgoogledatascience.com/2018/01/designing-ab-tests-in-collaboration.html.

Young, S. Stanley, and Allan Karr. 2011. "Deming, data and observational studies: A process out of control and needing fixing." *Significance* 8 (3).

Zhang, Fan, Joshy Joseph, and Alexander James, Zhuang, Peng Rickabaugh. 2018. Client-Side Activity Monitoring. *US Patent US 10,165,071 B2.* December 25.

Zhao, Zhenyu, Miao Chen, Don Matheson, and Maria Stone. 2016. "Online Experimentation Diagnosis and Troubleshooting Beyond AA Validation." *DSAA 2016: IEEE International Conference on Data Science and Advanced Analytics.* IEEE. 498–507. doi:https://ieeexplore.ieee.org/document/7796936.

# Index

*A/A tests*, 200
   how to run, 205
   uneven splits and, 204
Above the fold time (AFT), 88
Acquisition, Activation, Retention, Referral,
      Revenue, 91
Agile software development, 13
analysis
   automated, 76
   cohort, 241
   edge-level, 234
   logs-based, 129
   post-period, 242
   triggered, 159
analysis results
   review meetings, 62
analysis unit, 168
annotating data, 178
atomicity, 70
automated analysis, 76

backend algorithmic changes, 19
backend delay model, 87
Bayes rule, 186
Bayesian evalutation, 114
Bayesian structural time series analysis, 140
Benjamini-Hochberg procedure, 191
Bernoulli randomization, 231
bias, 191, 240
biases, 201
binarization, 197
blocking, 197
Bonferroni correction, 191
bootstrap, 169
bootstrap method, 195
bot filtering, 48

Campbell's law, 109
capping, 197
carryover effects, 74
cart recommendations, 17
causal model, 96
causal relationship, 96
causality, 8, 137
Central Limit Theorem, 187
centralized experimentation platform,
      181
churn rate, 8
click logging, 178
click tracking, 52
client crashes metric, 99
client-side instrumentation, 163
cohort analysis, 241
confidence interval, 30, 37, 187, 193
confidence intervals, 43
constraints-based design, 76
constructed propensity score, 143
Control, 6–7
cooking data, 77
correlation, 9
counterfactual logging, 73
cultural norms, 61

data
   annotating, 178
data analysis pipeline, 151
data collection, 121
data computation, 178
data enrichment, 178
data pipeline impact, 47
data sharing, 65
data visualization, 77
day-of-week effect, 33

deceptive correlations, 145
delayed experience, 237
delayed logging, 157
delta method, 169, 195
density, 199
dependent variable, 7
deploying experiments, 69
designated market area, 138
difference in differences, 143
driver metrics, 91

ecosystem impact, 231
edge-level analysis, 234
educational processes, 61
empirical evidence, 114
equipoise, 118
ethics, 116
    anonymous, 123
    corporate culture and, 122
    equipoise, 118
    identified data, 123
    risk, 118
exclusion restriction, 142
experiments
    long-term, 61
experiment
    objective, 6
    OEC, 6
    results, 181
experiment assignment, 71
experiment hypothesis, 112
experiment IDs, 67
experiment lifecycle, 67
experiment platform
    performance, 72
experiment scorecard, 179, 216, *See also:*
    visualizations
experimentation maturity model, 180
experimentation maturity models
    crawling, 59
    flying, 59
    running, 59
    walking, 59
experimentation platform
    centralizing, 181
experiments
    *A/A*, 200
    analysis, 67
    analytics, 177
    automated analysis, 76
    best practices, 113

bias, 191
browser redirects, 45
channels, 5
client-side, 153
client-side implications, 156
constraints-based design, 76
culture, and, 179
data collection, 121
deception, 120
deployment, 69
design, 32
design and analysis, 27
design example, 33
design platform, 58
determining length, 33
duration, 190
edge-level analysis, 234
evaluation, 128
failure, 226
generating ideas for, 129
historical data retention, 231
holdback, 245
human evaluation and, 130
IDs, 69
impact, 174
infrastructure, 34
instrumentation, 34, 121, 162
interference, 226
interleaved, 141
isolating shared resources, 231
isolation, 231
iterations, 67
just-in-time processes, 61
length, 42
long-term effect, 236
nested design, 76
observation, 127
offline simulation and, 188
organizational goals and, 112
paired, 198
performance testing, 17
platform, 66
platform architechture, 68
platform components, 67
platform for managing, 67
power, 34, 189
power-of-suggestion, 120
production code, 70
randomization, 114
raters, 130
replication, 176

experiments (cont.)
    replication experiment, 15
    reusing, 231
    reverse, 176, 245
    risk, 118
    sample size, 188, 197
    scaling, 73
    segments, 52
    sensitivity, 28
    server-side, 153
    short-term effect, 235
    side-by-side, 131
    slow-down, 81, 86
    traffic allocation, 33, 192
    trustworthiness, 174
    validation, 135
    vocabulary, 179
    when they are not possible, 137
external data services, 133
external validity, 33, 135

*factor. See* parameter
false discovery rate, 42
first-order actions, 230
Fisher's meta-analysis, 192
focus groups, 132

gameability, 100, 107
geo-based randomization, 232
goal metrics, 91
goals, 91
    alignment, 93
    articulation, 93
Goodhart's law, 109
granularity, 167
guardrail metrics, 35, 92, 159, 174, 219
    cookie write rate, 224
    *latency*, 81
    organizational, 35, 98
    quick queries, 225
    trust-related, 35

HEART framework, 91
heterogeneous Treatment effects, 52
hierarchy of evidence, 9, 138
holdbacks, 175
holdouts, 175
HTML response size per page metrics, 99
human evaluation, 130
hypothesis testing, 185, 189
    Type I/II errors, 189

*ideas funnel*, 127
independence assumption
    violation, 203
independent identically distributed samples, 193
independently identically distributed, 195
information accessibility, 180
infrastructure, 34, 66
innovation productivity, 114
institutional memory, 63, 111, 181
Instrumental Variable method, 231
Instrumental Variables, 142
instrumentation, 34, 59–60, 67, 72, 128, 151, 162, 177
    client-side, 163
    corporate culture and, 165
    server-side, 164
intellectual integrity, 63
interference, 174
    detecting, 234
    direct connections, 227
    indirect connections, 228
interleaved experiments, 141
internal validity, 43
Interrupted Time Series, 139
invariants, 35
isolation, 231

JavaScript errors, 99

key metrics, 14

latency, 99, 135, 156
layer ID, 75
leadership buy-in, 59
*learning effect*, 243
least-squares regression model, 142
lifetime value, 95
log transformation, 197
logs, 164
    common identifier, 164
logs, joining, 177
logs-based analyses, 129
long-term effects, 51
long-term holdbacks, 175
long-term holdouts, 175
long-term impact, 173
long-term Treatment effect, 235
lossy implementations, 46, 224

maturity models, 58
Maximum Power Ramp, 172

mean, 29
measuring impact, 61
meta-analysis, 78, 112
metrics, 14
    analysis unit, 169
    asset, 92
    binary, 197
    business, 92
    categorizing, 181
    clicks-per-user, 47
    client crashes, 99
    data quality, 92
    debug, 62, 92
    defining, 179
    developing goal and driver, 94
    diagnosis, 92
    driver, 91
    early indicator, 175
    engagement, 92
    evaluation, 96
    feature-level, 104
    gameability, 107
    goal, 62, 91
    guardrail, 35, 62, 81, 92, 159, 174, 219
    how they relate to each other, 114
    HTML response size per page, 99
    improvements, 60
    indirect, 91
    invariants, 35
    irrelevant metrics significance, 191
    JavaScript errors, 99
    logs-based, 164
    longitudinal stability, 170
    negative, 95
    normalizing, 105
    operational, 92
    organizational, 91
    organizational guardrail, 98
    pageviews-per-user, 99
    page-load-time, 18
    per-experiment, 179
    per-metric results, 181
    per-user, 179
    predictive, 91
    quality, 62
    related, 182
    revenue-per-user, 99
    sample ratio mismatch, 219
    sensitivity, 103, 114
    sessions-per-user, 18
    short-term, 239
    short-term revenue, 101
    sign post, 91
    statistical models and, 95
    success, 91
    surrogate, 91, 104
    taxonomy, 90
    true north, 91
    t-tests and, 187
    user-level, 195
    validation, 96
    variablity, 29
*minimum detectable effect*, 190
*model training*, 229
multiple comparisons problem, 42
multiple hypothesis testing, 42
*Multivariate Tests (MVTs)*, 7

nested design, 76
network effects, 237
network egocentric randomization,
    233
network-cluster randomization, 233
NHST. *See* Null hypothesis significant
    testing
normality assumption, 188
novelty effect, 33, 49, 174
    detecting, 51
Null hypothesis, 30, 106, 185, 192
    conditioning, 40
Null hypothesis significant testing, 40
Null test. *See* A/A test

*Objectives and Key Results*, 90
observational study, 139
    limitations of, 144
OEC. See overall evaluation criterion
    clicks-per-user, 47
offline simulation, 188
One Metric that Matters, 104
online conrtolled experiments
    website optimization example, 26
    backend algorithmic changes, 19
    benefits, 10
    key tenets, 11
operational concerns, 173
organizational goals, 91
organizational guardrail metrics, 98
orthogonal randomization, 176
orthogonality guarantees, 71
*Outcome, Evaluation and Fitness function*, 7
outliers, 196

overall evaluation critereon, 180
  for e-mail, 106
  for search engines, 108
  revenue-per-user, 109
  teams and, 112
  triggering and, 212
overall evaluation criterion, 5, 27, 102
  definition, 6
  purchase indicator, 32

page-load-time (PLT), 88
Page phase time, 88
pageviews per-user metrics, 99
paired experiments, 198
parameter
  definition, 7
parameters, 67
  system, 70
peeking, 42
perceived performance, 88
percent delta, 194
performance, 135, 156, 179
  impact on key metrics, 18, 82
performance testing, 17
per-metric results, 181
permutation test, 188
personal recommendations, 17
PIRATE framework, 91
platform architecture, 68
platform components, 67
platform tools for managing experiments,
  67
population segments, 52
post-period analysis, 242
power, 189
primacy and novelty effects, 33
primacy effect, 33, 49, 174
  detecting, 51
propensity score matching, 143
p-value, 30, 106, 178, 186, 193, 220
  misinterpretation, 40
p-value threshold, 181
p-value thresholds, 77

query share, 108

ramping, 55, 66, 113, 151, 171, 234,
  245
  Maximum Power Ramp, 172
  phase 1
    pre-MPR, 174

phase 2
  MPR, 174
phase 3
  post-MPR, 175
phase 4
  long-term effects, 175
randomization, 8
randomization unit, 65, 151, 195
  definition, 7
  functional, 170
  granularity, 167
reading list, 24
Regression Discontinuity Design,
  141
regression model, 142
related metrics, 182
replication, 176
replication experiment, 15
*Response variable*, 7
revenue-per-user metric, 99
reverse experiment, 245
reverse experiments, 176
rings of test populations, 174
risk mitigation, 173
Rubin causal model, 226

sample ratio mismatch, 45, 215,
  219
sample size, 188
sampling, 55
scaling, 73
  manual methods, 74
  numberline method, 74
  single-layer, 73
  single-layer method drawback, 74
scorecard, 7
scorecard visualizations, 180
search engine results page, 113
segments, 52, 178, 180
  poorly behaving, 180
selection bias, 158
sensitivity, 103, 114, 196
sequential tests, 42
server-side instrumentation, 164
sessionized data, 129
shared goals, 60
shared resources, 44
short-term revenue metric, 101
short-term Treatment effect, 235
side-by-side experiments, 131
significance boundary, 32

Simple Ratio Mismatch
  debugging, 222
simple ratio mismatch, 180
Simpson's paradox, 54
single-layer scaling, 73
skewness coefficient, 187
slow-down experiments, 81, 86
speed, 179
Speed Index, 88
speed, quality, and risk, 172
spurious correlations, 146
SRM. *See* sample ratio mismatch
Stable Unit Treatment Value Assumption, 43,
  168, 226
standard error, 29
statistical power, 30, 185, 190, 198
statistics, 178
  confidence interval, 187
  practical significance, 189
  two-sample t-tests, 185
surrogate metrics, 104
surveys, 132
SUTVA. *See* Stable Unit Treatment Value
  Assumption
system parameters, 70
system-learned effect, 243

Taylor-series linear approximation,
  83
technical debt, 72
thick client, 153
thick clients, 151
thin client, 153
time to first result, 88
time-based effects, 140
time-based randomization, 232
time-staggered Treatment, 244
time-to-successful-click, 89
timing effects, 47
traffic allocation, 174

Treatment, 6
Treatment effect, 41, 175, 214, 236
  learning, 243
  system-learned, 243
  time-staggered, 244
  user-learned, 243
Treatment effect dilution, 240
triggering, 40, 47, 72, 159, 180, 209
  attributes, 222
t-statistic, 186
Twyman's law, 39
type I error rates, 41
Type I errors, 201
Type I/II errors, 189

uber holdouts, 176
user experience research, 95, 131
User Ready Time, 88
user-learned effect, 243

validation, 135
value of ideas, 11
*variable. See also* parameter
variables
  Instrumental, 142
variance, 193
variance estimation, 236
variant
  definition, 7
  mapping, 7
variants, 6, 67
  allocation, 27
  assignment, 69
  balanced, 198
visualization tool, 181
visualizations, 180
  scorecard, 180

web beacons, 163
website performance, 84